I0471793

CHICAGO
ARTIST COLONIES

CHICAGO
ARTIST COLONIES

KEITH M. STOLTE

Foreword by Amy E. Keller & Zac Bleicher

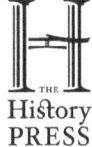

THE
History
PRESS

Published by The History Press
Charleston, SC
www.historypress.com

Copyright © 2019 by Keith M. Stolte
All rights reserved

Front cover, top left: *Chicago Daily News* (September 1924), Chicago History Museum, DN-0076733; *top center*: K.M. Stolte (2018); *top right*: Herman Miskin (1909), Metropolitan Opera Association; *bottom*: Photographer unknown, University of Chicago Photographic Archive, Special Collections Research Center, apf1-08072.

Back cover, top left: Carl Street Studios, east courtyard. K.M. Stolte (2018); *top center*: Dil Pickle Club Records, Newberry Library Special Collections; *top right*: Frank Fisher Studios. K.M. Stolte (2018); *bottom*: C.D. Arnold (1893), Chicago Public Library, Special Collections, WCE, CDA, Vol. 2, Plate 5.

First published 2019

Manufactured in the United States

ISBN 9781467143226

Library of Congress Control Number: 2019937042

Notice: The information in this book is true and complete to the best of our knowledge. It is offered without guarantee on the part of the author or The History Press. The author and The History Press disclaim all liability in connection with the use of this book.

All rights reserved. No part of this book may be reproduced or transmitted in any form whatsoever without prior written permission from the publisher except in the case of brief quotations embodied in critical articles and reviews.

Contents

Foreword

West Burton Place is a short cul-de-sac in the middle of Chicago containing an eclectic collection of the most fantastic homes you will ever see in the city—sturdy Victorian and Italianate homes situated between modernist jewel boxes of stained glass, decorative tile and carved wood. One of the city's most unique and interesting streets, the dozen or so buildings in this particular enclave are a mix of late-nineteenth-century flats and adaptively reused vernacular art deco and moderne buildings from the interwar period, where an artist colony and movement was created by artists most of the world has forgotten, even in Chicago. The original artists have since long passed, but the block, often colloquially referred to as the "handmade street," still attracts special residents—those committed to preserving the character, art and sense of community enshrined in these precious structures.

Many of Chicago's artist colonies, along with much of Chicago's historic real estate, has been lost to the wrecking ball. Occasionally, the demolition of the old makes way for impressive, forward-thinking architecture that pushes the envelope, encouraging us to collectively dream for more; all too often, though, the city bends to the will of developers, constructing the most generic, so-called luxury condominiums under the banner of "progress."

But West Burton Place—largely untouched since the last artist studio conversion in the 1940s—would not suffer the fate of architectural mediocrity. Instead, the community fought to ensure the block's protection.

It was July 2015, and we both received an urgent email blast declaring a state of imminent emergency from a resident of 155 West Burton Place, the site of Edgar Miller and Sol Kogen's historic artist colony called Carl Street Studios. A developer had purchased the adjoining property, was proposing to tear it down and wanted to replace it with a cheap facsimile of a craftsman-style structure. The developer, an outsider unfamiliar with the block but enamored with the idea of building on a cul-de-sac, had no idea what he had gotten himself into.

The community quickly sprang into action, launching a preservation effort that sought landmark status for the block in record time to save the property. One of the principals of that movement, Keith Stolte, provided a treasure trove of information about the block's intriguing history and importance in Chicago's cultural fabric. Over the summer of 2015, we became friends and trusted allies, quickly drafting and presenting a report to the Chicago Landmarks Commission, which paved the way for the block to be saved and legally protected as a designated landmark district in 2016.

But beyond the importance of the architecture, we were amazed to hear the stories of the artists who lived on the block, the communities they built and the many Chicago artist colonies—such as the Tree Studios, Towertown and the 57th Street Artist Colony, to name a few—that came before. Finding information about these periods of art history can be very difficult in Chicago. Local art is rarely discussed in Chicago's pop culture. Of course, nearly everyone in the city knows and has been to the Art Institute and is familiar with the many incredibly famous modernist European and American painters featured there (Picasso and Pollock), but there is an incredible dearth of knowledge (and representation) of Chicago's own artists, past and present, in the public realm.

Perhaps in Chicago's preoccupation with commerce, industry and technical innovation, we neglected other histories and consigned to oblivion the memories of earlier artistic movements that had a profound effect on the city and the greater American story. The reality is that this history is alive in the communities that remain extant throughout the city, and the city's stories are often best told through the residents and preservationists who fight so hard to protect them. Younger generations of artists, historians, creatives and scholars of all kinds are interested in learning more about Chicago's past and about artistic movements from which they can become inspired.

Through Mr. Stolte's meticulously researched and engrossing writing, we discover a time during Chicago's beginnings when thriving communities drew thousands of artists to the promise of creating something beautiful, unique and thought-provoking. We are thrilled that this new work pulls so much of the recorded accomplishments and milestones of Chicago's artists and their communities together into one brilliant, comprehensive book. For anyone interested in Chicago and its place in the history of American art, this resource will be a prized possession.

Amy E. Keller
Executive Vice President and Director of Preservation Advocacy
Chicago Art Deco Society

Zac Bleicher
Founder and Executive Director
Edgar Miller Legacy

Introduction

In 1916, a Chicago arts magazine published its September edition with the first twelve of twenty-eight pages completely blank. Not a word, not a picture appeared within these pages.[1] This was a dramatic and bold protest by the *Little Review* of what it regarded as the low quality of art and literature in the United States at that time. The *Little Review* was essentially signaling that there was little going on in the nation's art scene that was worth its ink, and the first twelve pages of the September issue were offered as a want ad for merit-worthy art. That this magazine had the presumptuousness to stage such a stunt is remarkable for two reasons: first, the *Little Review*, self-proclaimed arbiter of art and literature in America, was only about two years old at the time and still trying to gain traction among the cultured elite; second, Chicago, its home base, had been a cultural backwater a mere twenty-five years before, certainly not a place where critical judgments on the state of the arts were to be expected.

Artists in Chicago, with one or two notable exceptions, were virtually nonexistent prior to the Great Chicago Fire of 1871. From its incorporation in 1837 through the fire that all but decimated the city, only two artists of note worked in Chicago. Remarkably, one of those artists, George Peter Alexander Healy, was internationally famous and his works appear in some of the most prestigious art museums and civic institutions in the world. But even after the fire, Chicago had little time for art. Despite the fire's devastation, much of Chicago's infrastructure, particularly its transportation systems, remained intact. Reconstruction efforts immediately following the fire spurred great economic development, and the city's population rose from a pre-fire level of about three hundred thousand to more than one million in 1890. Chicago was racing to become a vast commercial center, where, ultimately, its role as an important transportation hub guaranteed its place as the nation's second-largest city by the turn of the twentieth century. Commerce, not art, ran through the city's veins at this time.

So how was it that this newborn Chicago publication, the *Little Review*, could presume to judge the state of the nation's arts and literature in 1916? By what authority did art critics in the most cynically commercial of all commercial centers in the United States claim the right to condemn the arts establishment of the country? The answers to these questions reside in the aftermath of the World's Columbian Exposition of 1893. Along with the 1871 fire, the Columbian Exposition constitutes one of the great historical milestones of Chicago. Indeed, the 1893 World's Fair, properly considered, is an important milestone of the cultural, technological and commercial development of the United States. The Fair provided the majority of its twenty-seven million visitors their first experience with electric lights—electric anything, for that matter. This was the advent of mass consumerism, and many visitors to the Fair had their first encounters there with soon-to-be staples such as Cracker Jack, Wrigley's chewing gum, Cream of Wheat and the zipper.

The Columbian Exposition also offered the vast majority of its visitors their first opportunity to view thousands of works of art by artists from around the country, and indeed the world, and to rub elbows with some of these artists who traveled to Chicago for the Fair. American sculptor Augustus Saint-Gaudens described the 1893 fair as "the greatest meeting of artists since the fifteenth century." This, in a city that could boast only a handful of artists two decades before.

The Palace of Fine Arts, a vast building designed to house these works of art, was one of the most popular sites of the Fair. And although works by Chicago artists constituted a very small portion of the art displayed (significantly less than 5 percent), Chicagoans, particularly wealthy businessmen and their wives, were proud that, for a few months at least, their city was the cultural center of the world.

It was true that Chicago was already home to the Art Institute, which had existed in one form or another since 1866, and a handful of very impressive private art collections owned by wealthy collectors. But the works in the Art Institute's collection and the collections of wealthy Chicagoans were almost exclusively by the hands of East Coast and European artists.

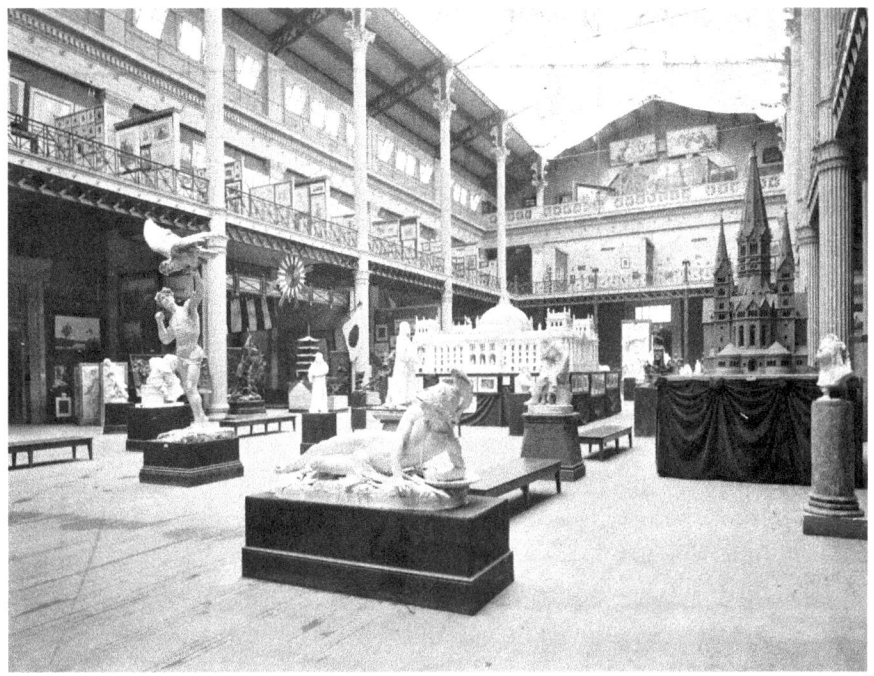

World's Columbian Exposition, Palace of Fine Arts, Main Hall. *C.D. Arnold (1893), Chicago Public Library, Special Collections, WCE, CDA, Vol. 8, Plate 61.*

The residual pride that the Columbian Exposition instilled in Chicagoans would ultimately change that.

During its first sixty years, Chicago focused its resources, financial and human, on transportation and commerce. After the Fair, Chicagoans started shifting resources to make the city a center of art and culture. The Chicago elite, adopting John Ruskin's view that the quality of a society manifests in its art, would ensure that the city's arts would be promoted and, indeed, conspicuous. Starting in 1896, the Art Institute began an annual month-long exhibition of art exclusively by artists from Chicago and vicinity. This annual event continued in one form or another until 1985. Wealthy Chicagoans and business institutions began sponsoring monetary prizes for noteworthy works by Chicago-area artists displayed at these exhibitions. A Chicago businessman bequeathed a large portion of his wealth to the Ferguson Monument Fund in 1905 to sponsor works of public sculpture by Chicago artists.

The Municipal Art League was formed in 1902 expressly to support the artists of Chicago, in part by purchasing works of noteworthy merit.

The Society of Associated Arts, also organized in 1902, was formed to promote a unity of purpose among artists in every field of art, thereby keeping them in close sympathy and cooperation. Both organizations had a hand in the periodic exhibition of art by Chicagoans. Chicago social clubs, such as the Union League and the University and Standard Clubs began purchasing large numbers of artworks by Chicagoans and sponsored art exhibitions and lectures within their premises. (The Union League Club currently owns probably the biggest and finest private collection of Chicago artists' works anywhere.)

The *Fine Arts Journal*, founded in 1899, was devoted to reporting on the art scene in Chicago and elsewhere. The *Little Review* and *Poetry Magazine*, the only periodical in the nation devoted exclusively to the poetic arts, were organized a little more than a decade later. At the turn of the century, Chicago's newspapers began employing art critics for the first time. The Palette and Chisel, a local art society, school and exhibition space, was founded in 1895. The Renaissance Society at the University of Chicago, founded in 1915, and the Chicago Arts Club, founded the following year, provided other important venues for local artists to exhibit their art, especially avant-garde and modernist works.

Thus, following the Columbian Exposition, there was a sweeping effort by Chicago artists and wealthy art patrons to consolidate and attract artists of all stripes to come and stay in Chicago and enhance the cultural life of the city. And the effort worked. The School of the Art Institute soon attracted some of the best art instructors in America and became one of the foremost art schools in the world, a distinction it still enjoys. Wealthy patrons donated significant, world-class works of art to the Institute, ultimately transforming that institution into one of the world's great art museums, and the second largest in the United States.

Within ten years of the Fair, Chicago boasted the most vibrant literary scene in America, claiming Theodore Dreiser, Henry Blake Fuller, Hamlin Garland and, a little later, Sherwood Anderson, Ben Hecht and Carl Sandburg. The city's architecture, already famous before the fair, was further strengthened by innovations created by the early modernist Louis Sullivan and his most astute pupil, Frank Lloyd Wright. No one could seriously dispute that Chicago was then home to the most progressive and influential architects in the world.

Chicago boosters lured conductor Theodore Thomas from New York in 1891 in anticipation of the World's Fair, where he served as conductor of the exposition orchestra. By the end of the century, Thomas would make the

Chicago Symphony Orchestra one of a half dozen of the most accomplished in the world. The city had dabbled with opera since the 1850s and had its first permanent Chicago Opera Company by 1910, essentially gobbling up the entirety of Oscar Hammerstein's Manhattan Opera Company. With that New York company came Mary Garden, by then a household name and soon to become Chicago's "Queen of Opera" for the next twenty-five years. In November 1910, Garden reprised her previous performances at Paris and New York of the title role in Richard Strauss's and Oscar Wilde's *Salome*, which one critic described as "a florid, excessive, unhampered tour de force, lawless and inhuman." Garden performed her shocking Dance of the Seven Veils in a body stocking. Musically, Chicago was fertile ground; it came as no surprise that, when the great jazz musicians were squeezed out of New Orleans after 1917 by government forces (at the behest of the U.S. Navy), it was to Chicago that they came and took refuge. From that time forward, the city and the development of jazz were intertwined.

The arts in Chicago were so advanced by 1913 that, following its inaugural exhibition in New York, the famously notorious Armory Show of international avant-garde art traveled to Chicago, where more than twice the number of patrons attended the exhibition than in New York. Within twenty years after the Columbian Exposition, critic H.L. Mencken, always with his finger on the pulse of American culture, was able to claim:

> *Out in Chicago, the only civilized city in the New World, they take the fine arts seriously and get into such frets and excitements about them as are raised nowhere else save by baseball, murder, political treachery, foreign wars and romantic loves…almost one fancies the world bumped by a flying asteroid, and the Chicago River suddenly turned into the Seine.*[2]

So it was, by 1916, that Margaret Anderson, the publisher of the *Little Review*, could claim with some authority to critically assess the state of art in America. By the time those twelve blank pages appeared in the *Little Review* as an admonishment to American art and literature, Chicago had transformed itself from a cultural backwater to one of the country's foremost centers of art, architecture, music and literature. One of the post-Fair phenomena that made it so, and that has not yet been mentioned, is the development and evolving tradition of artist colonies in Chicago and surrounding areas.

The first artist colony was founded by Anna and Lambert Tree, a wealthy judge, within a year following the close of the Columbian Exposition. The Trees, impressed by the success of the 1893 Fair in attracting art

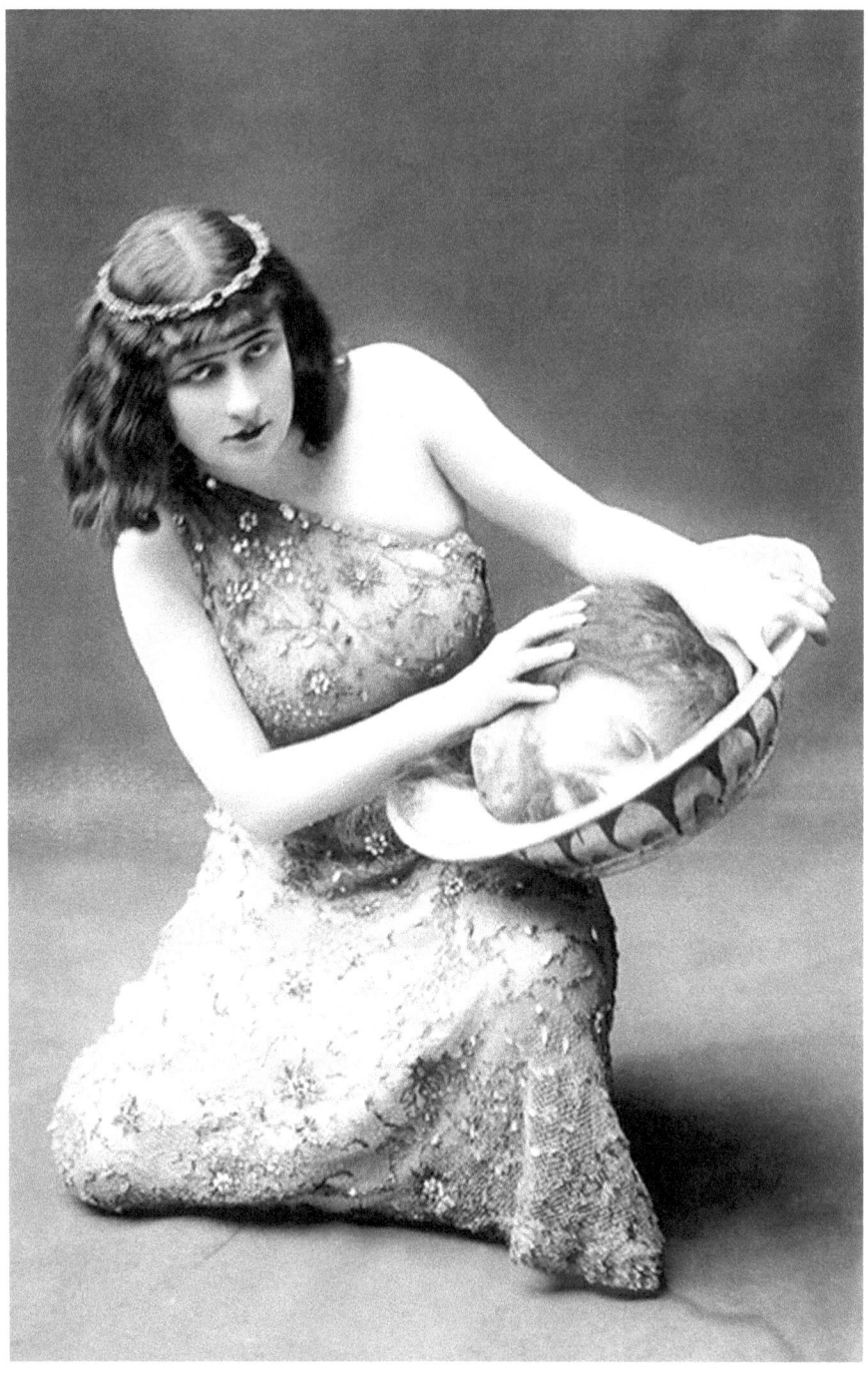

Mary Garden performing in Richard Strauss's *Salome. Herman Miskin, (1909), Metropolitan Opera Association.*

and artists to Chicago, decided to help make Chicago a magnet for artists going forward. In 1894, the Trees constructed a three-story, block-long brick building on State Street to provide low-cost housing and studio space to artists. A few years later, a large artist colony took hold in the old Studebaker Building on Michigan Avenue, renamed the Fine Arts Building. The *Little Review* was founded at and operated out of the Fine Arts Building for several years, and many of its contributors were artists and writers associated with the Fine Arts Building artist colony.

By the early 1900s, an influential artist colony formed on the South Side in a series of small single-floor buildings originally built to serve as souvenir and concession shops for the Columbian Exposition. A few blocks away, Lorado Taft, the city's most prominent sculptor, created his Midway Studios across the old Midway Plaisance from the newborn University of Chicago. Within a decade of the Fair, Chicago artists had established two artist colonies, the Eagle's Nest Camp and the Ox-Bow artist colony, in

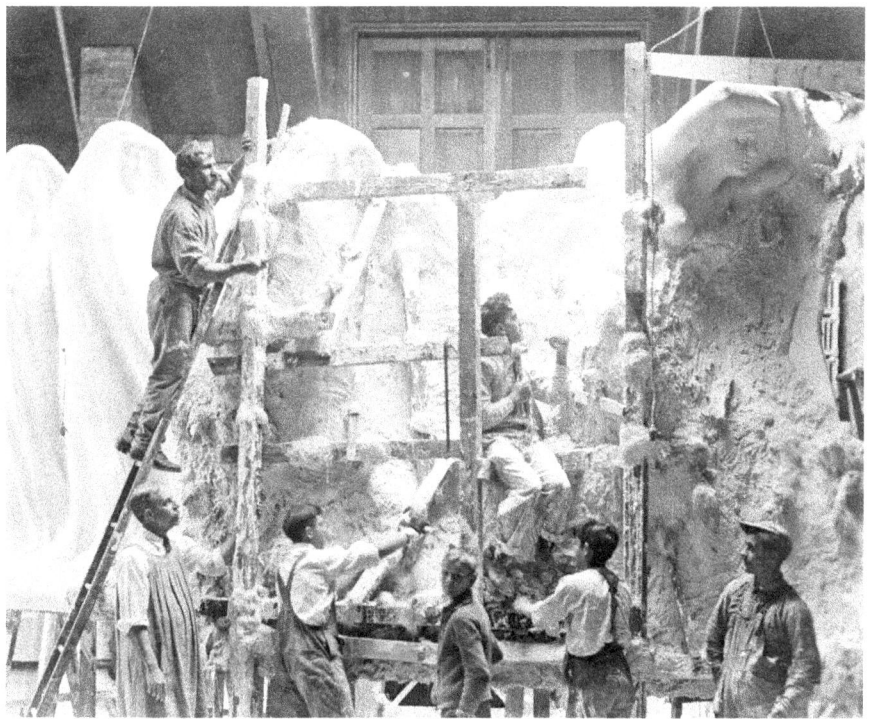

Lorado Taft and apprentices sculpting a portion of the *Fountain of Time* at Midway Studios, circa 1919. *Photographer unknown, University of Chicago Photographic Archive, Special Collections Research Center, apf1-08073.*

more picturesque, bucolic settings in order to escape the city during the oppressive Chicago summers.

Still later, in the 1910s and 1920s, the Towertown neighborhood on the Near North Side of the city, which encompassed the Tree Studios, was populated by numerous artist ateliers, bookstores, tearooms, speakeasies and other bohemian establishments. There, the charming Italian Court Building attracted better-established artists and the Three Arts Club was built to provide affordable housing and studio space for struggling female artists. Eccentric hobohemian John "Jack" Jones opened his Dil Pickle Club off a small alley across from Bughouse Square in 1917. There, artists and bohemian hangers-on would have discussed feminism, free love, homosexuality and other taboo topics with the likes of uber-lawyer Clarence Darrow, anarchists Dr. Ben Reitman and Emma Goldman and professors from the University of Chicago.

The opening of the Michigan Avenue Bridge and the development of the North Michigan Avenue corridor as a major retail and commercial thoroughfare in the mid-1920s made Towertown economically unattractive to artists, who consequently migrated to the cheaper, run-down Old Town neighborhood farther north and west. There these artists created unique, ad hoc studio communes on West Burton Place and Wells Street in the late 1920s, 1930s and 1940s. In 1936, Frank Fisher, a Marshall Field's executive, employed progressive architect Andrew Rebori and artist Edgar Miller, both pioneer artist colonists on West Burton Place, to design an artist studio building on State Street in the Gold Coast. This studio building represents probably the best example of art moderne architecture in the Midwest.

Born out of civic pride inspired by the World's Columbian Exposition of 1893, the artist colonies of Chicago thrived for many decades and became home or work space or both for hundreds, if not thousands, of artists of every field of endeavor. The Fine Arts Building is still home to dozens of artist studios, art publications and other art-related organizations. Artists continuously occupied the Tree Studios for more than one hundred years, prior to the building being redeveloped in the early 2000s into a more general office and retail space. Both of the summer artist colonies are still in operation, now under the auspices of institutions of higher education. The funky, "handmade" artist studio buildings on West Burton Place and Wells Street have always been home to artists or people associated with the arts in some fashion.

Alas, time has taken its toll on other Chicago artist colonies. The 57th Street Artist Colony was the center of "bohemia" in Hyde Park for sixty years before being torn down in 1963, a victim of urban renewal. The much-beloved Italian Court Building on Michigan Avenue met its end in 1968 to make way for an office tower. The Three Arts Club ceased as a residence for female artists in the 2000s and is now a high-end Restoration Hardware store.

The story of Chicago's artist colonies is integral to the city's historic role as a major cultural center in the United States throughout the twentieth and twenty-first centuries. The city's most famous and influential artists were members of at least one, and most were members of several, of these artist colonies. Oliver Dennett Grover, probably the most well-known Chicago painter at the time of the Columbian Exposition, later painted his landscapes and portraits in studios at the Fine Arts Building, Tree Studios and Eagle's Nest Camp. His contemporaries Lorado Taft and Nellie Walker, Chicago's most prominent sculptors, both created their art at the Fine Arts Building, Midway Studios and, during summers, at the Eagle's Nest Camp. Frederic Milton Grant, one of the most successful artists during the interwar period, painted his still lifes and colorful village scenes at the 57th Street Artist Colony, Tree Studios, Eagle's Nest Camp, Ox-Bow colony and the Italian Court Building. Edgar Miller, a Renaissance man who mastered the arts of virtually everything he touched—oil and watercolor painting, sculpture, wood carving, textiles, ceramics, mosaics and stained glass—had a hand in creating the Carl Street Studios and other studio buildings on West Burton Place, the Kogen-Miller Studios on North Wells Street and the Fisher Studios in the Gold Coast.

Chicago's rich history of artist colonies continues to this day. As stated already, some of the oldest artist colonies are still in operation. Small communal artist enclaves have been established in the Wicker Park and Logan Square neighborhoods. Ragdale, the Lake Forest home of early Chicago architect Howard Van Doren Shaw (who designed the handsome Fisheries Building at the Columbian Exposition), has been transformed into an artist colony that provides fellowships and temporary residential and work space for writers, composers, visual artists and choreographers. Chicago's artist colonies helped to establish, and continue to enhance, Chicago's role as a world cultural center.

Part I

Chicago in the Nineteenth Century

A Cultural Backwater Striving to Catch Up

1

The Arts in Chicago Before the Fair

On the evening of October 8, 1871, a fire broke out in a barn on the southwest side of Chicago. Within two days, the fire quickly spread and destroyed extensive portions of the city, razed 17,000 buildings and caused an estimated $200 million in damages. The fire left more than 300 people dead and more than 100,000 homeless. It destroyed all the belongings of poor and rich alike, without distinction. That was the bad news. The good news was that the Great Chicago Fire provided Chicagoans with a unique opportunity to remake their city into a better, safer and more habitable place, which they did with gusto within weeks following the conflagration that leveled the city.

One thing the fire did not destroy in any appreciable degree were works of art made by artists in Chicago—because there was very little art made in the city between the time of its incorporation in 1837 and that fateful and fiery October evening. The paintings and prints hanging on the burning mansion walls of Chicago's wealthy citizens did not come from Chicago, they came from New York, Boston, Philadelphia, Paris, London, Munich and the ancient cities of Italy. Prior to the fire, city directories identified only a few dozen residents as artists, but most of these were not engaged with the creation of fine art. They were more likely involved in the day-to-day commercial industries of sign-making, interior millwork and decoration, and rendering graphics for newspapers, periodicals and what little product packaging existed at the time.

GEORGE PETER ALEXANDER HEALY

The only painter of any more than a piddling reputation who lived and worked in Chicago before the fire had already left the city a few years before and was residing in Europe, not to return on a permanent basis for more than two decades. Fortunately, he took many of his paintings with him or otherwise sent them elsewhere in the United States, so they survived the Great Fire and now grace the walls of the White House, the U.S. Capitol and some of the nation's most respected art and history museums. George Peter Alexander Healy was born in Boston in 1813, grew up in near poverty and had little early formal instruction in art. Nevertheless, at age nineteen he persuaded Mrs. Harrison Gray Otis, the reigning queen of Boston society, to sit for a portrait. That portrait at once made his reputation in Boston, and he was soon exhibiting his paintings, mainly portraits, at the Boston Athenaeum.[3]

The following year (1834), Healy sailed for Paris and entered the studio of Baron Antoine-Jean Gros. By 1840, Healy had become a fashionable portrait painter in a city full of artistic talent, and he was given sittings by the French king, Louis Philippe. The king was so pleased with his portrait that he sent young Healy to England to copy some of the paintings in Windsor Castle and later to America to copy Gilbert Stuart's full-length portrait of George Washington and portraits of other prominent Americans.[4]

Healy became a quasi-official painter to Louis Philippe's court until the revolution of 1848 put an end to the French monarchy (for the second time) and Healy's royal patronage. By that time, the collection of Healy's portraits at Versailles, either copies of earlier works or his original paintings, included portraits of such luminaries as Queen Elizabeth I, King George III, William Pitt, Admiral Horatio Nelson, George Washington, John Adams, Thomas Jefferson, Alexander Hamilton, Andrew Jackson, John Quincy Adams and Henry Clay.[5]

Healy remained in Paris following the revolution, but his subject matter was decidedly American, capturing famous statesmen in historic and dramatic scenes. For example, in 1851, Healy painted his monumental picture of Daniel Webster replying to Senator Robert Hayne on the powers of the federal government, regarded by many as one of the most eloquent speeches ever delivered in Congress, which hangs in Faneuil Hall in Boston.

Healy's painting representing Benjamin Franklin exhorting Louis XVI for alliance and resources during the American Revolution won a gold medal at the exhibition of 1855, the highest honor yet awarded to an American artist.[6]

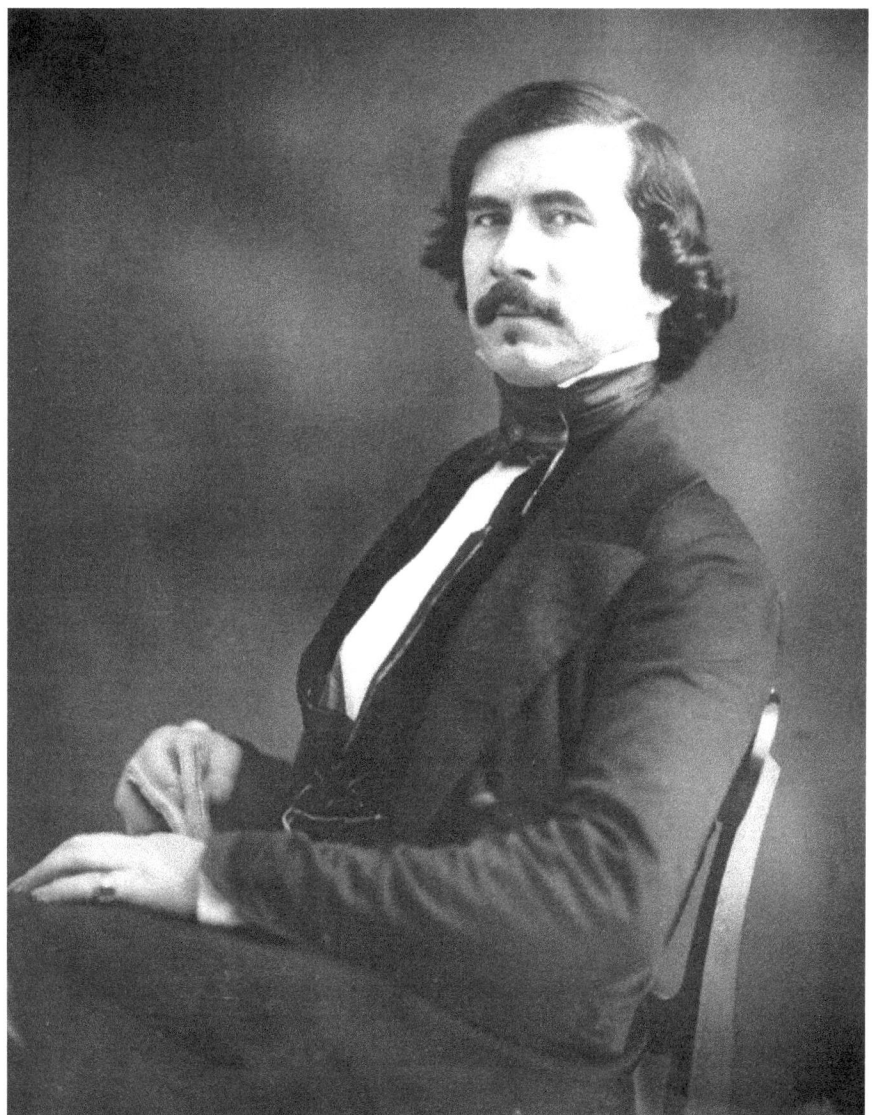

George Peter Alexander Healy. *Southworth & Hawes (1852), Boston Museum of Fine Arts.*

So, George Healy's international reputation was already firmly established when, at about the same time, he made the acquaintance of William Butler Ogden, an early settler to Chicago, builder of railroads, real estate magnate and the city's first mayor—and, of course, the subject of a Healy portrait.

Ogden, the son of a successful lumber merchant, had been trained in the law and served in the New York legislature in 1834. The next year, he was sent to Chicago by a consortium of eastern investors to supervise large parcels of landholdings in the area. Chicagoans found this handsome newcomer from New York urbane, educated, charming and quick-witted. He was also ambitious. Upon the city's incorporation in 1837, the citizenry elected William Ogden as their first mayor. His real estate management work led Ogden to the management of the Illinois and Michigan Canal and, later, to the region's burgeoning system of railroads. He was a founder of the Galena and Chicago Union Railroad, Chicago's first rail line, and the Chicago and Northwestern Railroad. He was appointed the first president of the Union Pacific, which Ogden used to extend the reach of Chicago's rail lines to the West Coast. Ogden's impressive accomplishments were largely fueled by his ability to persuade New York investors and Midwest farmers to part with millions of dollars to fund his real estate and transportation enterprises.

Having made a large fortune early in his career, Ogden then involved himself in every civic and cultural endeavor worth joining in Chicago until he died in 1877. He also amassed a large and valuable art collection, starting in the 1850s. His collection came to include works by prominent East Coast artists such as Frederic Edwin Church, Hiram Powers, John Frederick Kensett, Jasper Cropsey and Asher Durand. The latter's 1852 painting *Landscape After a Shower* was probably the first work by a major American artist that graced a Chicago home. Ogden also collected Old Master paintings from Europe.

When William Ogden sat for his portrait in the Paris studio of George Healy in 1855, the famous expatriate painter could not have anticipated the powers of persuasion that this silver-tongued Chicago pioneer and businessman could unleash in the name of civic pride. Over several meetings with Healy, Ogden made the clarion call for Healy to abandon his successful portrait studio in Paris and take up digs in the young, rough frontier city of the Midwest badly in need of art and culture.

Ogden succeeded in persuading Healy to visit Chicago in the fall of 1855. In short order, several leading Chicagoans commissioned Healy to paint their portraits and those of their families. In his *Reminiscences,* Healy wrote that he intended to stay in the city only a short time, but the pressure Ogden and other prominent Chicagoans exerted on him, and the professional and pecuniary success he almost immediately enjoyed in Chicago, finally led Healy to move his family from Paris and make Chicago his new home.[7]

Healy remained in the Chicago area for fourteen years. For the first two years, Healy and his family lived in a house in the city, but in 1857, he erected a large home in what became the suburb of Elmhurst, reportedly the first house ever built there, and maintained a studio on Lake Street in Chicago.

Healy moved his family back to the city in 1863, to a house located at the intersection of Washington Street and Wabash Avenue, where he remained until 1869.[8]

In 1857, the U.S. Congress commissioned George Healy to paint a series of portraits of American presidents. During the next two or three years,

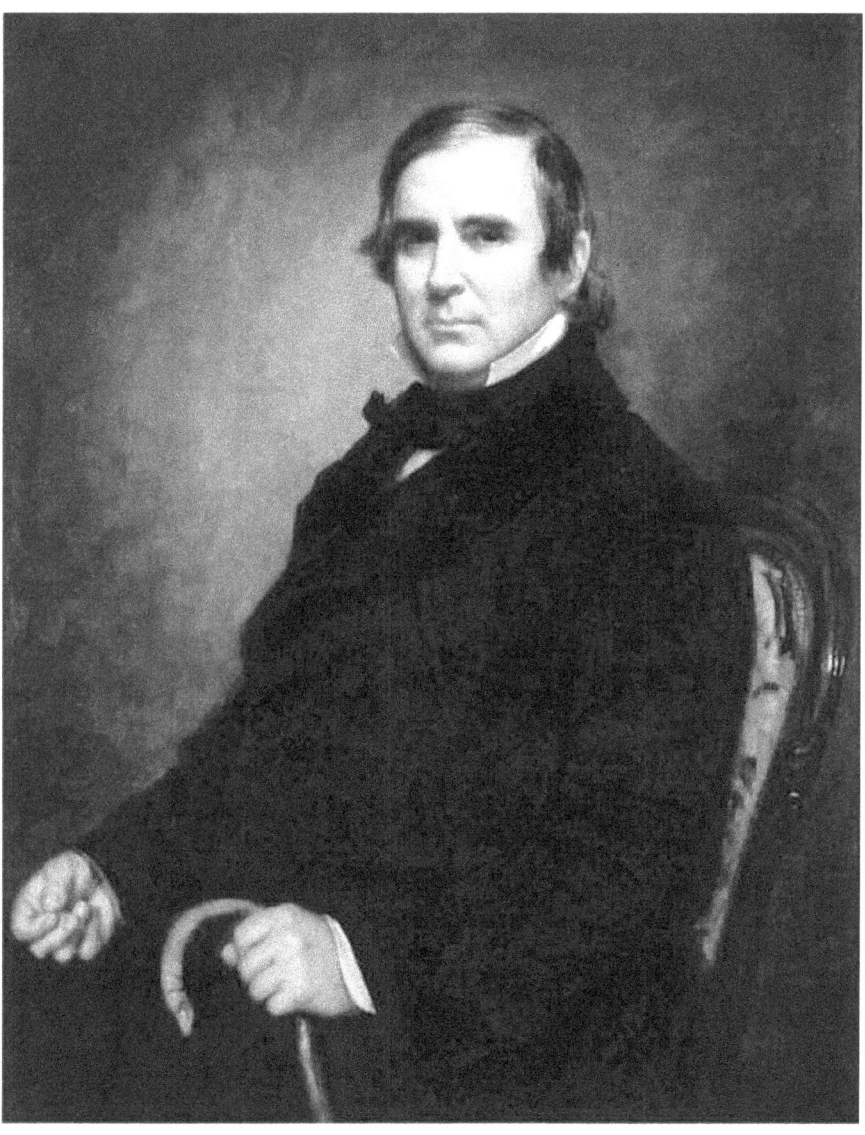

Portrait of William Ogden, painted by George P.A. Healy (1855). *Chicago History Museum.*

Healy traveled extensively throughout the United States and painted his presidential portraits as well as dozens of other commissioned portraits of prominent Americans. The presidential series included paintings of John Quincy Adams, Andrew Jackson, Martin Van Buren, John Tyler, James Polk, Franklin Pierce, Millard Filmore and James Buchanan. In 1860, Healy was commissioned to paint the first of many portraits he would ultimately make of Abraham Lincoln, who had recently been elected president. This was his famous portrait of Lincoln, beardless, painted in Springfield. Although Healy would paint many of the most well-known portraits of Lincoln, his 1860 painting was the only one for which Lincoln would actually sit.

During his fourteen years living and working in Chicago, Healy was to paint six hundred canvases of a veritable who's who of American society, politics and culture. In addition to those Americans identified so far, Healy painted portraits of most members of Chicago's Blue Book, including Mayor John "Long John" Wentworth, businessmen William Blair, E.W. Blatchford, Cyrus McCormick, Martin Ryerson and their wives. He painted Civil War generals U.S. Grant and William Sherman and U.S. politicians Daniel Webster, John Calhoun, Henry Clay, William Seward and Elihu Washburne. His work included portraits of writers Nathaniel Hawthorne and Henry Wadsworth Longfellow. Europeans Franz Liszt, Otto Von Bismarck, a handful of British nobles and the King and Queen of Romania were portrayed in his prodigious opus.

LEONARD WELLS VOLK

George Healy was not just the North Star of Chicago culture during his decade-and-a-half residency in the area; he was virtually the only star. The only other artist of note prior to the Great Fire was Leonard Wells Volk, a sculptor. Born in Wellstown, New York, in 1828, Volk was first a marble cutter, together with his father, in Pittsfield, Massachusetts, where the family had moved. In 1855, Volk married Emily King Barlow, whose maternal cousin was Stephen A. Douglas of Illinois, a powerful leader of the U.S. Senate and participant in the famous Lincoln/Douglas debates of 1858. Douglas was a wealthy landowner in Chicago and a founder of the Illinois Central Railroad. Through Douglas's benevolence, Volk was able to travel in 1855 to Rome to study sculpture.[9]

Returning to the United States two years later, Volk and his family settled in Chicago. During a visit by Abraham Lincoln to the city in the spring of 1860, Volk asked the candidate for the Republic nomination for president to sit for a bust. Volk then made one of two life masks of Lincoln (the other was made by Clark Mills in 1865). Lincoln was quite pleased with the final bust, declaring it to be "the animal himself." The life mask (and casts of Lincoln's hands Volk made in the summer of 1860) gave Volk a creative advantage—he used the life mask, hand casts and finished bust to create later versions of Lincoln after his death, including a life-sized statute.

During his years in Chicago, Volk executed several statues or busts of famous Chicagoans and others. For example, he made a life-sized statue of his wife's cousin, Senator Douglas, which was ultimately placed on a tall pedestal near Thirty-Fifth Street over Douglas's tomb. Volk created statutes of Douglas and Lincoln for the Illinois State Capitol in Springfield, Illinois, and a statue of General James Shield for the U.S. Capitol.[10] Likenesses of local dignitaries Elihu Washburne, David Davis and Zachariah Chandler also took form under Volk's chisel.[11]

Although they had opened and operated successful studios in Chicago, both George Healy and Leonard Volk decried the paucity of art and culture in their newly adopted city. Healy said he intended to make "an art center" in Chicago, but, apart from the prodigious outpourings of portraits by his own hand, there is little evidence that he or the city succeeded in attracting other painters of any consequence. Before 1860, there were no art schools, exhibition halls or art dealers. Wealthy Chicagoans purchased (or brought with them when they settled in the city) paintings, prints and sculptural works of East Coast and European artists. Therefore, when in 1858 Leonard Volk encouraged the city fathers to consider staging a major public art exhibition in Chicago, it was generally acknowledged that the art to be displayed would be loans of works of East Coast and European artists from the private collections of wealthy citizens.

THE ART EXHIBITION OF 1859

Following a meeting at the Chicago Historical Society on March 22, 1859, the organizing committee issued a notice of a plan for an art exhibition "to consist of such select and approved paintings and sculptures as are in the possession of our citizens, in order to afford to the public, and especially to all persons interested in the Fine Arts, an opportunity to gratify and improve their taste in art matters."[12] A board of directors was appointed, and Volk was selected as curator with primary responsibility for exercising control over the standards of art established by the directors and Volk. On April 12, newspaper advertisements seeking contributions of art appeared and formal invitations were sent to persons "whose wealth and good taste have put them in the possession of choice pieces of statuary or well-conceived and well executed paintings."

Landscape architect Frederick Law Olmsted addressed certain reservations of some of Chicago's elite that levels of good taste among the general citizenry might be too lacking for a high-quality exhibition: "Having all migrated to the West while young and lived for a while on the very frontier…you might expect them to be very different from what they are. In fact, the[ir] children are clever and well-bred. They are rather sensitive about the West and Chicago, lest anyone should think that people are not likely to be as informed and cultivated as anywhere."[13] Editor and critic James Spencer Dickerson pointed out that the elite of Chicago had always been formed of people of education and culture, even in its earliest days. "Among the earliest settlors of Chicago, even in the 1830s, were people of refinement." Many early settlers, such as William Ogden, Walter Newberry, Eliphalet Blatchford and John Wentworth, came from wealthy cultured families in the East and received good liberal educations, before migrating to the new city on the prairie. Indeed, even the first permanent white settler, fur trader John Kinzie, brought his violin when he and his small family came to Chicago in 1803.

Paint and chemical manufacturer Alexander White became the biggest contributor of art to the exhibition. White moved to Chicago in 1837 and, after making a fortune from his chemical business and real estate investments, traveled the East Coast and Europe, amassing an impressive collection of art. He loaned as much as 10 percent of the art displayed at the exhibition, including the well-known, monumental painting *Washington Crossing the Delaware* by Emanuel Leutze, now one of the most memorable paintings in the collection of the Metropolitan Museum of Art in New York. (Fortunately, White sold his formidable art collection, including the Leutze painting, in New York before the Great Fire.)

All told, 369 works of art (about 320 oil paintings, 20 sculptures and 20 works of crayon or watercolors) were loaned by over 70 Chicagoans.[14] The exhibition opened at Burch's Building on the corner of Wabash and Lake on May 9, 1859, and was expected to run for a month. It was attended by over 12,000 visitors, out of a city population of about 110,000, and was so successful the organizers decided to extend the exhibition. At least three editions of the exhibition catalogue were printed to accommodate a larger-than-expected visitorship. The 1859 Art Exhibition was deemed such a success and so important to the cultural life of Chicago that art patrons held four additional exhibitions (1860, 1863, 1865 and 1866). Alas, most of the artworks displayed at these five exhibitions were later destroyed as the Great Fire engulfed the city during those two days in October 1871.

The Chicago press summarized the interest and pride that the public exhibited in the city's first foray into the public art scene. The *Chicago Tribune* announced that the 1859 Art Exhibition negated the unfair assumption that the city was "entirely devoid of all taste and culture in art."[15] The *Daily Chicago Times* described the exhibition "as an object of wonder and gratification" in a city that "twenty-five years ago was only an Indian trading post."[16] And yet, such pride merely exalted the taste and financial wherewithal of seventy out of more than one hundred thousand citizens who had the good fortune to own meritorious works of art created largely by eastern and European artists. Some thought it was now high time that Chicago started generating its own art, as well as exhibiting the works of artists from other cities.[17]

FROM THE CHICAGO ACADEMY OF DESIGN TO THE ART INSTITUTE OF CHICAGO

In November 1866, a group of artists met in Chicago to discuss the formation of an art school and gallery space to exhibit art and present musical, literary and dramatic events. Among this group were Walter Shirlaw (destined to leave Chicago and become a noteworthy painter in the East), Sheldon Woodman and Charles Peck, the latter two of whom remained relatively unknown. Shortly afterward, this group created the Chicago Academy of Design. Six months later, on May 3, 1867, the academy opened its first exhibition and offered an entertainment event in the Crosby Opera House. The program for this inaugural (and sadly, only) event included the performances of the *William Tell Overture* by Rossini and some chorus portions of Wagner's *Tannhauser*.[18]

Although the entertainment event was quite successful, the art exhibition met with a lukewarm reception by the public, and conflicts among the artist members of the academy seemingly resulted in an early death of the organization.

The carcass of the Chicago Academy of Design was exhumed in late 1867 by a group of the principle artists of the city, including Healy, Volk, Shirlaw and James Farrington Gookins, with Volk being selected as president of the reorganized institution, a position he held until 1878.[19] "Life," "antique" and "rudimentary" drawing classes were offered in a room at the Crosby Opera House beginning in January 1868. The following year, the organization was incorporated as a nonprofit, so as to avoid taxes on the acquisition of artworks. After the Crosby Opera House declined to continue leasing space to the academy, it leased a new marble-faced building on Adams Street between State and Dearborn. This five-story structure featured two exhibition galleries, a hall and lecture room, several schoolrooms and sixteen commodious art studios.[20] The new Academy of Design Building opened to the public on March 22, 1870, and it burned to the ground a year and a half later, a victim of the Great Chicago Fire. But the academy, as an institution, survived.

Three years after the fire, classes resumed in leased spaces in a new, grand, three-story structure built at the southwest corner of Michigan Avenue and Van Buren Street. The building also housed artist studios, including that of the academy's president, Leonard Volk. It was after the fire that the Academy of Design began attracting instructors and administrators of significant talent. Harvard-educated engineer William Richardson French moved to Chicago in 1867 as a civil engineer. Soon after, French was lecturing and writing articles on artistic matters.

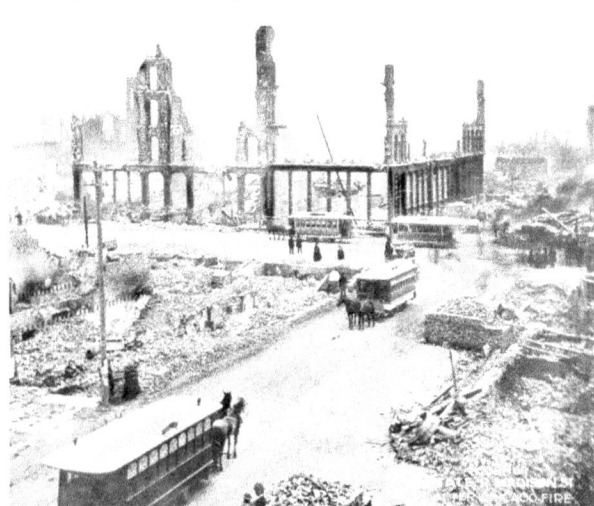

State and Madison after the Great Chicago Fire. *L.J. Labeau (October 1871).*

In 1878, he became secretary of the Chicago Academy of Design. The following year, the academy was once again reorganized as the Chicago Academy of Fine Arts, with its aims as "the maintenance of schools of art and design, the formation and exhibition of collections of objects of art and the cultivation and extension of the arts of design by appropriate means."[21]

The academy changed its name in 1882 to the Art Institute of Chicago, and William French became its first director in 1885 and remained in that post until his death almost thirty years later. In the 1880s, wealthy Chicago businessmen and art patrons joined the Board of Trustees of the Art Institute, including banker Charles Hutchinson, who became the institute's president, and lumber/steel magnate Martin Ryerson, who became a longtime benefactor. In 1885, the trustees ordered the erection of a new fireproof building designed by Burnham and Root located at the corner of Michigan Avenue and Van Buren Street. The new building, designed to incorporate a Richardsonian architectural style then prevalent in the Chicago Loop, featured gallery spaces, administrative offices and twelve schoolrooms.

By the time of the Columbian Exposition of 1893, the School of the Art Institute had become one of the foremost art schools in the United States, and its faculty boasted some of the most accomplished instructors in the country. In the 1880s, the school appointed painters John Vanderpoel and Oliver Dennett Grover, both of whom had attended the Chicago Academy of Design and studied in Europe under leading painters Gustav Boulanger, Jules Lefebvre and Jean-Paul Laurens. Sculptor Lorado Taft, who had studied at the École des Beaux-Arts in Paris, founded the school's sculpture department in 1886. In that same year, enrollment was 360 students, some of whom would become prominent practitioners of the arts in cities throughout the United States and Europe. By the time of the 1893 fair, enrollment would grow to about one thousand. Within thirty years, the museum arm of the Art Institute was to become a repository of the cream of the most formidable art collections amassed by wealthy Chicago collectors.[22] In time, only the Metropolitan Museum of Art in New York could claim a more impressive collection of art in America.

THE 1890s GAVE BIRTH TO OTHER
ENDURING INSTITUTIONS

Other enduring educational and cultural institutions had their genesis in Chicago in the early 1890s. Anticipating the need for orchestral resources for the World's Columbian Exposition, a group of Chicago's leading businessmen (with illustrious names such as Pullman, Armour, Field, Ryerson, McCormick and Potter) created the Chicago Orchestral Association in 1891 and offered the baton to Theodore Thomas of New York, then the foremost conductor in the United States.[23] Thomas conducted his first concert in Chicago in 1869, leading his small New York–based Central Park Garden Orchestra.[24]

The Orchestral Association formed the Chicago Symphony Orchestra, destined in a short time to become one of the most distinguished orchestras in the world. Due to the paucity of local talent in Chicago, Thomas recruited 60 of 84 musicians who constituted the early Chicago Symphony from East Coast cities.[25] Thomas would later be appointed music director of the Columbian Exposition Orchestra, a body of 120 musicians and 300 singers that gave numerous symphonic performances of the standard repertoire during the fair.[26]

By the time the Chicago Symphony Orchestra came into existence, Chicago could already boast what was the country's best and grandest music venue. In 1886, Chicago merchant Ferdinand Peck, whose parents arrived in Chicago in 1831, hired the newborn architectural firm of Adler & Sullivan to design a fabulous music hall and theater to be housed in the most imposing structure yet built in the city. (Indeed, after construction was completed in 1889, the Auditorium Building would for a time hold the record as the tallest building in the United States.) This complex would also incorporate a first-class hotel and a large block of offices that, Peck and his fellow investors intended, would help defray the costs of theatrical and musical performances. The Auditorium Building's theater contained 4,300 seats and, through Dankmar Adler's engineering genius, featured acoustics that were and still are unmatched anywhere in the world. Thus, by the time the Chicago Symphony Orchestra began performing at the Auditorium, Chicago concertgoers could not hope for a better musical experience.

At about the same time and six miles away, in Chicago's newly absorbed Hyde Park neighborhood, a young academic theologian from Yale was busy using Rockefeller millions to collect what, within a decade, would become the most accomplished academic faculty in the country. In 1891, William

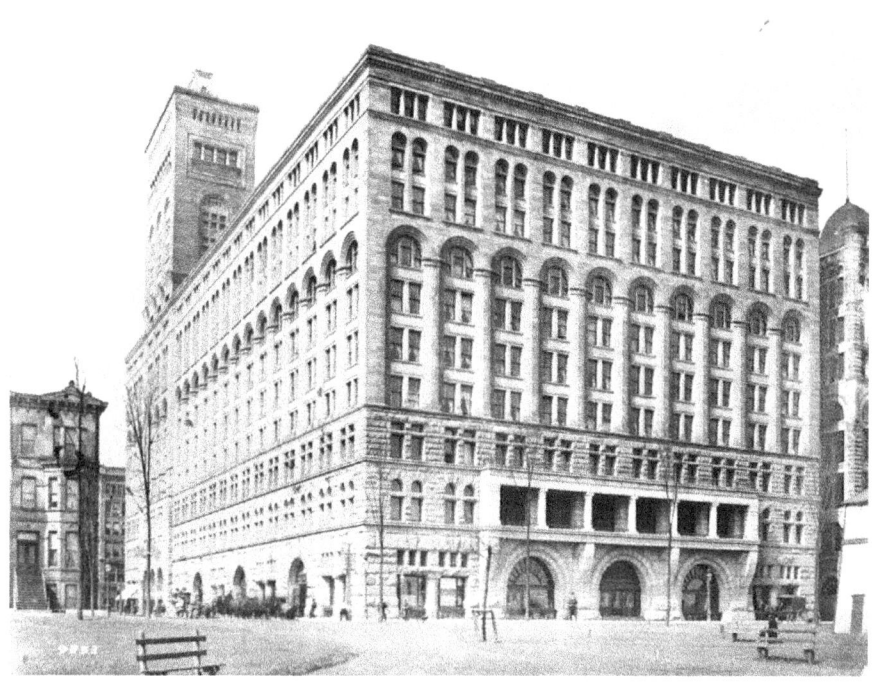

Auditorium Building, east and south façades. *J.W. Taylor (1890), Library of Congress, Historic Buildings Survey, HABS Ill, 16-CHIG, 39-75, Photo No. 9853.*

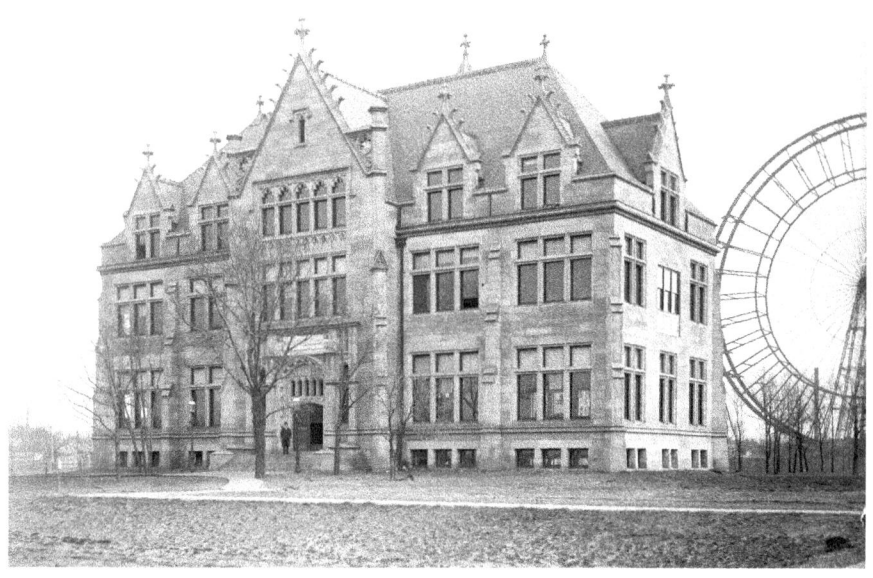

University of Chicago Walker Museum and Ferris wheel. *Photographer unknown, (1893), University of Chicago Photographic Archive, Special Collections Research Center, apf6-00075.*

Rainey Harper, a Baptist biblical scholar, was appointed as the first president of the University of Chicago, incorporated the previous year by Baptist interests. The country's richest Baptist, and citizen for that matter, was John D. Rockefeller, oil magnate and notorious monopolist. Rockefeller initially pledged a matching donation of $600,000 (more than $25 million in today's money) to found a major university on land donated by Chicago's leading merchant, Marshall Field. Harper's incessant cajoling over the next decade would ultimately lead Rockefeller, and to a much lesser extent several wealthy Chicago businessmen, to part with scores of millions of dollars that Rainey used primarily to attract the most prestigious academics in the United States.

By 1900, Rainey's herculean toil and Rockefeller's cash built a world-class institution whose professors and students over the next 120 years would receive more Nobel Prizes than any other institution in the world. The university's imposing gray Gothic towers were being built in 1892–93 on land adjacent to the site of the World's Columbian Exposition, whose Venetian-like lagoons and canals, gleaming white buildings of the spectacular "White City" and monumental Ferris wheel on the Midway were simultaneously being constructed a few blocks away.

The World's Columbian Exposition Puts Chicago on the Cultural Map

N o one could legitimately question that Chicago had made great strides in its educational and cultural development in the period between the Great Fire and the World's Columbian Exposition. Attracted to the city by the architectural void caused by the fire, the nation's foremost architects relocated to Chicago and designed the world's first skyscrapers, utilizing several groundbreaking engineering innovations. The city's downtown in 1893 must have offered visitors a sense of what a few years later Frank Baum had in mind when he wrote of the Emerald City in his *The Wizard of Oz.*[27] Besides the Chicago Public Library, the city could claim two soon-to-be world-class private libraries: the Newberry Library, devoted to the humanities, and the John Crerar Library (opened to the public a year after the Fair), devoted to the sciences.

But at the time the World's Fair National Commission was determining the site for a major exposition to mark the 400th anniversary of Christopher Columbus's maiden voyage to the New World, the city still suffered from a prevailing belief, particularly held by non-Chicagoans, that it remained a cultural backwater. This belief acted as an impediment, for a while at least, to Chicago being selected as the fair's host city.

Much fear was expressed during the first preparations for the Exposition that the department of Fine Arts would be the weakest of all. It was said that the location of the Exposition at Chicago was immensely unfavorable to the prospects for a fine display in this line. It was said that Europe would not contribute its art collections, or any considerable portion of them, for the reason that Chicago was generally believed abroad to be a city far removed from the center of education and culture in the United States.[28]

To the extent that this concern had any merit at the time, what Chicago may have lacked in culture and refinement relative to its sister cities in the East was far outbalanced and overcome by the city's civic pride, energy and, most important, money.

CHICAGO GETS ITS FAIR

As for an appropriate situs, the National Commission's biggest concern, Chicago boosters pointed to a three-mile tract of beautiful, largely unoccupied and unimproved land on the shores of Lake Michigan in the city's recently annexed South Side. Chicago also claimed to have the country's best architects, who could be prevailed upon to help design and build the fairgrounds. (Ironically, most of the Fair's buildings were actually designed by architects from other cities, with a few quite notable exceptions.) But when Chicago's elite pledged to raise $10 million (almost $265 million in today's dollars) for the exposition and to take heroic measures to erect an architectural and landscape fantasy within a few short years, they walked away with the prize.[29]

Chicagoans fully lived up to their promises. Through titanic efforts and the devotion of much of the city's treasure, both material and human, the city fathers made the World's Columbian Exposition of 1893 one of the most spectacular civic, educational, technological and cultural milestones of world history. This seemingly hyperbolic sentiment echoes the straightforward assessment of many in 1893 that "after the end of the Exposition all the world may be divided into two great classes—those who have attended the Fair and those who have not."[30] And what a fantastic spectacle the former class, which numbered more than twenty-seven million, must have witnessed!

The Exposition covered about seven hundred acres and featured more than two hundred buildings, most designed in the neoclassical idiom with their plaster exteriors painted white. All but a handful of buildings were intentionally designed to be temporary and were constructed using wood and iron framing with exteriors deceptively covered with an inexpensive lath

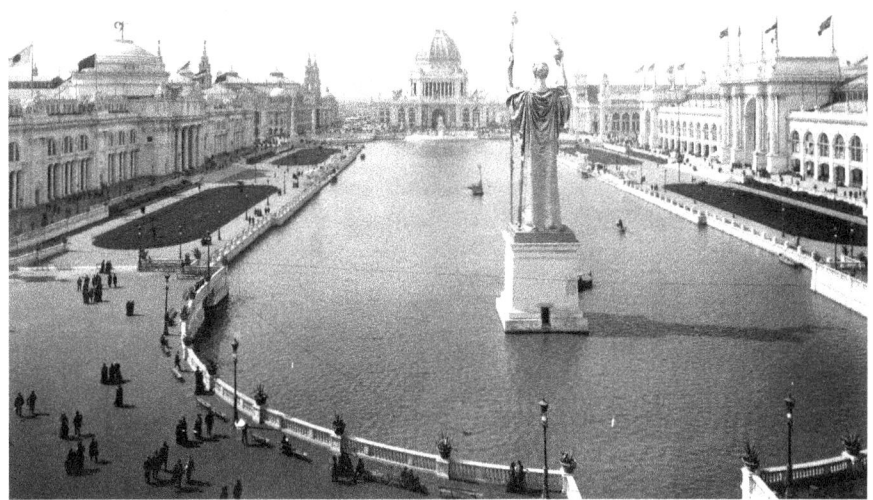

World's Columbian Exposition, Grand Basin and Court of Honor. *C.D. Arnold (1893), Chicago Public Library, Special Collections, WCE, CDA, Vol. 2, Plate 5.*

and plaster combination painted white to emulate marble and stone. Daniel Burnham, whose firm was appointed to oversee the design and construction of the Fair, believed that the Beaux-Arts style would emphatically inform America and the world that Chicago was indeed refined and heir to the cultural traditions of Europe. The Grand Court (see accompanying image) and the gleaming, white neoclassical palaces that lined the Venetian-style lagoons and canals, led *Harper's Magazine* to exclaim, "The first impression which takes possession of the beholder of the White City, for if he is at all susceptible to these emotions which are excited by the creation of art, he will be so overcome with astonishment and admiration as to make it a difficult effort for him to tear himself away from the contemplation of the exterior of the wonderful assemblage of palaces to enter one of them."[31]

In striking contrast, Chicago architect Louis Sullivan, of the alliterative "form follows function" fame, designed his Transportation Building in a more sleek, geometric modernist style for which he had by then become associated. Sullivan distained his fellow architects' aping of European architectural styles and ensured his massive Transportation Building struck a self-consciously dissonant cord, both in style and color. Years later, in his autobiography, Sullivan famously complained that the Fair's emphasis on the Beaux-Arts style to apply a sheen of high culture to the event had actually held back American architectural thought by forty years. American cities' and towns' adoption of Burnham's City Beautiful movement in the 1890s through the 1910s tends to prove Sullivan right. But what the Beaux-Arts style lacked of America's innovative and progressive spirit at the Fair, it made up for in the breathtaking drama of the sweeping views and vistas visitors encountered at the Exhibition, especially at night.

A vast majority of the Fair's twenty-seven million visitors had never seen light emanating from an electric light bulb prior to their arrival at the Exposition in the spring or summer of 1893. The Westinghouse Company outfoxed Thomas Edison, winning the contract to wire the Exposition with alternating current, ultimately at a financial loss. Every night, the Exposition's buildings, terraces and walkways were lit by 160,000 light bulbs to the sheer astonishment of fairgoers, who theretofore had lived their lives

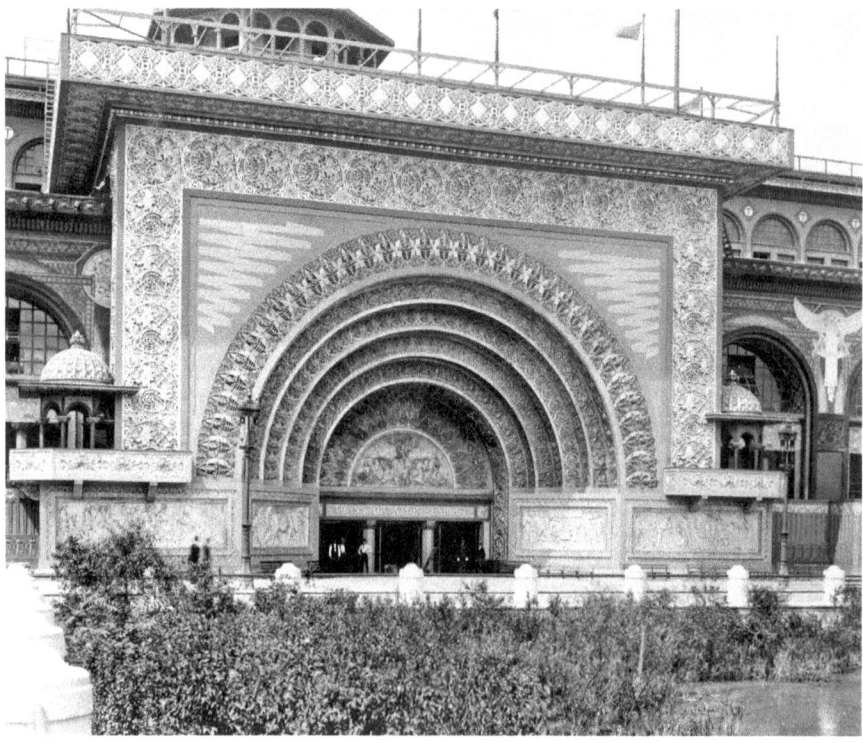

World's Columbian Exposition, Transportation Building, designed by Louis Sullivan. *C.D. Arnold (1893), Chicago Public Library, Special Collections, WCE, CDA, Vol. 2, Plate 21.*

under gas lamps or candles. Fairgoers were awed by large searchlights that lit up the skies over the White City. Thousands of light bulbs, together with the use of moving color filters, rendered magical the enormous dancing electric fountains that dotted the fairground's canals and lagoons.

The light bulb was not the only electrical contrivance these visitors encountered at the Fair. Generally accessible electricity, especially for household use, was several years in the future for most Americans. Although Edison had invented the incandescent light bulb in 1879 and introduced the light bulb and his massive electric dynamo at the Paris Electrical Exposition of 1881, there still existed no practical infrastructure to deliver electric current to homes and businesses in most places in 1893. Electric plants were very expensive and operated in small local areas at this time, which were limited for the most part to portions of New York City. Therefore, visitors to the Fair were fascinated and astonished when they encountered for the first time the workings of Edison's phonograph, Alexander Graham Bell's telephone, an early form of motion pictures and even a rudimentary dishwasher.

The intrigue of most fairgoers continued in the halls containing foreign and anthropological exhibits. Americans, who constituted the vast majority of visitors to the Columbian Exposition, were an isolated population. By and large, they rarely visited distant cities within their own country, and a miniscule portion of the American population who had been born in the United States had ever traveled overseas. For most, their glimpse into the cultures and lifestyles of exotic foreign peoples at the Exhibition would be their first, and very possibly their last.

The 1890s ushered in an epoch, still going strong, of mass production and consumerism in the United States. Apart from the electric devices already mentioned, some enduring consumer products that most fairgoers would first encounter at the 1893 Fair and later purchase for the rest of their lives included Wrigley's chewing gum, Cracker Jack, Cream of Wheat, Shredded Wheat, Aunt Jemima pancake mix, Pabst Beer (which, some dubiously claim, won a blue ribbon at the Fair), hamburgers and carbonated soda. The concession stands and vendors on the Midway encouraged rampant consumption by fairgoers and netted millions of dollars. In short, the Columbian Exposition was a sort of dry run for the emerging mass-marketing consumerism that prevailed in the United States throughout the twentieth and twenty-first centuries. First and foremost, however, the World's Columbian Exposition positioned itself as a major cultural event, and so it was.

ART FROM EVERYWHERE BUT CHICAGO

One of the handful of buildings at the 1893 World's Fair that was not intended to be temporary was the Palace of Fine Arts, designed by Charles Atwood. As the exhibition space for valuable works of art loaned by artists and cultural institutions from cities throughout the United States, fourteen countries of Europe, and Japan, Brazil, Costa Rica and Mexico, the structure had to be well-built and fireproof. It was constructed with a brick substructure under its lath and plaster façade, on a brick basement that rose to a height of nine feet. Its outer decorative motif was classical Greek and featured a series of imposing Ionic columns on each of its façades with several statuary works reflective of ancient Greece. Atwood designed the Palace of Fine Arts to fit squarely within Daniel Burnham's panoply of neoclassical behemoth palaces surrounded by picturesque lagoons and canals.

The structure of the Palace of Fine Arts formed an oblong 500 feet in length and 320 feet in width, covering an area of nearly five acres.[32] At the center of the building was a rotunda capped by a dome 60 feet in

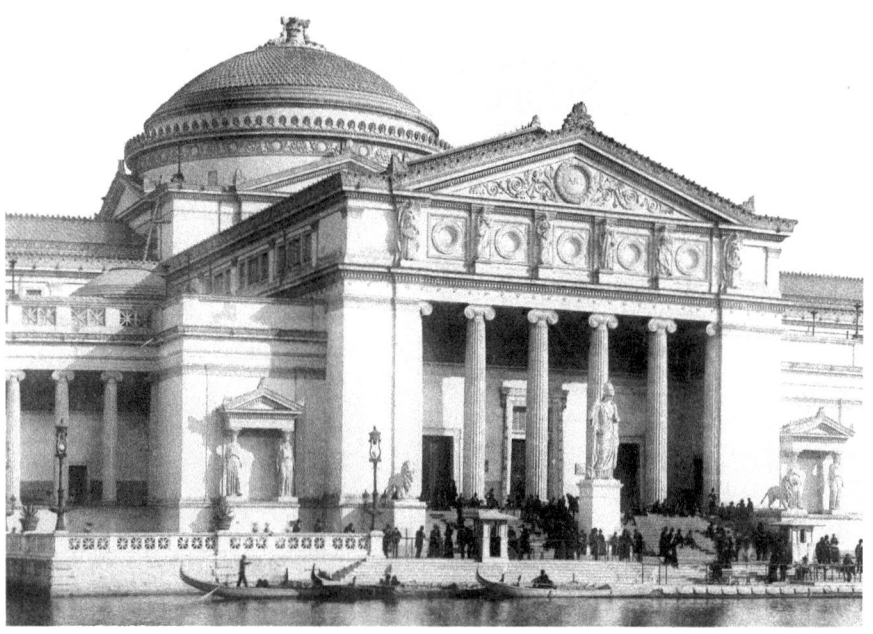

World's Columbian Exposition, Palace of Fine Arts, south porch facing North Pond. *C.D. Arnold (1893) University of Chicago Photo Archive, Special Collections Research Center, apf3-00069.*

diameter that rose to a height of 125 feet.[33] The general plan of the building constituted a longitudinal east/west court, a latitudinal north/south court and a continuous series of compartmented exhibition spaces accessible from the longitudinal court, with east and west pavilions emanating at the northeast and northwest corners of the building.

The structure had a generally flat roof about fifty feet high (excepting the central dome) and skylights to illuminate the artwork below. Some of the gallery spaces that ran along the main courts were lofted, providing for open exhibition compartments on a second floor. Sizable sculptural works were typically placed within the large open spaces in the longitudinal and latitudinal axes of the central courts. Framed artworks were generally assigned to exhibition compartments according to their national origin.

The United States was assigned fifteen exhibition compartments, France sixteen compartments, Great Britain and Germany seven compartments each and the other fifteen or so countries that loaned artworks were assigned between one and six compartments each.[34] A confusing anomaly arose because, if a collection of paintings came from an institution or art collector located within the United States and included works of foreign artists, the foreign works were displayed within the compartments assigned to the United States. Thus, the catalogue of American artworks on exhibit at the Columbian Exposition included a fair number of works created by European-based artists.

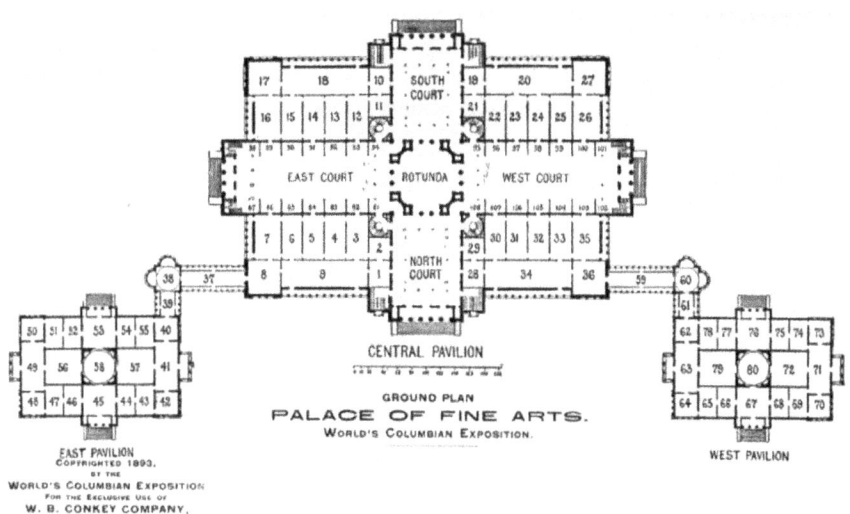

World's Columbian Exposition, Palace of Fine Arts Floor Plan. *W.B. Conkey Co. (1893).*

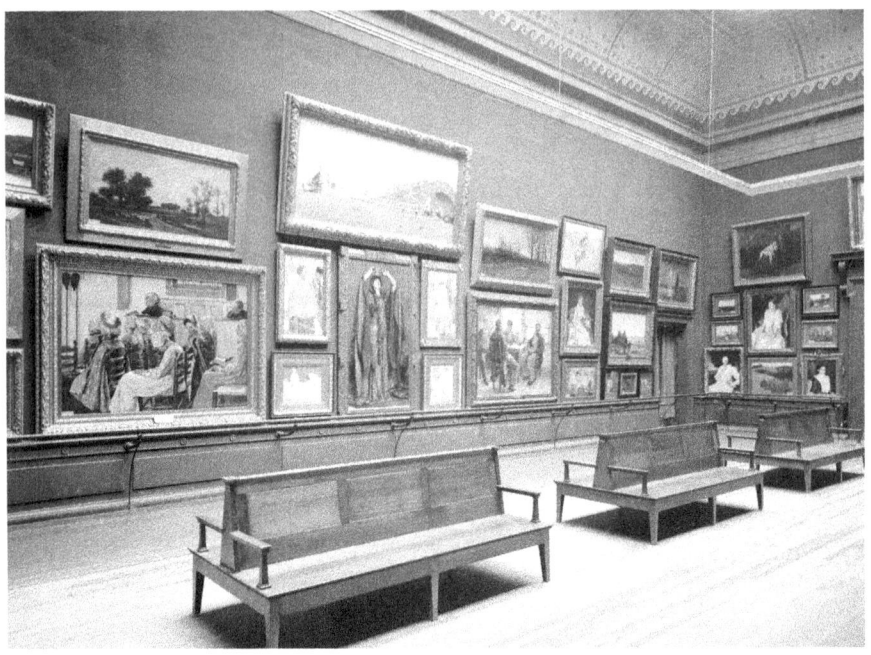

World's Columbian Exposition, Palace of Fine Arts, Gallery 3. *C.D. Arnold (1893), Chicago Public Library, Special Collections, WCE, CDA 8, Plate 61.*

According to the Official Catalogue of artworks, about 8,100 works of art were displayed in the Palace of Fine Arts alone,[35] while unknown numbers of artworks were displayed in other venues such as the Administration and Women's Buildings and the individual state and national buildings. In addition, the Fair organizers invited several artists from around the country to paint decorative murals and to sculpt statuary in or near most of the primary buildings. Few, if any, visitors to the Exposition had ever encountered art on this scale before.[36] Of the 8,100 works exhibited, almost 2,500 were on display in the American galleries.[37]

Fairgoers were treated to such American artistic achievements as Thomas Eakins's *Gross Clinic*, John Singer Sargent's *Portrait of Ellen Terry as Lady Macbeth*, Winslow Homer's *Eight Bells*, Eastman Johnson's *The Cranberry Harvest*, Walter Shirlaw's *Toning the Bell* and other works now in the pantheon of American art.

Some of the most august artists in American history displayed their art at the Columbian Exposition, including, in addition to the greats identified above, sculptors Paul Bartlett and William Partridge and painters Cecilia Beaux, Frank Benson, Edwin Blashfield, William Merritt Chase, Kenyon

Cox, Charles Curran, T.W. Dewing, Frank Duveneck, Frank Fowler, Childe Hassam, George Innes, John LaFarge, Gari Melchers, Elizabeth Nourse, Abbott Thayer, Louis Comfort Tiffany, Elihu Vedder and James McNeill Whistler. These artists were almost all based in cities on the East Coast or in Europe and were represented by multiple works in the Palace of Fine Arts.

The presence of works by Chicago artists at the Fair was a mixed bag, but mainly disappointing. Fifty-eight artists loaned 148 sculptural works on display in the American galleries of the Palace of Fine Arts.[38] Eleven of those sculptors (about 19 percent) listed Chicago as their home, not a bad showing statistically. By comparison, New York–based sculptors sent 16 works. European-based sculptors exhibited in the American section had 11 works. But when it came to oil paintings, by far the dominant art medium at the Palace of Fine Arts, the contribution by Chicago artists was paltry by any measure.[39]

About 447 artists contributed slightly over 1,000 oil paintings in the American galleries. Only 20 (4.5 percent) of those artists resided in the Chicago area. By contrast, 147 artists (33 percent) contributing oil paintings in the American galleries came from New York. If one counted the number of actual oil paintings contributed by Chicago artists relative to the overall

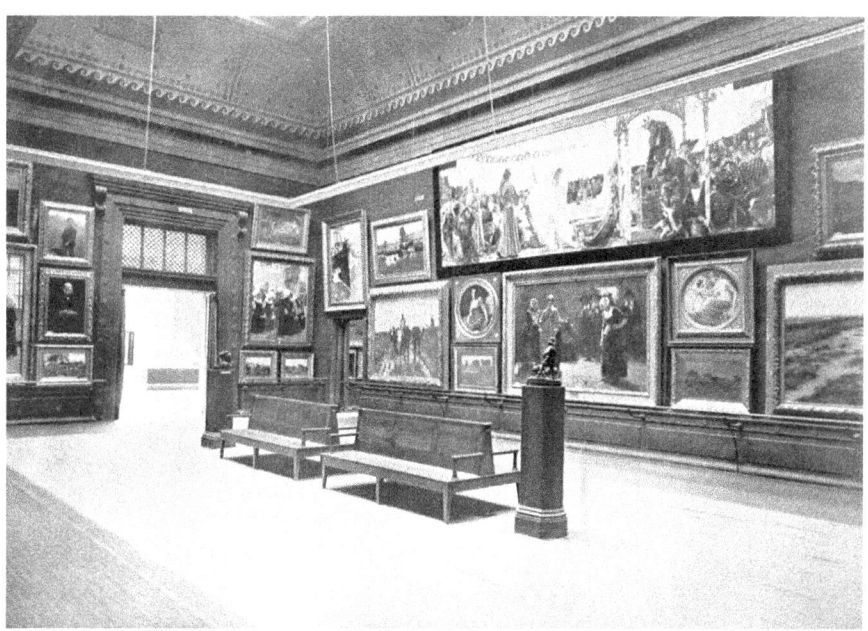

World's Columbian Exposition, Palace of Fine Arts, Gallery 7. *C.D. Arnold (1893), Chicago Public Library, Special Collections, WCE, CDA 8, Plate 87.*

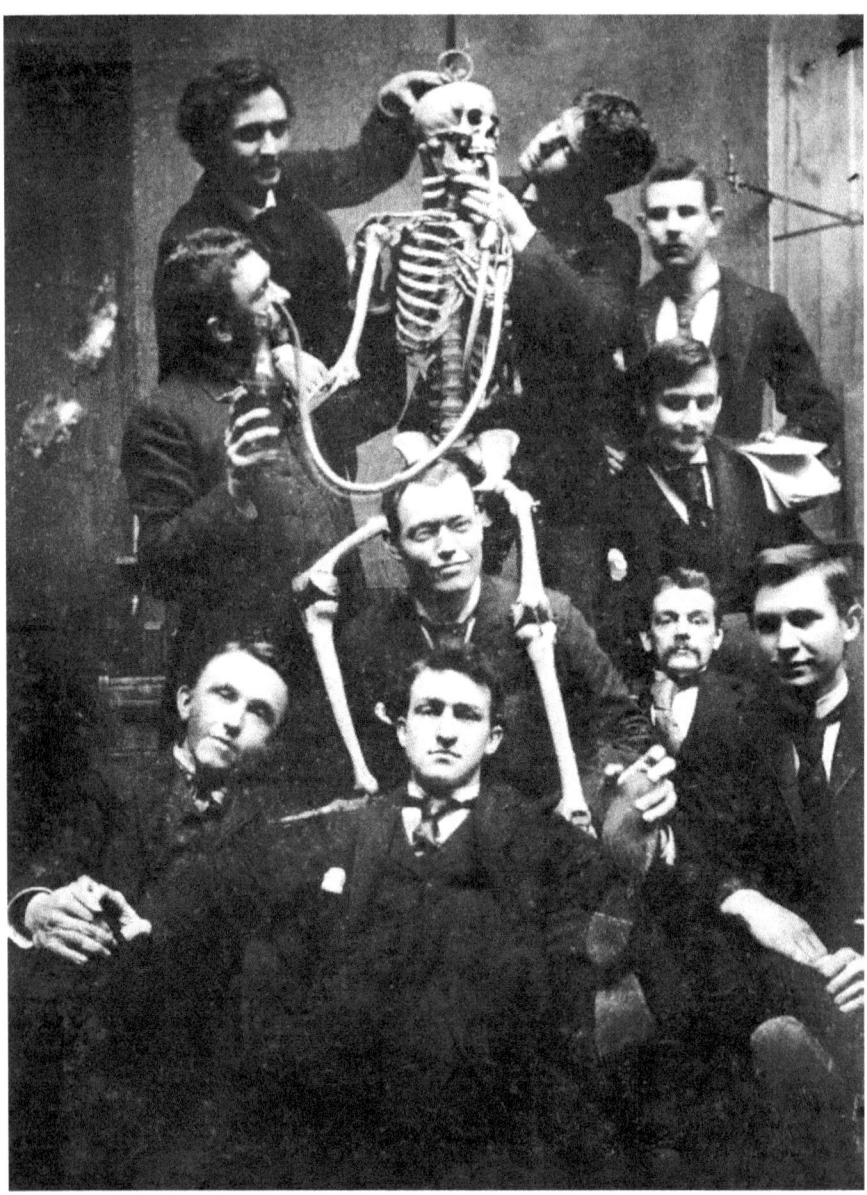

John Vanderpoel with his figure drawing class. Vanderpoel appears at the right of the skeleton's left knee, with mustache. *Photographer unknown (circa 1895). Burnham & Ryerson Archives, The Art Institute of Chicago.*

total exhibited in the American galleries, the result is even more dismal—27 paintings out of 1,006, which constituted about 2.7 percent of all works exhibited. As would be expected, New York–based artists and American expatriates residing in European cities heavily dominated the oil painting medium in the American galleries. The combined contributions of only two East Coast oil painters, Winslow Homer and George Innes, admittedly considered among the leading lights of American art then and now, exceeded by two the total contributions of all Chicago oil painters, most of whom were only allowed a single entry.

One exception was John Henry Vanderpoel, who contributed five oil paintings, almost 20 percent of the total Chicago entries. Born in the Netherlands in 1857, Vanderpoel immigrated to the United States with his family in 1869 and settled in Chicago, where he studied at the Academy of Design. Between 1886 and 1888, he traveled to Europe and studied at the Académie Julian in Paris with Boulanger and Lefebvre. Prior to his sojourn to Paris and after he returned, Vanderpoel taught at the Art Institute, becoming one of that institution's most respected instructors. Among his students were Frederick Carl Frieseke, Joseph C. Leyendecker and Georgia O'Keeffe, who would characterize Vanderpoel in her autobiography as "one of the few real teachers I have known." His book *The Human Figure*, published in 1907, became and remained a standard text at art schools everywhere through much of the twentieth century. He was so beloved as an instructor by generations of students that two years after Vanderpoel's death in 1911, many of his former pupils and colleagues established the Vanderpoel Memorial Art Collection, a cultural gem now housed in a gallery in the Beverly neighborhood on the far south side of Chicago. That the collection now numbers over five hundred pieces by many prominent artists is a testament to the esteem that he enjoyed.

OLIVER DENNETT GROVER

Based on contemporary publications, few took much notice of the contributions of Chicago artists. William Walton, in his *World's Columbian Exposition Official Illustrated Publication, Art and Architecture*, devoted twenty-five pages to American art displayed at the Palace of Fine Arts and mentioned dozens of artists and their works, but not a single reference is made to a Chicago artist. Another official publication, the voluminous *World's Columbian*

Exposition (Monarch Book Company, Philadelphia, 1893), also largely ignored works by Chicago artists, with a notable exception: Oliver Dennett Grover's *Thy Will Be Done*.[40] This oil painting stood out among Chicago artworks and, indeed, was one of the star attractions in the Palace of Fine Arts by reason that it had just won the first Yerkes Prize in a major art competition, conducted less than a year before by the Chicago Society of Artists.

Utilities and transportation magnate Charles Yerkes, a man who was reviled far and wide for his shady business dealings, offered $500 (about $14,000 in today's dollars) to be awarded as prizes for the first- and second-best works of art displayed at the society's fourth annual exhibition. The night after the exhibition's opening on April 25, 1892, a fire destroyed the entire inventory of artworks then on display. Undaunted, the society rescheduled the exhibition for May 30, 1892. Some sixty-nine artists entered 118 works in the exhibition. The three-man jury comprised Lewis Henry Meakin, a noted art professor from Cincinnati; Charles Kurtz, who had been appointed as second in charge of the impending fine arts exhibition at the Columbian Exposition; and the venerable George Peter Alexander Healy, who had returned to Chicago earlier that year after living twenty-three years abroad.

The jury unanimously conferred the first Yerkes Prize on the thirty-two-year-old Oliver Dennett Grover for his life-sized portrait of a young woman. One need not know the painting's suggestive title, *Thy Will Be Done*, to understand that the woman had just received notice of a personal tragedy. She looks forlornly upward, but with courageous resolve, while clutching a letter or telegram in her left hand and the envelope lays discarded at her feet. Her right hand, tightly clenched in a fist, is raised to her breast. Almost in anticipation of the tragic event, whatever it is, the young woman appears to wear mourning clothes—or a dress appropriate at the time for an expectant mother—thereby heightening the pathos of the scene.

Grover was born in Earlville, Illinois, in 1860 and later moved with his family to Chicago, where he would attend the Academy of Design. He traveled to Munich in 1879 to study at the Royal Academy and later to Paris to study at the Académie Julian, the foreign art school of choice for so many of his Chicago colleagues. When he returned to Chicago in 1887, Grover was appointed as an instructor at the Art Institute. Early in his career, Grover became a muralist, contributing to large murals in 1889–90 at the new Auditorium Building and painted several lunette murals for the Auditorium hotel's dining room. He would paint other large murals in buildings at the Columbian Exposition, a downtown bank and a library in the Hyde Park area.

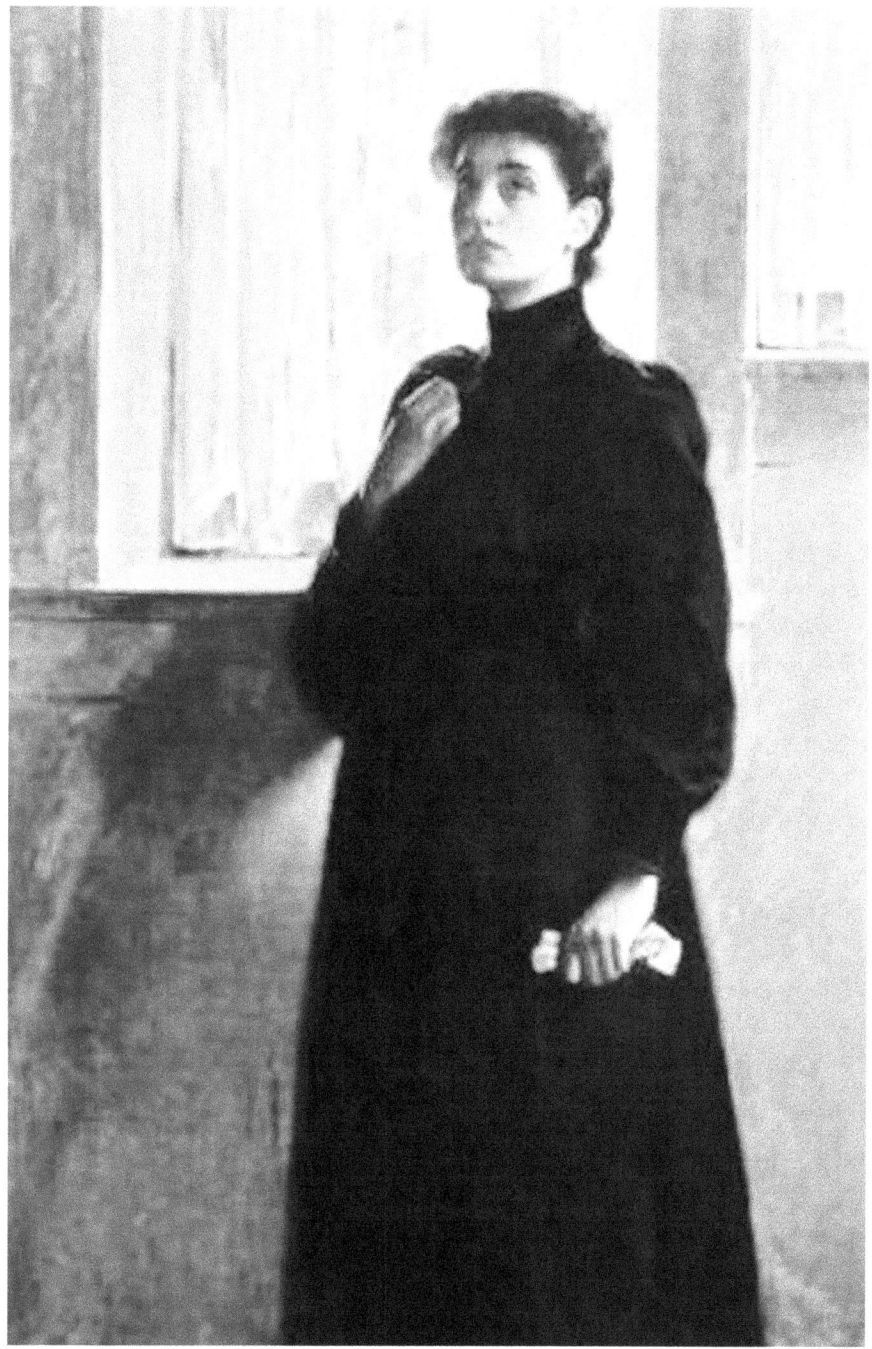

Thy Will Be Done, Oliver Dennett Grover, oil on canvas. First exhibited at the Art Institute of Chicago in 1892; winner of the first Yerkes Prize. *Courtesy of the Illinois Art Project.*

As an oil painter, he chose as his primary subject matter society portraits, landscapes, cityscapes of Venice and other Italian cities and towns and, later in his life, the American West, in particular Glacier National Park in Montana. He exhibited his paintings perennially at the Art Institute's annual Exhibition of American Art and annual Exhibition of Artists from Chicago and Vicinity, and he had a one-man show in December 1912. He would have a posthumous memorial exhibition there a year after his death in 1927. Grover also exhibited his work in other American cities, including the Pennsylvania Academy and the National Academy of Design, where he was elected an associate member in 1913. Grover was a member of the leadership of the Chicago Society of Artists, a founder of the Western Art Association, a member of the National Society of Mural Painters and an instructor at the Chicago Art Academy.

By the early 1900s, Grover, together with sculptor Lorado Taft and painter Ralph Clarkson, formed a triumvirate that dominated "almost dictatorially" the art scene of the city.[41] For the first quarter of the twentieth century, all three men, joined by their friend Charles Francis Browne, would have prominent and leading roles in several institutions established to promote, encourage and enhance the production of fine art in Chicago, including several artist colonies and social societies. All four artists essentially came to define the artist colony formed in 1898 in the Fine Arts Building, where each had a studio. All four men would be founding members of the Eagle's Nest Camp on the Rock River in Oregon, Illinois, established at about the same time. Grover and Clarkson later opened and maintained studios in the Tree Studios complex, established the year after the World's Columbian Exposition, and Browne would be associated with the 57th Street Artist Colony formed in the early 1900s in a series of small concession buildings located at the north entrance of the Exposition. In 1906, Taft would open the Midway Studios a few blocks away on the Midway Plaisance, the mile-long boulevard that was home to the carnival arm of the 1893 Fair dominated by the enormous Ferris wheel.

The World's Columbian Exposition closed on October 30, 1893, six months after it opened. Most of the Fair buildings perished in a large fire the next year. The Palace of Fine Arts survived and became the Field Museum of Natural History, which continued to display numerous natural and anthropological exhibits left over by the Fair. Today, the building houses the Museum of Science and Industry. The day following the Fair's closing day, the *Chicago Tribune* announced that "the influence of art at the Columbian Fair will reach far into the

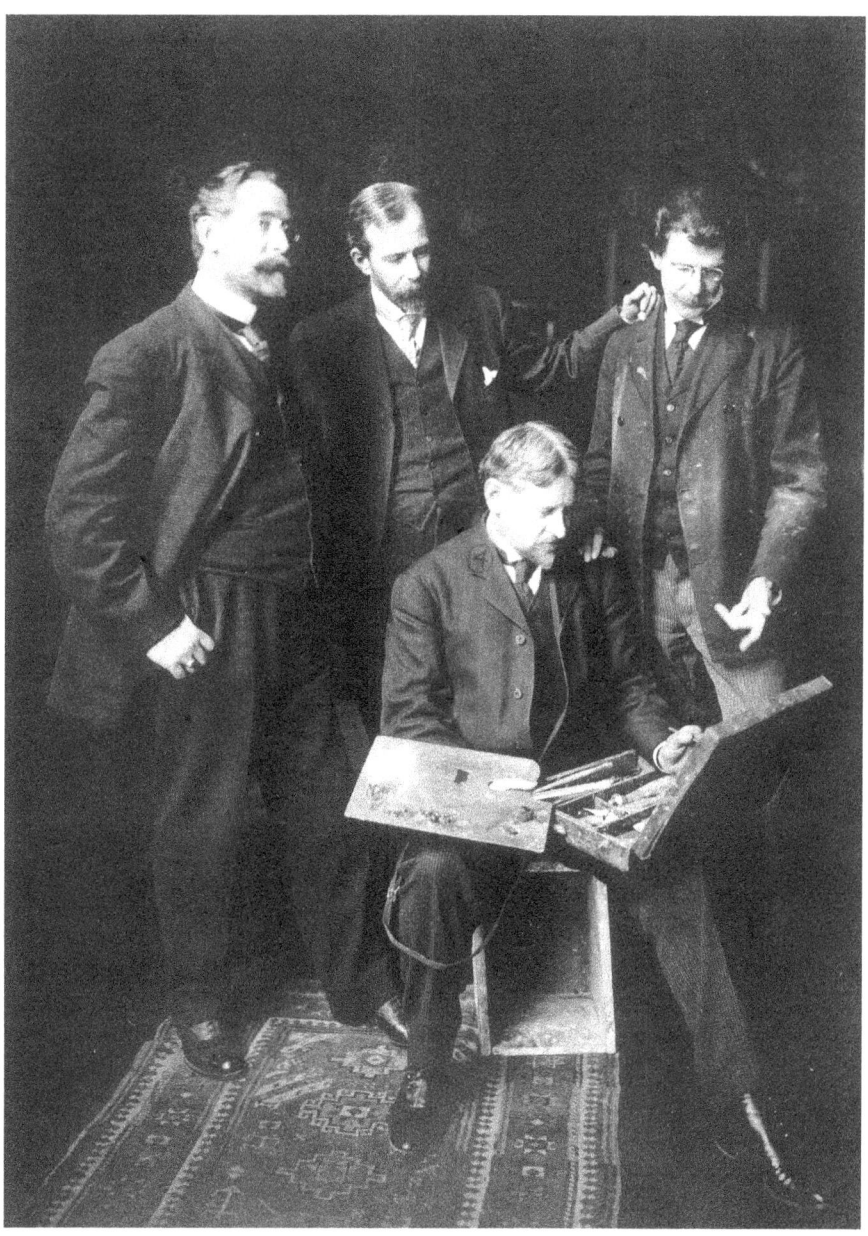

The Triumvirate: Oliver Dennett Grover, Lorado Taft and Ralph Clarkson, together with their friend Charles Francis Browne. *Photographer unknown (circa 1895), Courtesy of the University of Illinois Archives, Lorado Taft Papers, Box 30, No. 130.*

future."[42] Many of the works exhibited at the Columbian Exposition went on to become "icons of American art, emblematic of national achievement in the aesthetic arena."[43]

Although the Fair was gone, it had left something important and indelible in the soul of Chicago. The city, having possessed and enriched itself for a few months with the greatest contemporary art in the world, was resolute to make itself a major cultural center, the Florence to New York's Rome, so to speak. Local art patrons and artists almost immediately sought ways to attract and keep artists in the city and to promote and encourage an environment where art and culture could thrive. One of the means by which to accomplish these goals was the establishment of several communal artist colonies within a decade of the Chicago World's Fair.

Part II

Artist Colonies of the Chicago Area

3

What Is an Artist Colony?

When the artists and art patrons in the 1890s sought to establish discrete communities dedicated to the promotion and enhancement of the arts, they had few models to guide them. Although artist colonies had existed for several years in Europe, especially in Paris, Barbizon, Provence, Pont-Aven and the American Academy in Rome, few existed in the United States at that time.

The only art colony of consequence in America in the early 1890s was the Tenth Street Studio Building in New York, constructed in 1857. It was the first building in the country expressly designed (by Richard Morris Hunt) to provide residential and studio spaces for artists and was, at various times, home to painters Winslow Homer, Frederick Church, Albert Bierstadt, William Merritt Chase and Chicago-born Walter Shirlaw. Artists occupied the Studio Building until it was razed in 1956 to make way for a large apartment building. The now-famous art colonies of Provincetown and Woodstock were established after the first Chicago enclaves were formed, in 1899 and 1902, respectively. Artists began coalescing at Carmel-by-the-Sea in 1905. The colonies at Taos, Santa Fe and Laguna Beach were established even later. So, with respect to artist colonies, Chicago artists and art patrons were more or less pioneers.

But what, precisely, is an artist colony? The concept of the "artist colony" escapes easy definition. Is it a single locus, say, a building such as the Tenth Street Studio Building in New York, where a circle of artists lives and works? Or is it a looser collection of artists united by similar interests or styles who have taken up residence within a town, such as Gloucester, Provincetown, New Hope, Taos, Santa Fe or Carmel? Or something in between, such as a much smaller neighborhood, perhaps a handful of blocks, within a larger city, such as Greenwich Village or SoHo? Some may even consider an "artist colony" to be a tiny but tightly knit fraternity of artists who congregate within a single studio, such as Joseph Stieglitz's 291 Gallery, or an arts organization, such as the Salmagundi Club in New York or Palette and Chisel in Chicago. The idea of the "artist colony" is elastic and has encompassed all of these things. How artist colonies establish themselves and regulate their memberships, to the extent they do, are questions that are equally problematic. The question of why they exist at all may be the most elusive.

Everyone knows that Claude Monet lived and painted his impressionistic canvases in a small bucolic town in the French countryside named Giverny. Many are vaguely aware that an artist colony later formed in Giverny. Some may assume, quite reasonably, that Monet, master of a revolutionary new style of painting, invited a group of close disciples to congregate within his environs to learn and emulate his technique, much as Frank Lloyd Wright would do at Taliesin (near Madison, Wisconsin) a generation later. In fact, the origins and purpose of the art colony that established itself in Giverny are not quite as one might assume.

When Monet settled in Giverny in 1883, he was already established as a leading painter in France whose reputation was beginning to spread in Europe and America. His impressionistic technique had previously provoked the Parisian art community then dominated by the Beaux-Arts idiom, but it intrigued some. With the first Impressionist Exhibition, held in 1874, Monet and his impressionist adherents freed themselves of the constraints of the Paris Salon, and the movement took root and flourished, first in France, and later throughout Europe and in American cities.

Several artists began to converge on the small town of Giverny in 1887. They were not, as one might assume, invited by the great impressionist master, and they were not French or even European.

The origins of the Giverny colony date to 1887, when a small band of artists, including Willard Metcalf, Louis Ritter, Theodore Wendel and John Leslie Breck "discovered" the village. Claude Monet (by then, known to the American artists through both Parisian and American exhibitions) had settled there in 1883. After the initial discovery, other American artists soon followed and many had begun to expand their visits beyond the summer months. Monet was initially receptive of the arrival of the artists, but soon tired of the invasion. Although he never offered himself in any teaching role, his presence in the village ensured the steady growth of the colony and accounted for the new luminosity and coloristic richness in the paintings of the Americans who worked there.[44]

Thus, the artist colony at Giverny did not form as a bright, nourishing sun around which a group of lesser satellites spun, as one perceives the relationship between master architect Frank Lloyd Wright and his group of aspiring supplicants at Taliesin to have been. Any mentor-pupil relationships between Monet and these American invaders, to the extent such relationships existed at all, were strictly informal. Indeed, due to the increasing number of new artists at Giverny, Monet gave serious consideration to leaving the village, where he had settled precisely to find peace and quiet. A few Americans were able to pierce through Monet's protective barrier and enter into his circle of close friends, and one American painter from Ohio, Theodore Earl Butler, went so far as to marry Monet's stepdaughter, Suzanne Hoschedé. But most members of the Giverny artist colony were kept at bay.

Nor, as one might expect, was the artist colony monolithic with respect to the style or subject matter of the artists who settled there. Many focused on the natural beauty of the village and the surrounding region and painted picturesque village scenes and landscapes to capture the expression of outdoor light and atmosphere. Others depicted genre scenes, especially featuring fashionable middle- to upper-middle-class females in private settings of homes and beautiful gardens. Some painted in the misty, loose and ethereal style of the purist French impressionists, while others adopted a hybrid impressionism, painting with a more characteristically American technique that imposed a stronger underlying structure with classical academic draftsmanship. Still others did not adopt the impressionistic technique at all. Even technique and subject matter, then, did not unify the art of the American Giverny colonists.

If the Americans who visited or settled in Giverny did not do so to receive formal instruction in impressionism from Claude Monet himself or to work with Monet and fellow artists painting in the same style or subject matter, what accounts for their traveling thousands of miles at great expense to a tiny village in the French countryside? Is there a unity of purpose behind why artists, and in particular American artists, are drawn to communal enclaves populated by other creative types? A sense of camaraderie and fraternity may be a motivating factor. The close and intimate friendships among Oliver Dennett Grover, Lorado Taft, Ralph Clarkson and Charles Francis Browne, together with their shared conservative, academically inclined sensibilities, certainly accounted for their taking up professional digs together at the Fine Arts Building, summering together at the Eagle's Nest Camp and joining the Cliff Dwellers Club, a social and dining club. Economic circumstances are very much a factor in other cases. Many of the artists who settled in Greenwich Village in the 1910s were drawn to the neighborhood because of its cheap rents. As we shall see, the same was true for the artists who first occupied the Tree Studios or set up ateliers in the attics, garrets and coach houses of Towertown.

Perhaps an even more compelling explanation is that artists truly are a breed apart. During the late Middle Ages and Renaissance, it was common for persons engaged in the same line of work, so to speak, to be members of a guild and to live and work within a small common geographical area. But that communal way of life largely went by the wayside when the guilds declined in the late sixteenth and early seventeenth centuries. The only categories of persons still generally engaged in communal living and working relations include students at colleges, universities and boarding schools, the clergy of certain religions, members of the armed forces and, possibly, some lawyers at the English Inns of Court. But with the possible exception of the last category, sound, practical and self-evident reasons exist for the communal live/work arrangements for those groups.

What is it about artists that lead many of them to join collectives with other creative persons, especially those working in mediums different from their own? One critic, trying to explain several artist colonies in fin-de siècle Paris and early-twentieth-century New York, opined that such groups

> *came together as a small fraternity that posited the artist as outside, not inside, his own culture and envisioned art as a rarefied and enlightened activity that would serve as an antidote to, and therapy for, a money-driven, bourgeois society. Such groups formed to shelter and shield one another from the pollution of the materialist world, and to bolster one another's faith in art as a form of aesthetic activism. For it was not just art for art's sake that motivated these artist circles, but art to save the world from enslavement to things and emotional starvation. Their art would, if embraced, help people to transcend the baseness of modern existence and live, if only momentarily, in the wholesomeness of beauty.*[45]

Heady stuff. In *Brideshead Revisited*, Evelyn Waugh penned a less-exalted view of artist colonies: "There was an institution in my day called a 'sketching club'—mixed sexes (snuffle), bicycles (snuffle), pepper and salt knickerbockers, Holland umbrellas and, it was popularly thought, free love (snuffle); *such* a lot of nonsense."[46] Perhaps what motivates most artists to join artist colonies are certain ideals and intangibles that fall somewhere in between these two views.

Floyd Dell, a leading Chicago critic and writer of notable originality, commented on the evolutionary nature of art and the influence of the different artistic mediums on each other in that evolution at the time of the Armory Show in April 1913. "The arts do fertilize each other; they liberate each other from their own tradition....The artistic effects characteristic of one medium of expression awakens a fruitful envy in the imagination of workers in another medium."[47] It was just about this time that Dell and his wife settled in two separate units at the 57th Street Artist Colony, purportedly, in part, to experiment in free love of the type condemned in *Brideshead*. Dell may have come closest to explaining why artists of disparate mediums converge in geographically close and socially and professionally intimate groups—to reap the benefit of multidisciplinary stimulation and the exchange of new ideas and trends among fellow creative souls.

Keeping the Artists in Chicago

The First-Generation Artist Colonies

As has been shown, works generated by Chicago-based artists constituted a tiny fraction of the enormous amount of art displayed at the Palace of Fine Arts of the World's Columbian Exposition. But the Exposition had attracted and commissioned scores, if not hundreds, of artists to assist in constructing and decorating the buildings and grounds of the Fair. Murals and sculptures abounded throughout the fairgrounds, and many of the artists who contributed to these artworks remained in the city. The Exposition also attracted other artists and writers from throughout the United States to record the exhibitions and happenings of the Fair in books, newspapers and periodicals. Finally, artists came from all over to see one of the world's largest collections of art in a single space. Some Chicagoans meant to keep as many of these artists in the city as possible. Two of those Chicago residents were Judge Lambert Tree and his wife, Anna.

LAMBERT AND ANNA TREE BUILD THEIR ARTIST STUDIOS

The Lambert Trees resided in a large home, which they built in 1884, at the corner of Cass Street (later renamed Wabash Avenue) and Ontario Street. The Trees owned the entire block bordered by State Street on the west, Cass Street on the east, Ohio Street on the south and Ontario Street on the north. They had inherited this land from Anna's father, one

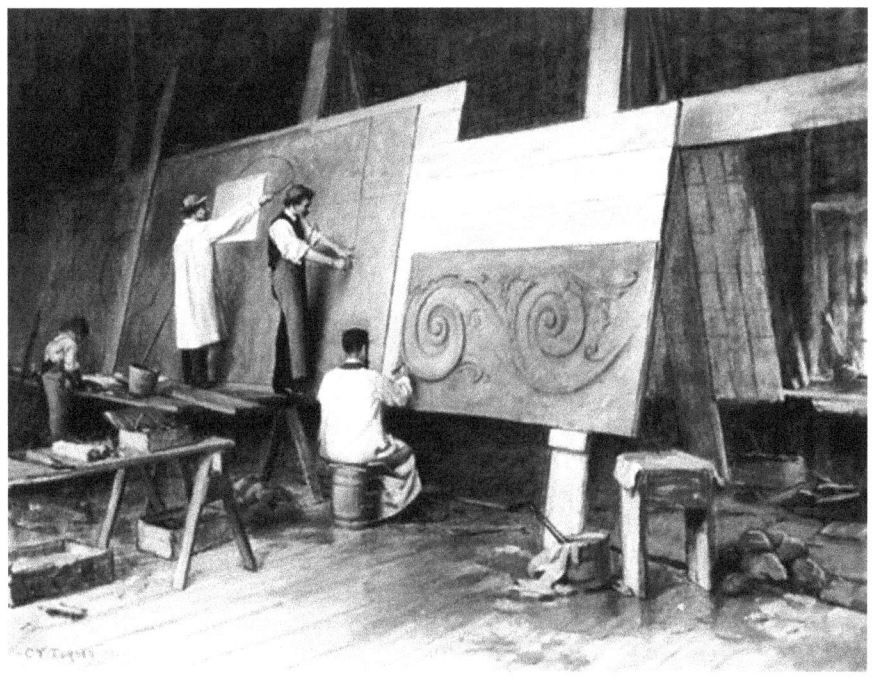

Artists Executing Designs for the Worlds Columbian Exposition, Chicago, 1893. Charles Yardley Turner (1894), oil on canvas. *Christies.*

of the earliest settlers in Chicago, who owned the property since 1840. In 1894, the Trees decided to build a grand structure to house artists in their own backyard.[48]

Lambert Tree was born in 1832 in Washington, D.C., the son of a postal clerk. He was educated at private schools and studied law at the University of Virginia. In 1859, Lambert married Anna Josephine Magie, who developed an interest in art and became an artist herself. They had a son, Arthur, in 1869. Arthur later married a daughter of Marshall Field and moved to a large estate in Great Britain, to his father's chagrin. Arthur's son Ronald served several terms in the House of Commons in Parliament.

On the advice of Senator Stephen Douglas, Tree settled in Chicago in 1856 and practiced law until 1870, when he was elected judge of the Cook County Circuit Court. As a judge, Tree was especially notable for taking a strong stand against corruption in city government. Following several unsuccessful campaigns for a seat in the U.S. Congress in the 1880s, Tree was appointed ambassador to Belgium in 1885. He held this position until 1888, when he was appointed ambassador to Russia. He returned to

America in 1890 and spent the next two years in Washington, D.C., as a member of the Intermonetary Commission.

After Tree returned to Chicago in 1892, he and his wife became involved in the cultural life of the city, contributing to the newly established Newberry Library and the Chicago Historical Society. He also donated two sculptures to Chicago parks and, together with Mayor Carter Harrison, funded an award program in 1887 to honor heroic firemen and policemen that still exists today.

When Judge Lambert Tree and his wife, Anna, determined to build what became known as the Tree Studios, their catchphrase was not "build it and they will come." Instead, it was "build it and they will stay." Out of the pride that inspired many well-heeled Chicagoans after the World's Columbian Exposition, the Trees planned to erect a three story, block-long studio building precisely to attract artists who were already in Chicago and who had worked at or visited the Fair.[49] They intended that rents would be low enough for most artists to be able to afford and planned for a series of retail spaces on the ground floor to help offset the costs of maintaining the building. The Trees were inspired by a building they saw on Madison Avenue in New York and contracted the Parfitt Brothers architectural firm of New York as primary architects to replicate the Madison Avenue building, which they had designed.[50] They also appointed Hill & Woltersdorf as local architects to supervise the actual construction.

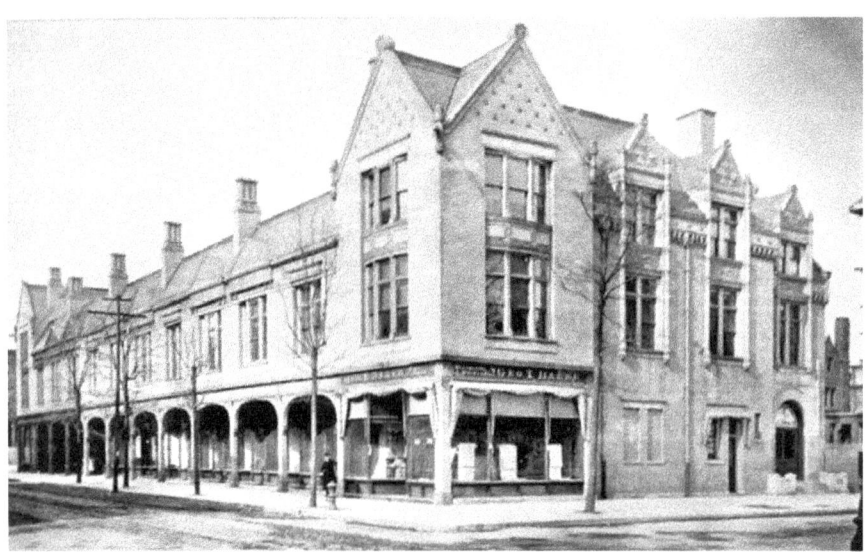

Lambert Tree Studios, west façade (1894). Inland Architect *(May 1895)*.

The initial building that constituted the Tree Studios complex was constructed in 1894–95. It was designed in a picturesque, modified Queen Anne style and featured relatively simple but elegant artist studio spaces with lofted sleeping spaces above. There were shared bathrooms in the central hall, and to prevent awkward moments, a sign cautioned, "In consideration of visitors, all models are required to wear a garment when leaving the studio to walk to the bathroom."[51] The original leases also declared that "[n]o cooking of strong odors or foods as fish or cabbage" and "no playing of the piano or any loud music until after 5:00 [p.m.]."[52]

The west façade of the Tree Studios was composed of a full-length cast-iron arcade at the ground level for small stores, reminiscent of the arcaded buildings on the Rue de Rivoli in Paris.[53] The second and third stories are covered in buff-colored Roman brick with large windows for the thirty-five artists' studios contained within. Decorative features include dormers, chimneys with clay pots and a cast-iron frieze below the roof soffit. The idealized heads of Lambert and Anna Tree are carved into the stone ornament. The building was designed to promote interaction among artists by the use of connecting doors between studios. The architects also built display cases in the central hallway to permit residents to display their work. In March 1895, *The Arts*, a local magazine, commented that "Chicago can at last boast of a studio building, wherein the artist may have as many comforts as his more favored brother, the office man."

Anna Tree died in 1903, and Lambert died seven years later on his return voyage to Chicago after visiting his son Arthur in England. Tree's estate sold the family home and adjacent land to the Temple of the Mystic Shrine (the Shriners), which, in 1912, built the Medinah Temple where the Tree mansion once stood. The trust Lambert Tree established to oversee the Tree Studios specifically dictated that only bona fide artists were allowed to rent apartments at the Tree Studios. The rents were kept low as the Trees intended from the beginning.

The studio complex was a success from the outset. A continual waiting list of artists desiring space within the building later led the trustees to build two annexes attached to the original 1894 building.[54] In 1912, the trustees commissioned Hill & Woltersdorf to design a three-story structure of very dark red brick in the English arts and crafts idiom for the Ohio Street annex. This structure contained four spacious studio apartments, significantly larger than the studios of the original building, with private bathrooms. Owing to the southern exposure, these apartments have much smaller windows on the exterior façade than the original building but include bowed windows.

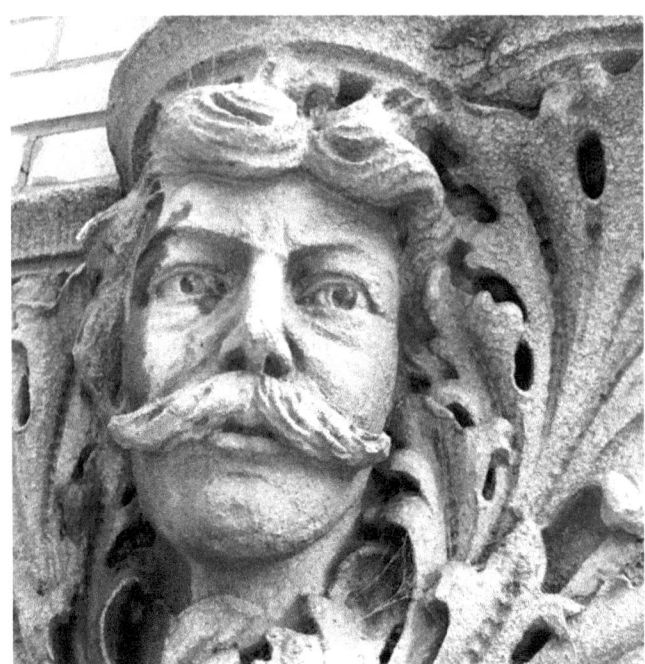

Tree Studios, south façade doorway, decorative element depicting Lambert Tree. *K.M. Stolte (2018).*

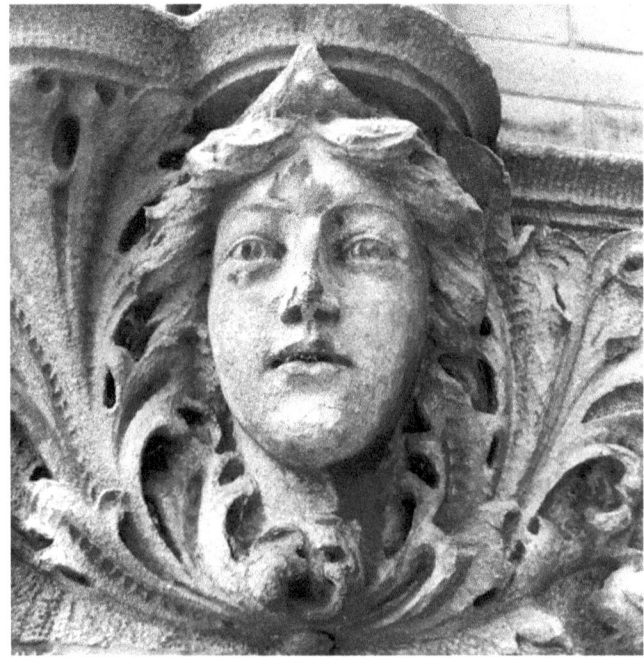

Tree Studios, south façade doorway, decorative element depicting Anna Tree. *K.M. Stolte (2018).*

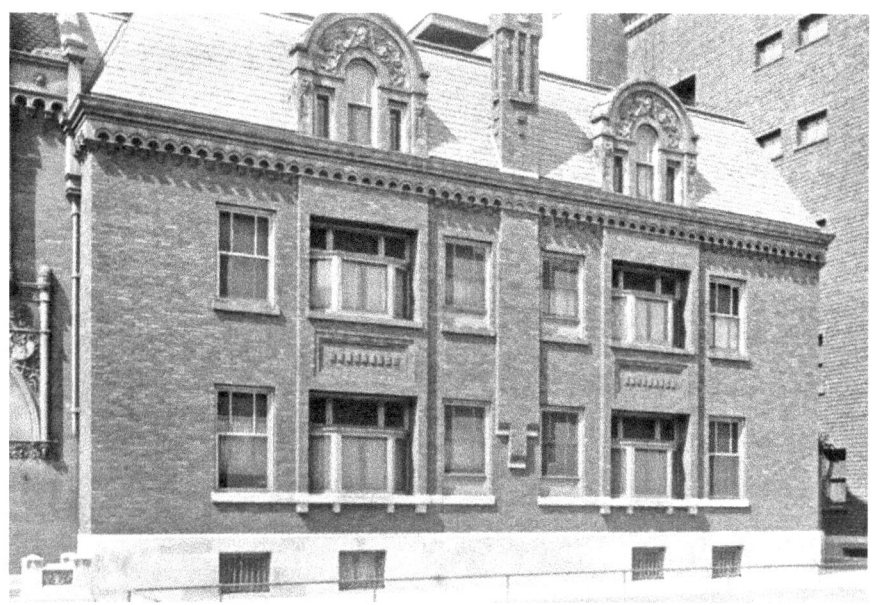

Tree Studios Annex 1, south façade (1912). Architectural Record *51 (1922)*.

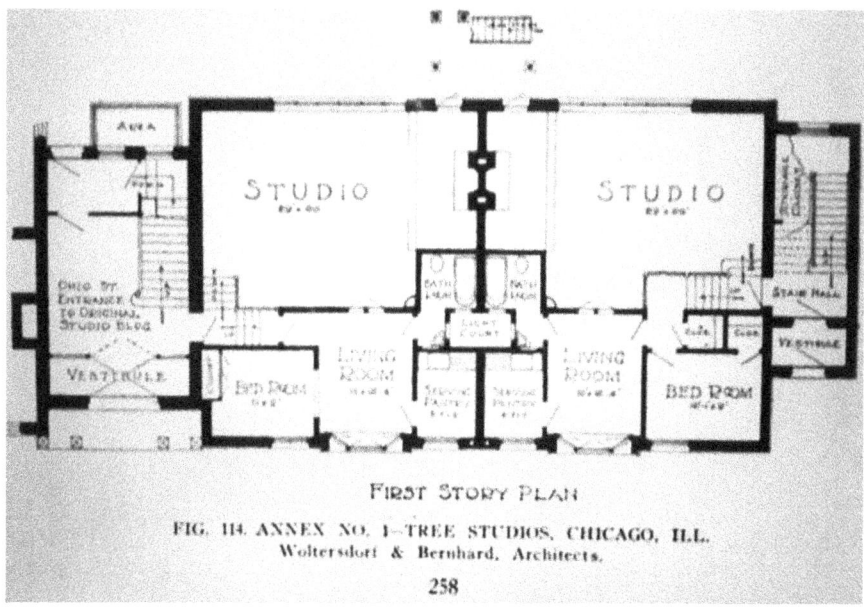

Tree Studios Annex 1, floor plan. Architectural Record *51* (1922).

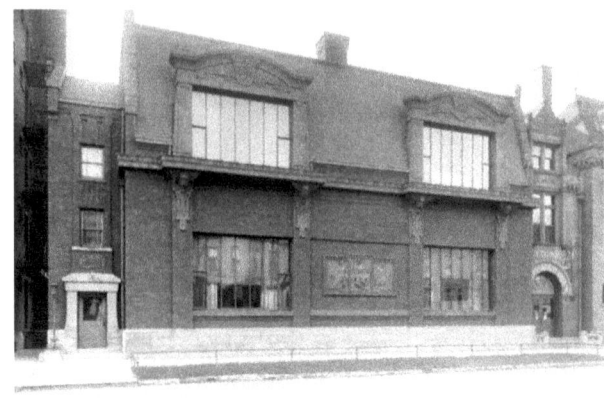

Tree Studios Annex 2,
north façade (1913).
Architectural Record *51*
(1922).

The façade incorporates decorative brickwork and a terra-cotta panel depicting an artist's palette and brushes. Each of the two dormer windows is a Palladian composition of three parts framed by terra-cotta panels and topped by an arch decorated with holly, berries and a woman's head.

The next year, Hill & Woltersdorf designed the Ontario Street annex in a European modern style, somewhat reminiscent of the primary façade of the Glasgow School of Art designed by Scottish architect Charles Rennie Mackintosh. From the exterior, it appears to constitute only two floors, but in fact the four apartments inside feature mezzanines, thus creating duplex units. Each studio boasts a very large window (ten feet high and fourteen feet wide) on the north-facing wall, flooding the unit with the sort of muted light favored by artists. These windows are actually a series of lengthy vertical panes of glass separated by thin mullions. Between the windows on the first floor appear three terra-cotta panels depicting Greek female figures representing painting, sculpture and architecture.

The second floor of this annex slopes back, forming a mansard-type roof, with the two windows standing out as dormers. Over the windows are curved stone pediments, each of which incorporates a tree on a shield, in honor of the building's benefactors, and lines from a poem by Wordsworth: "Art is long / Time is Fleeting / So be up and doing / Still achieving still pursuing." Below each of these windows are stone brackets featuring the faces, it is believed, of Lambert and Anna Tree. It is generally accepted that the Greek figures on the façade at the first floor of the Ontario annex and the decorative brackets and pediment reliefs on the façade at the second-floor level were the work of Richard Bok, a Chicago sculptor who is best known as the artist who produced sculptures for several buildings designed by Frank Lloyd Wright, Louis Sullivan and Dwight Perkins.[55]

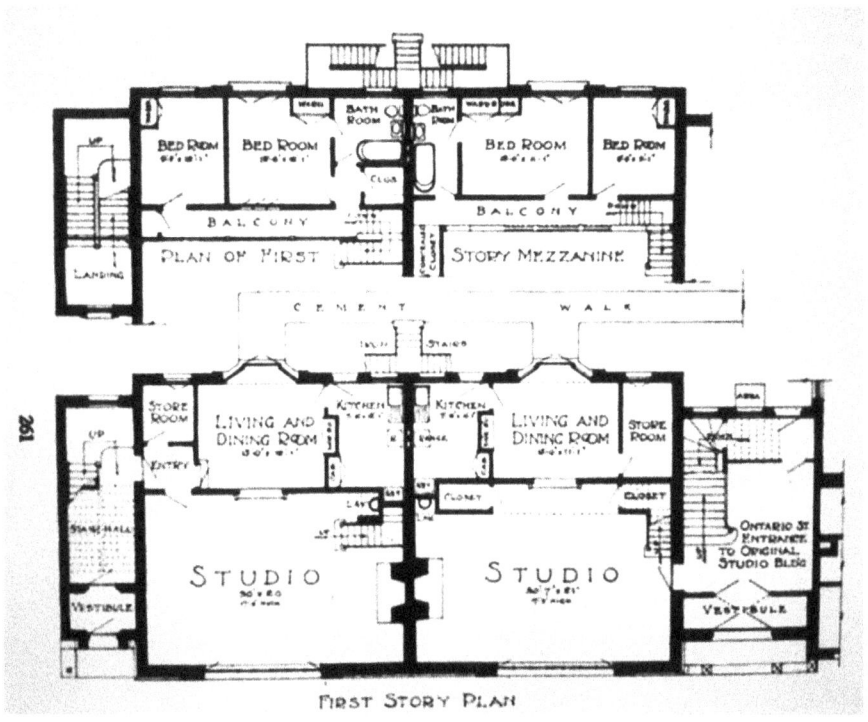

Tree Studios Annex 2, floor plan. Architectural Record *51 (1922)*.

After the Shriners' Medinah Temple and the Ohio and Ontario annexes were constructed in 1912–13, these buildings enveloped a courtyard at the rear of the original studio building. This courtyard, referred to by the architects as the Garden Court, incorporated a decorative fountain, walkways, trees and several stone benches. The open courtyard permitted light and fresh air into the windows and the French doors on the inner façades of all three components of the Tree Studios complex. The courtyard promoted social interaction among the artists who resided in the studios. It also provided outdoor space in which the painters among them could render scenes on their canvasses under indirect, ambient light.

The layout of the original studio structure was straightforward. The first floor comprised twelve discrete rooms running on an east–west axis along the width of the structure that were intended to be used, and throughout the building's history were used, for commercial shops. The two end units were slightly larger, in terms of both width and length, than the others. Each shop had a public access doorway on the State Street side. Originally, the lower front façade, facing State Street, included an open arcade-like

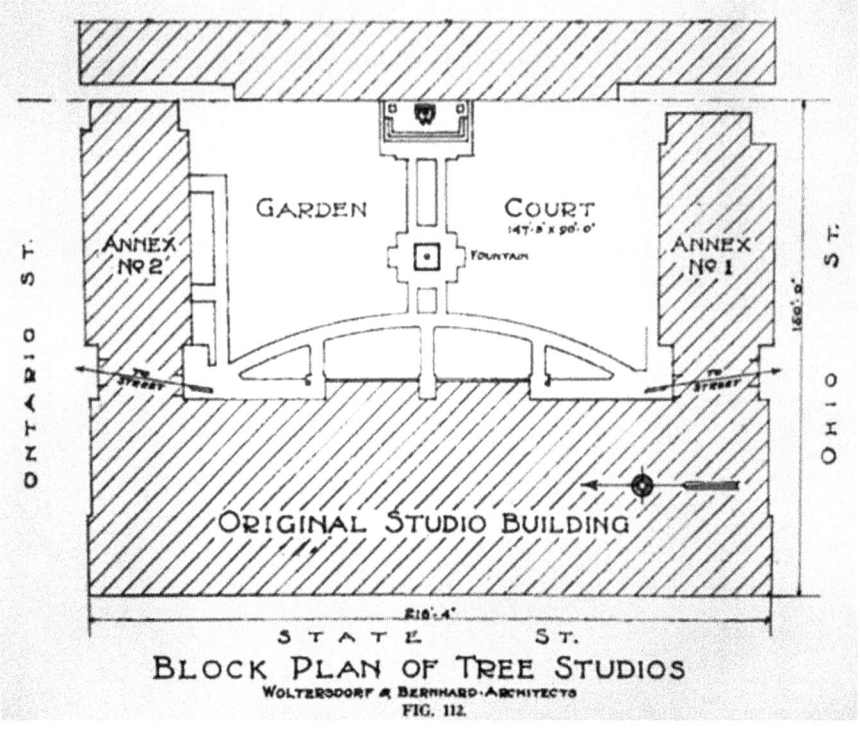

BLOCK PLAN OF TREE STUDIOS
WOLTERSDORF & BERNHARD·ARCHITECTS
FIG. 112

Tree Studios courtyard diagram. Architectural Record *51 (1922).*

loggia supported on the west perimeter by nine columns. (This loggia has now been incorporated within the shop spaces by the insertion of windows on the western perimeter.) At the back of the structure on the first floor, there was a hallway running on the north–south axis that permitted rear access to the shops. At the northeast and southeast corners, two staircases led to the second floor. At these two rear corners were the entryways, one on Ohio and the other on Ontario, by which the artist residents could access the building.

On the second floor of the original building were twenty-seven artist studios with a central hallway running on a north–south axis and two small east–west hallways at either end of the building running between the upper stairwells and the central hallway. Each studio had an access door opening to one of these hallways and a window facing the street or the courtyard. At the center rear of the structure were two common bathrooms, one for men and one for women. Ceilings were twenty-five feet high and featured skylights with northern exposure, a light preferred by artists. Every studio had a fireplace and was connected by doors to the adjacent studios through which the artists could view each other's art and visit one another.[56]

The studios in the 1912 Ohio Street annex measured twenty-one feet by thirty feet, and sixteen feet in height. They featured fireplaces and alcoves with stairways leading thereto for storage of artist materials. A bedroom, private bathroom and serving pantry adjoined each of these studios, completing the suite.[57] Addressing the advantages of the new Ohio Street annex studios, one contemporaneous writer explained:

The studio building scheme has in Chicago's instance proved a success, artists being anxious to form a community of their own and to be of mutual service to each other, as well as finding in this plan, rooms and surroundings adapted to their work. It is rarely that the studio buildings thus far completed have not had a waiting list and the four studios and their respective apartments in the new building on Ohio Street, have already found their lessees in Mr. and Mrs. Oliver Dennett Grover, Signor and Signora Andrew Rebori [a prominent architect], *Mr. and Mrs. Marshall Clark and William J. Reynolds. The building in its various details is highly artistic and is the culmination of studio planning in Chicago.*[58]

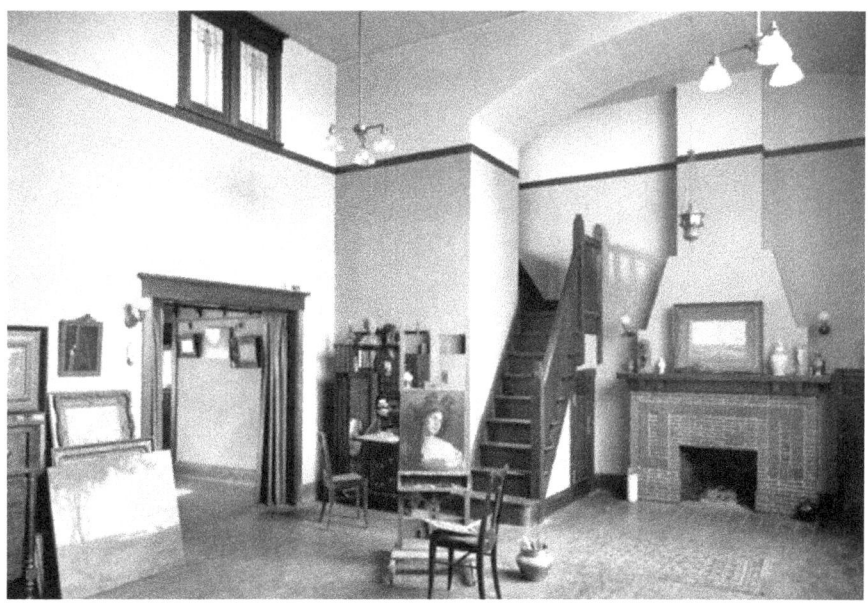

Tree Studios Annex 1, second-floor studio interior (1912). Architectural Record *51 (1922)*.

The four studios in the Ontario Street annex were even larger and more luxurious. Each measured about 30 feet by 33 feet and included a large studio work space (21 feet by 30 feet) dominated by enormous windows, a kitchenette (11 feet by 18 feet), a dining room (15 feet by 12 feet), two bedrooms (15 feet by 12 feet) and a private bathroom. The north half of each studio in the Ontario Street annex extends the full height of the apartment, while the southern half contains a lofted mezzanine floor containing the two bedrooms and a balcony overlooking the studio space below. Each apartment had terrazzo and wood floors and a large fireplace. The total cost of the annex was between $30,000 and $35,000 ($770,000 and $890,000 in today's dollars, respectively).[59]

From the outset, the Tree Studios attracted many of Chicago's most accomplished artists and continued to do so until the complex was redeveloped into a general office building in the early 2000s. Despite the low turnover historically,[60] it is estimated that more than four hundred artists have lived and worked in the Tree Studios.[61] As already noted, Oliver Dennett Grover was the original lessee of a studio in the Ohio Street annex. Husband-and-wife painters John F. and Anna Lee Stacey occupied one of the spacious apartments in the Ontario Street annex. Prominent painter Louis Ritman, who made frequent pilgrimages to Giverny, leased Studio No. 10 of the original building. John Storrs, a well-known modernist sculptor whose work included the statue of Ceres atop the Board of Trade Building at the foot of LaSalle Street, also lived there.

Painters of significant consequence who lived and worked at Tree Studios over the years include Boris Anisfeld, Frederic Milton Grant, Pauline Palmer, Louis Betts, Karl Albert Buehr, Martin Hennings, Gerald Frank, Ruth Van Sickle Ford, Walter Marshall Clute, Frederick Freer, Lucie Hartrath, Macena Barton, Rowena Fry, Anna Lynch, Leonard Seyffert and Richard Florsheim.

Prominent sculptors occupying studios at the complex included Louis Grell, Albin Polasek, Michael Murphy and Emil Zettler. Muralists included John Warner Norton, Edgar Cameron and Frances Badger. Other residents of Tree Studios were modernist architect Andrew Rebori, art critic C.J. Bulliet and actors Burgess Meredith and Peter Falk.

PAULINE LENNARDS PALMER

An early Tree Studios resident who was also one of the most popular painters in Chicago in her day was Pauline Lennards Palmer. (Palmer occupied Studio A.) She was born in McHenry, Illinois, in 1867 to parents who were immigrants from Prussia. She studied at the Art Institute of Chicago with John Vanderpoel and under impressionist masters William Merritt Chase, Frank Duveneck, Gari Melchers and Richard Miller. Palmer later traveled to Paris for training at the Académie Colarossi, École des Beaux-Arts and the Académie de la Grande Chaumiere. She spent some time at the artist colony at Giverny as well.

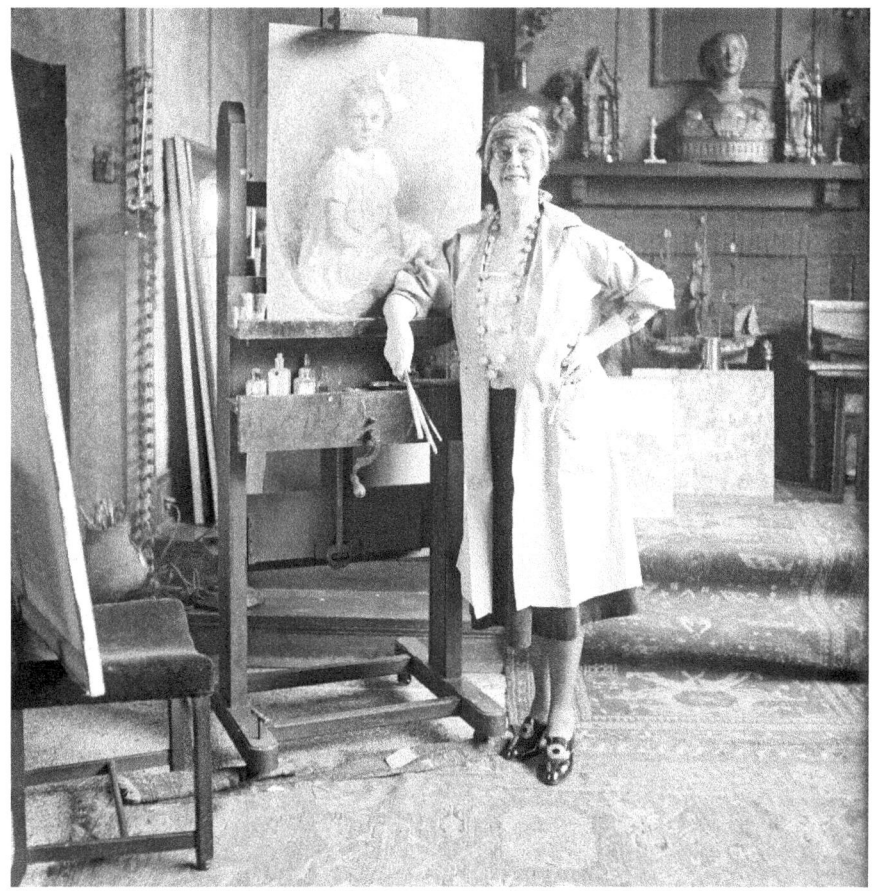

Pauline Lennards Palmer in her Tree Studio apartment. Chicago Daily News *(1928)*, *Chicago History Museum, DN-0085825.*

Palmer's work is characterized by the romantic, sun-drenched and colorful style typical of the American impressionists. In 1899, her paintings were compared favorably to the work of William Merritt Chase by a critic in *Arts for America*.[62] The same critic predicted that "among the younger artists, there is no one with a more promising future."[63] Palmer exhibited works at the Paris Solon in 1903, 1904, 1905, 1906 and 1911. She exhibited her paintings in numerous cities in the United States and won several awards at the Art Institute's annual American Art Exhibition and Chicago and Vicinity Exhibition, three prizes in 1907 alone. She was also in high demand as a juror of these and other exhibitions.

On March 24, 1913, the Art Institute honored Pauline Palmer with her first solo exhibition of sixty-eight of her paintings. The same day saw the opening of the massive and controversial Armory Show of international avant-garde artworks. William French, the director of the Art Institute at the time, worried that the modernist show would detract from the quiet integrity of Palmer's paintings. In fact, critics pointed out that, far from being overwhelmed by the Armory Show, Palmer's exhibition provided a needed counterbalance of sanity. One critic explained, "Instead of eclipsing the delicate art of Mrs. Pauline Palmer, [the Amory Show] has indirectly aided in giving her a veritable triumph."[64] The critic added that for people who were dazed by the "garishness of the revolutionaries," Palmer's paintings offered a welcome "rest and serenity."[65] Another critic enthused, "This exhibition gives Mrs. Palmer a strong push forward to a high place among American Painters." The notoriety of the Armory Show no doubt provided a substantial boost to Palmer's overall artistic exposure; a significant portion of the 180,000 visitors who came to see the Armory Show likely saw her show, and Palmer's exhibition probably experienced greater press coverage than it would have without the simultaneous modernist exhibition.

In 1919, Palmer was unanimously elected (for a three-year term) the first female president of the Chicago Society of Artists, by then the premier artist organization in Chicago. As president of the society, Palmer tried to keep an open mind about modern art, requesting a "well-known eastern adherent of the Modernist school to coach her in its 'mysteries.'" To no avail; following the instruction on modern art, Palmer found it even more mysterious.[66] In 1923, Palmer withdrew in protest from the Chicago Society of Artists over its decision to exhibit a series of abstract paintings by Flora Schofield, after which she and other traditionalists founded the Association of Chicago Painters and Sculptors.[67]

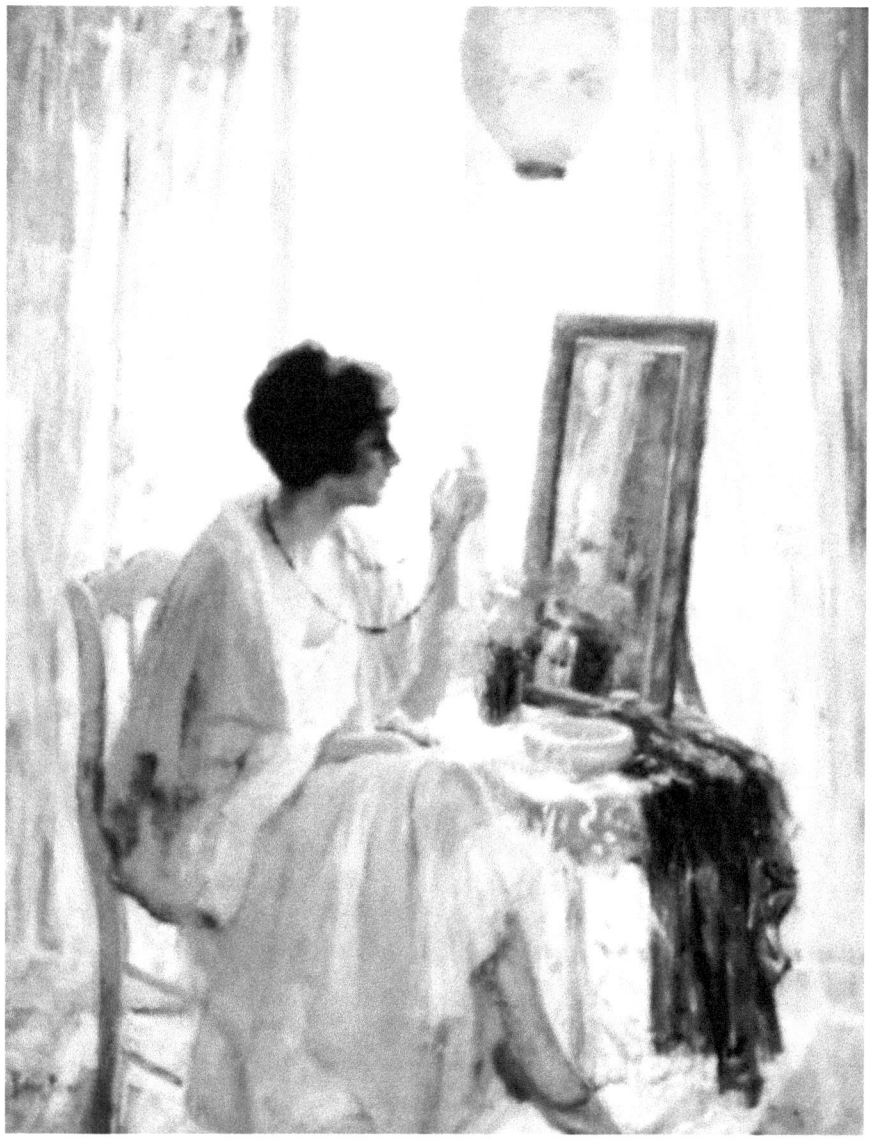

Pauline Palmer, *The Morning Sun*, 1920. *Rockford Art Museum.*

Throughout the 1910s, '20s and early '30s, Palmer's paintings continued to gain honors at exhibitions in Chicago and elsewhere.[68] However, by the mid-1930s, the forces of modernism began taking stronger root in the American Midwest, which theretofore had been entrenched in conservatism. (During the 1913 Armory Show exhibition in Chicago, Art Institute instructors and students alike burned copies of Matisse paintings in effigy following a mock trial of Matisse on the charge of artistic crimes.) Adherents to the old impressionist school, such as Pauline Palmer, were more and more overlooked and commercially less viable as time went by. Despite being one of the most accomplished, honored and popular female painters in America during the first third of the twentieth century, within thirty or forty years after Palmer's death in 1938, her art had become relics of an earlier era, her name virtually forgotten. Fortunately, in the past fifteen years or so, early twentieth-century Chicago artists have enjoyed a renaissance of sorts, and renewed interest in Palmer's work and that of her traditionist colleagues is on the increase.

THE MAGNIFICENT FINE ARTS BUILDING

If the artist colony established at the Tree Studios was the result of civic pride inspired by the Columbian Exposition, Chicago's second art colony was born, in part, out of a drive for corporate profits. In 1884, the Studebaker Company, a wagon and carriage manufacturer based in South Bend, Indiana, commissioned Chicago architect Solon S. Beman to design a building on South Michigan Avenue (now 410 South Michigan) that would serve as the company's retail showroom as well as a carriage manufacturing facility. Beman is best known as the architect who designed George Pullman's company town south of Chicago. Beman's design for the Studebaker Building, constructed in 1885, was strongly influenced by the then-popular Romanesque style pioneered by Henry Hobson Richardson.

The building's eight-story load-bearing walls were supported by rusticated granite and limestone piers. Beman ornamented the Michigan Avenue façade with a pair of granite columns framing the center bay at the ground floor and another larger pair just above at the third and fourth floors, with five arches at the fifth-floor accommodating oriel windows. The façade at the three uppermost floors feature rows of smaller windows. The building was capped by two decorative dome-like structures over the corner bays and peaked roofs over the bays in between, providing a unique Moorish touch. At street level were two heavy arched entrances at the north and south ends of the building and three enormous plate-glass windows appropriate for showcasing Studebaker's newest carriage models. The interiors featured granite and marble walls, trim and floors and grand barrel-vaulted ceilings in certain areas.

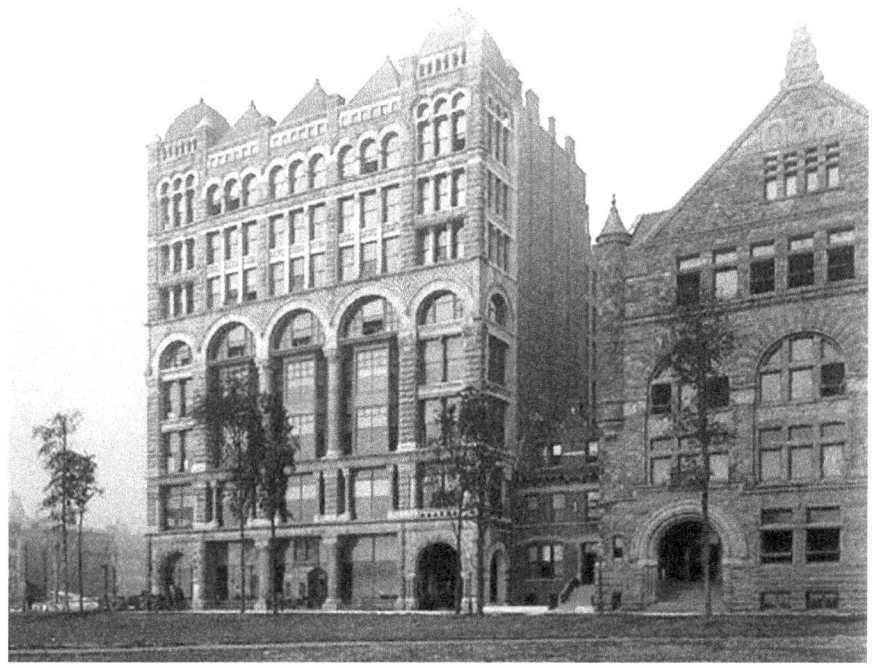

Studebaker Building and former Art Institute Building, eastern façades. *Photographer unknown (1885), Rare and Manuscript Collections, Cornell University Library, Accession Number 15/5/3090.00166.*

Within ten years, the Studebaker Company outgrew the building, despite the addition of an adjacent annex to the north. Accordingly, the company commissioned Beman to design another building on South Wabash Avenue. Ralph Fletcher Seymour, a painter, illustrator and publisher who occupied offices in the Fine Arts Building for decades, had a differing view as to why the Studebaker Company moved its operations to Wabash Avenue.[69] According to Seymour, "Farmers were accustomed to buy their farm wagons on Wabash Avenue and not on Michigan [Avenue]. They refused to walk a couple of extra blocks just to look at the Studebaker line and the building became a white elephant."[70]

One man had a unique idea of what to do with this white elephant. Charles C. Curtiss, music publisher, real estate developer and the son of a former mayor of Chicago, persuaded the Studebaker Company, which would retain ownership of the building well into the twentieth century, to renovate, modernize and repurpose the building. Curtiss became the driving force in transforming the Studebaker factory and showroom into a prototypical arts center, where practitioners of all the arts and related interests could

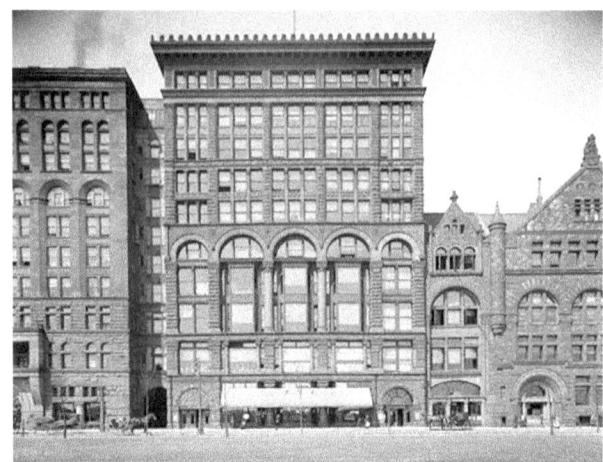

Fine Arts Building, eastern façade. *Photographer unknown (1900), Detroit Publishing Company, Library of Congress Prints and Photographs Division, Digital ID: det 4a08711.*

work and, just as importantly to Studebaker, pay rent. In 1897, the company commissioned Beman to remodel the building by removing the Moorish domes and peaked roofs at the top of the building and replace the top floor with three new stories, capped by a more standard cornice.

The primary Studebaker showroom on the first floor was converted into two theater venues, the larger Studebaker Theater (later referred to as the Fine Arts Theater) and the seven-hundred-seat University Theater. The remaining floors were adapted for use as artist and musician studios, galleries, offices and shops. On the fourth floor, the beautiful Venetian Court, complete with fountains and mosaic flooring, occupies the central light and airshaft. Above one of the entry doors in the main hall was inscribed "All Passes—Art Alone Endures," echoing the motto engraved on the façade of the Tree Studios. By the time the remodeling was complete, the newly renovated Fine Arts Building immediately attracted painters and illustrators, sculptors, musicians, music and drama schools, architects, small publishers and printers, several art-related clubs and a bevy of progressive social organizations. Whereas the intimate and elegant Tree Studios could house dozens, the ten-story Fine Arts Building could cater to hundreds. Curtiss, however, imposed certain standards for new tenants:

> *The city was full of more or less idle artists, left a little deflated with the conclusion of the first Chicago World's Fair. And a promoter, Mr. Charles C. Curtiss, secured the building and was given permission to remodel it into a home for the arts. As a primary qualification (perhaps just a trifle heartless), for admission as a tenant he required a high moral and financial standard, and still another, (desirable but not essential) a reasonable high*

aesthetic ability. Having admitted them, he brow-beat them into compliance with his standards. Nevertheless, about all the artists with enough financial strength to pay the rent gathered there. Musicians and workers in the allied arts filled the lower floors. Two or three theaters, book lovers and literary clubs, rare book dealers, art dealers, dramatic and dancing schools and semi-public institutions took space. Some of Bernard Shaw's plays had their first American presentation in this building. Transients connected with all of these activities frequented its galleries and rooms.[71]

The top floor (the tenth) was reserved for artist studios because they were equipped with skylights. Over time, the walls opposite the elevators on several floors and in the stairwells were graced with paintings or murals by the building's original tenant painters. Some of these works still exist there.

In short order, the Fine Arts Building was a hive buzzing with artistic genius. The triumvirate arbiters of the Chicago arts scene—Oliver Dennett Grover, Ralph Clarkson and Lorado Taft—took studios on the tenth floor, joined by their friend and colleague Charles Francis Browne. The gravitas this must have conveyed to the Fine Arts Building's drawing power was surely significant. Additional painters, illustrators and sculptors who rented studio space in the building included brother illustrators Frank Xavier and Joseph Leyendecker (who would execute scores of cover illustrations for the *Saturday Evening Post*, *Vanity Fair*, *Vogue* and other popular periodicals); painter/illustrator/publisher Ralph Fletcher Seymour; sculptor Nellie Walker; painters Frederick Clay Bartlett and Martha Baker; and illustrator/cartoonist John T. McCutcheon, a Pulitzer Prize recipient who worked for decades at the *Chicago Tribune*.

But it was not these noteworthy painters and sculptors alone that made the Fine Arts Building the center of gravity, culturally speaking, for the next thirty years. Frank Lloyd Wright had an office on the tenth floor. He also designed three spaces in the building for other tenants: Francis Fisher Browne's bookstore on the seventh floor in 1907; the Thurber Art Galleries in the north annex in 1909; and the Mori Oriental Art Studio on the eighth floor in 1914. Another prairie school architect, Dwight Perkins, also had an office in the Fine Arts Building. Fellow modernist architect Andrew Rebori would redesign the Studebaker Theater in 1917.

The Fine Arts Building was also a literary magnet. It was the birthplace of Harriet Monroe's *Poetry*, a magazine founded in 1912, the only national periodical devoted exclusively to verse. It still exists. During its earliest years,

Poetry published the first or early poetic works by T.S. Eliot, Carl Sandburg, Robert Frost, Langston Hughes, Edna St. Vincent Millay, Ezra Pound, e e cummings, Marianne Moore and Gwendolyn Brooks. Margaret Anderson's revolutionary and acerbic *Little Review* was launched in the building two years later. The influential, more established *Dial Magazine* was also published out of the Fine Arts Building, as was the Chicago edition of the *Saturday Evening*

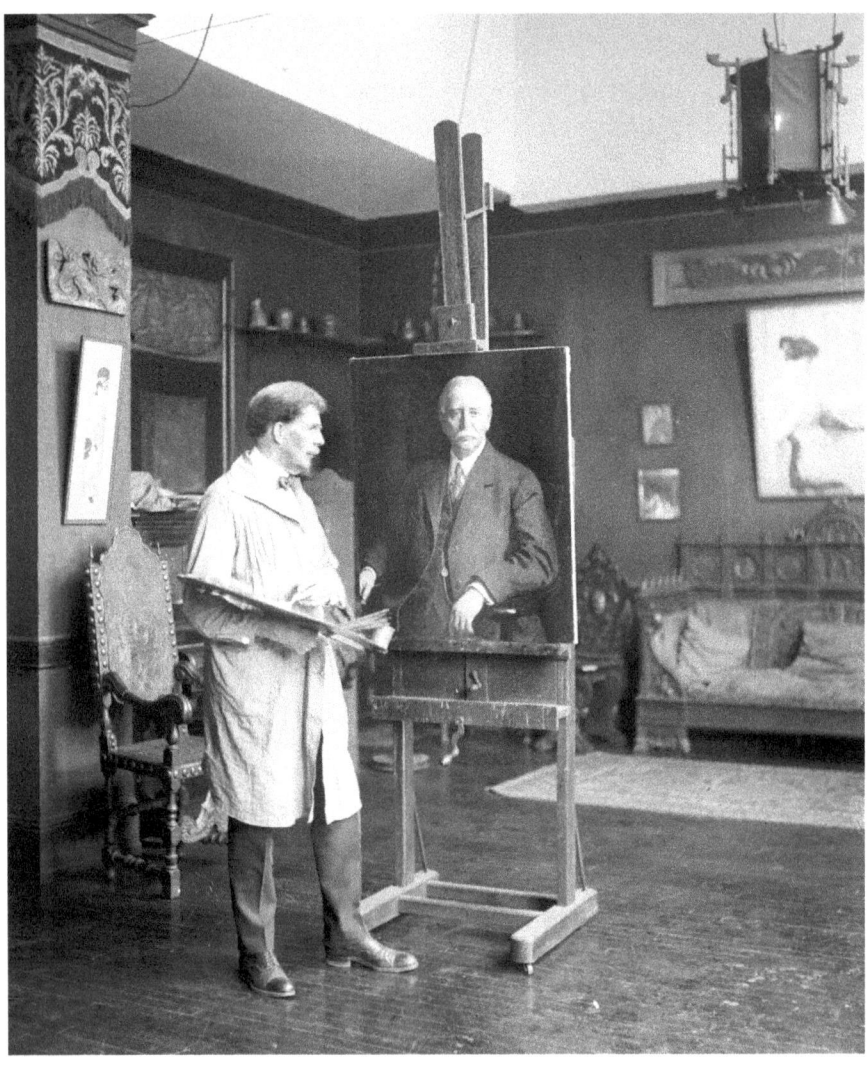

Ralph Clarkson in his Fine Arts Building studio. Chicago Daily News *(September 1924)*, *Chicago History Museum, DN-0076733*. The famed Little Room group met each week in Clarkson's studio for almost three decades.

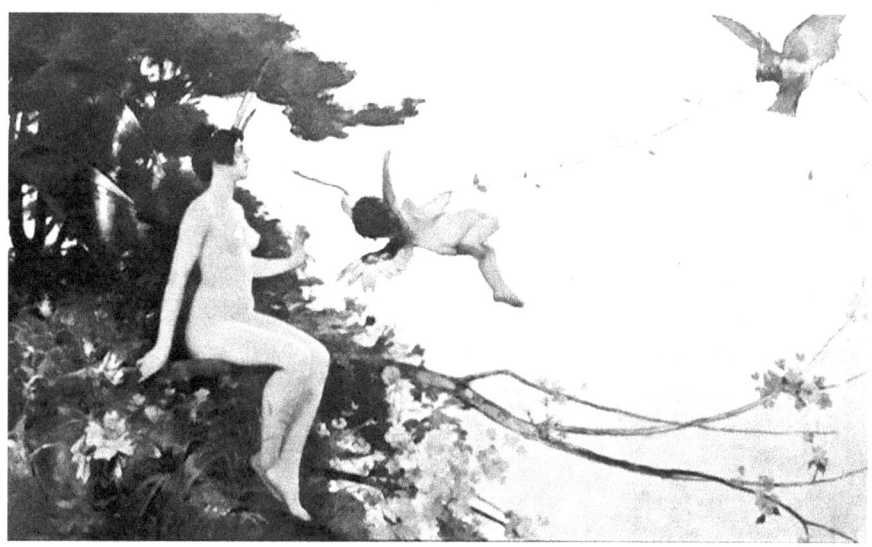

Oliver Dennett Grover, mural of a nymph, tenth floor, Fine Arts Building, circa 1910. *K.M. Stolte. (2018).*

Post. Chicago authors Theodore Dreiser, Hamlin Garland, Henry Blake Fuller, Ben Hecht and Sherwood Anderson either occupied studios in the Fine Arts Building or frequently caroused in the studios of other writers and artists who did. L. Frank Baum, who wrote *The Wizard of Oz* and thirteen other Oz books, had an office in the building, as did the illustrator of his books, William Denslow.

Controversies among the artist colony's literary set occasionally flared. After *Poetry* published newcomer Carl Sandburg's now-famous poem *Chicago* ("Hog butcher for the world," "city of the big shoulders") in 1914, the editors at the *Dial* mocked the poem, the poet and the magazine, calling the latter "a futile little periodical." In a withering reposte published in *Poetry*, the normally mild-mannered Harriet Monroe struck back with characteristic wit:

> *It is possible that we have ventured rashly in "discovering" Mr. Sandberg and others, but—whom and what has* The Dial *discovered? We have taken chances, made room for the young and new, tried to break the chains which enslave Chicago to New York, America to Europe and the present to the past. What chances has* The Dial *ever taken? What has it ever printed but echoes? For thirty years it has run placidly along in this turbulent city of Chicago, gently murmuring the accepted opinions of such leaders of*

thought as "The Athenaeum" and "The Spectator." During all that third of a century it has borne about as much relation to the intellectual life of this vast, chaotically rich region as though it were printed in Glasgow or Caracas. Not only has it failed to grasp great opportunity—it has been utterly blind and deaf to it, has never known the opportunity was there. Is its editor competent to define the word "futile?"[72]

Ironically, the *Dial* moved its editorial offices to New York in 1918 and was sold the following year, after which, under new management, it changed its subject matter and format. It became defunct in 1929. The "futile little periodical" *Poetry* is still extant, still published in Chicago and awash with cash, having received a bequest of $200 million in 2003 from Ruth Lilly, whose family founded Eli Lilly pharmaceuticals.

The Fine Arts Building was (and still is) home to the one-hundred-member Chicago Youth Symphony and the Anderson School of Music. Several music teachers and musical instrument manufacturers occupied studios. The building's annex housed Florence Ziegfeld's Chicago Musical College. A small opera company and several dramatic organizations maintained studios there and offered performances in the building's theaters. In 1912, husband and wife Maurice Brown and Ellen Van Volkenberg formed the Chicago Little Theater, which spearheaded the little theater movement in the United States. The company could not afford the rents charged for use of the building's Studebaker or University Theaters, so it converted a space on the fourth floor into a ninety-one-seat performance venue. The Little Theater performed experimental works by contemporary playwrights, Greek classics and plays by controversial European writers such as Wilde, Ibsen, Strindberg and Shaw. It also dabbled in experimental puppetry.

Anna Morgan, a prominent actress known for her naturalistic style in Shakespeare and Greek tragedies, relocated to Chicago from New York in the 1880s. When she retired from the stage in 1898, Morgan opened a studio in the Fine Arts Building, where she taught drama, speech and elocution. Her studio's curriculum included instruction on theatrical and political history, playwriting, literature, etiquette, acting and stagecraft. Morgan became close friends and companions with many of the leading lights of the Fine Arts Building colony and offered her studio space for periodic afternoon teas, social dances and small theatrical productions. Portions of her 1918 autobiography, *My Chicago*, offers some colorful glimpses of the social interactions and revelries among the Fine Arts set.

But perhaps it was the social organizations that arose from the unique congregation of the city's most prominent artists, writers, photographers, architects, actors, musicians and other cultural torchbearers at the Fine Arts Building that gave the artist colony that established itself there its greatest cohesion and enduring influence. The most vibrant of these social clubs was the Little Room, which met weekly in the large tenth-floor studio of Ralph Clarkson.

> *The Little Room was a Friday afternoon affair which grew out of the habit of the denizens of the Fine Arts Building and their friends of gathering in Ralph Clarkson's studio for tea and conversation after the afternoon concert of the Theodore Thomas orchestra in the Auditorium, which was next door to the Fine Arts Building. Among the "Little Roomers" were Henry B. Fuller, the writer, A.B. and I.K. Pond, the architects, Hamlin Garland, Floyd Dell, Emerson Hough, Keith Preston, Ralph Fletcher Seymour, Lorado Taft, Clarkson himself, and numerous other eminences in the cultural life of Chicago. Visiting luminaries in art and the theater were feted at The Little Room, Isadora Duncan once waltzing ecstatically with the 80-year-old [Irving Kane] Pond and rewarding him for his expert Terpsichore with a resounding kiss, after which the octogenarian architectural genius did a series of acrobatic back-flips which amazed everybody.* [73]

Irving Kane Pond, a talented Chicago architect and president of the American Institute of Architects, specialized in a unique American arts and crafts style and was active in Jane Addams's reforming efforts. He and his brother Allen designed most of the buildings associated with Hull House. Pond also had the distinction of scoring the very first touchdown for the University of Michigan football team, in May 1879. Perpetually good-natured and playful, he was a tumbler, back-flipper, hand-walker and avid circus fanatic whose 1937 book, *Big Top Rhythms*, detailed many circus acts. As world-renown dancer Isadora Duncan learned to her delight at the Little Room, Pond's amazing physical dexterity remained with him into his eighties. Pond's autobiography, published posthumously in 2009, seventy years after his death, is extraordinarily, in parts even shockingly, frank and honestly describes his compatriots at the Fine Arts Building and the Little Room. [74]

The Little Room provided a forum for its members to investigate and discuss new trends in the fine arts, literature and music. The writers, artists

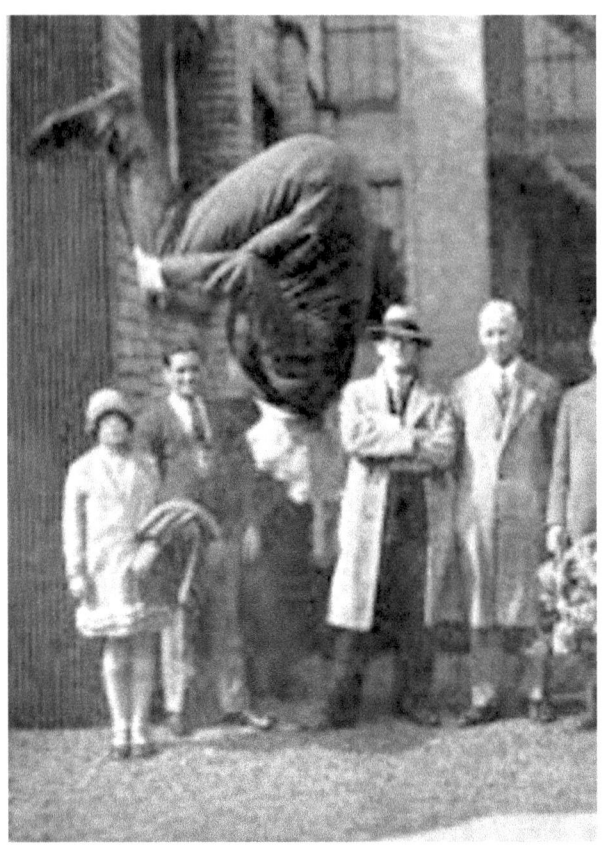

The acrobatic septuagenarian architect Irving Kane Pond in a backflip. *Michigan Alumnus Magazine 34, no. 2 (October 15, 1927), University of Michigan Library, Bentley Historical Library, BL012560.*

and architects who converged on Ralph Clarkson's studio each Friday afternoon periodically amused themselves and others by performing little plays, sometimes late at night, such as George Ade's *Captain Fry's Birthday Party*, which the Little Roomers elaborately staged in 1904.[75] Dancing by members and guests into the wee hours was not uncommon. The Little Roomers' afternoon teas and midnight dramas generally fostered an atmosphere of convivial and playful camaraderie while also offering opportunities for serious intellectual discussion on social and aesthetic issues. Irving Pond called the Little Room "the choicest gathering of kindred and congenial spirits Chicago has ever known."

The club played host to numerous distinguished visitors to Chicago over the years and became renowned throughout the United States, and even abroad, among the intelligentsia and cultured circles. Prominent Chicagoans visiting New York or London would be asked if they were members of the famous Little Room. And if the response was negative, they would fall perceptibly in the estimation of the inquirer, as if to suggest that they "could

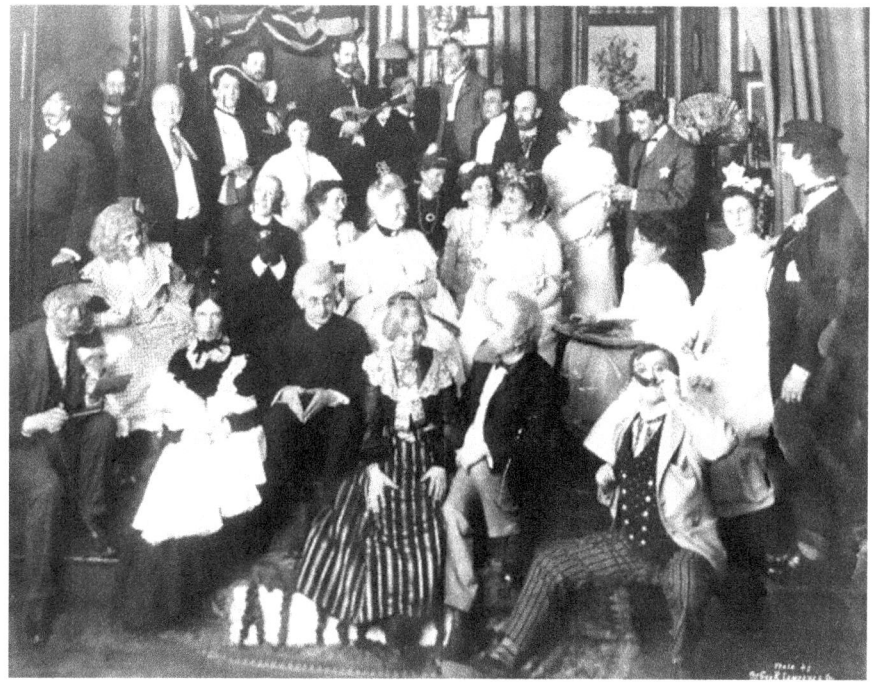

Little Room members performing *Captain Fry's Birthday Party* by George Ade in 1904. *The Bookman (Dodd, Mead & Co. Aug. 1912)*. Featured in the photograph are architects Irving and Allen Pond, Hugh Garden, Howard Van Doren Shaw; artists George McCutcheon, John McCutcheon and Ralph Clarkson; actress Anna Morgan; and writers/poets Melvin E. Stone Jr., Harriet Monroe and her sister Lucy.

not have much standing in Chicago if they were not a member of The Little Room."[76] The club became defunct in 1931.

Other clubs that took root in the Fine Arts Building were the Chicago Literary Club; the Caxton Club, a literary and bibliophilic society that still exists; the Fortnightly Club, a women's society for the enlightenment of the intellect, also still existing; and the Chicago chapter of the Daughters of the American Revolution.[77] Inspired by the controversial Armory Show, several artists and art patrons established the Arts Club of Chicago in the Fine Arts Building. Its primary mission was to exhibit avant-garde art, and true to that aim, the club presented the first solo exhibitions of the works of Picasso and Brancusi in the United States. The Municipal Art League was also founded and managed in the building. Its aim was the promotion and encouragement of Chicago artists, whose works it would purchase for public institutions.

In 1907, Pulitzer Prize–winning novelist Hamlin Garland founded a gentlemen-only dining club on the top floor of the Fine Arts Building, originally called the Attic Club.[78] Garland later rechristened it the Cliff Dwellers, a name he borrowed from the title of a controversial 1893 novel portraying Chicago in an unflattering light authored by his good friend and confidant Henry Blake Fuller. In addition to writing several critically acclaimed, but only modestly successful, novels, Fuller enjoyed the distinction of having written in 1891 (but published five years later) the first play in America to deal explicitly with male homosexuality.[79] A little less than three decades later, he would write what may be the first novel published in the United States featuring homosexual characters and themes treated sympathetically.[80]

Fuller was a son of Chicago, the scion of a once prosperous family of early settlers. Born in 1857, he was a highly cultured, intelligent and unusually well-read man who was an early adherent of literary realism; a genteel realist in an ungenteel city. In early diaries, Fuller acknowledged his homosexuality during his late teens.[81] He never married and was a shy, retiring man who maintained a high degree of privacy, despite enjoying a large coterie of close friends among Chicago's writers, artists and architects. (Although Fuller and Garland had been close friends and confidants for over thirty-five years, Garland was invited into Fuller's home on a single occasion: the death of Fuller's mother.[82]) Before Garland began courting Zulime Taft, Lorado Taft's sister, in 1898, he was under the misconception that Fuller and Zulime were a romantically attached couple because they spent so much time together.[83] Fuller corrected that mistake by encouraging his friend to woo Zulime, whom Garland eventually married. It was only many years later that Garland learned of his closeted friend's sexual proclivity and even reluctantly tolerated it.[84] As a point of moral and legal reference, in 1895, Oscar Wilde, a writer far more successful and internationally famous, was sentenced to serve a two-year term of hard labor in an English prison for suspected homosexual conduct. Midwestern mores of the time were hardly more progressive.

Ironically, Fuller never joined the Cliff Dwellers, but many writers and artists associated with the Fine Arts colony did, including Garland's two brothers-in-law, sculptor Lorado Taft and painter Charles Francis Browne; painters Ralph Clarkson, Oliver Dennett Grover, Ralph Seymour and John Warner Norton; architects Irving Pond and his brother Allen, Louis Sullivan, Frank Lloyd Wright and Howard Van Doren Shaw; landscape architect Jens Jensen; several prominent Chicago businessmen; and Mayor Carter Harrison II. In 1909, the Cliff Dwellers membership consisted of sixty non-artists, thirty-six architects, thirty-three musicians, twenty-five painters, nineteen writers and four sculptors.[85]

By 1909, the Cliff Dwellers had abandoned the Fine Arts Building for handsome digs on the penthouse floor of Orchestra Hall, a block north on Michigan Avenue. It remained in that space until the Chicago Symphony Orchestra management summarily expelled the club in 1996. It then moved to the far less clubby but more streamlined quarters atop the Borg-Warner Building. The club, which finally opened its membership to women in 1984, has remained a much-beloved meeting place for artists and art patrons and continues to offer dining facilities, exhibitions, lectures and other arts-related programs, as it has throughout much of its 110-year history.

The Fine Arts Building remains a haven for artists. The murals painted by Oliver Dennett Grover, Ralph Clarkson and the Leyendecker brothers still grace the walls and stairways. After a fifteen-year hiatus of nonactivity, the Studebaker Theater once again provides a venue for music and dramatic performances. Walking its halls, one still hears the murmur of a cello, someone playing a Liszt piano sonata or a soprano singing a song from *My Fair Lady*. The building was designated a Chicago Historic Landmark in 1978.

MARGARET ANDERSON

Two remarkable women dominated the intellectual life of the artist colony that nested in the Fine Arts Building. Both women founded literary journals that would come to have a significant impact on the culture of the United States. Harriet Monroe, publisher and editor of *Poetry*, was mature, serene, quiet, intelligent and determined. She had exceptionally good taste and excellent judgment and introduced a virtual who's who of poets to the world, names that still endure in an era when poetry is rarely read for pleasure. Although Monroe came of age a decade before the turn of the twentieth century, she was one of only a handful of art critics in America who wholeheartedly welcomed modernism in the visual arts when it finally arrived a generation later. The indomitable Monroe continued to edit and publish poetry until her death at age seventy-five while mountain-climbing in Peru in 1936.

The other woman, Margaret Anderson, was a whirlwind of imaginative energy, volatile, eccentric, impetuous, unpredictable, courageous, bold, beautiful and one of the most original thinkers in the city's history. Anderson was born in Indianapolis in 1886. She attended the Western College for Women in Oxford, Ohio, for one year, leaving in 1906 to become a pianist. In 1908, Anderson traveled to Chicago, where she became the book editor for a small Presbyterian magazine called the *Interior*. Her tenure was terminated by the magazine when she failed to sufficiently attack the morality of one of Theodore Dreiser's novels she had reviewed.[86] Anderson soon began working as a clerk at Francis Fisher Browne's bookstore on the seventh floor of the Fine Arts Building. In time, she also reviewed books for the *Dial*, which was owned and published by Browne. That arrangement lasted until Browne, forty-three years her senior, attempted to seduce his attractive young employee, and Anderson resigned her dual positions.

Ben Hecht, who admired Anderson's beauty and genius (his word) noted that "[d]uring the years I knew her she wore the same suit, a tailored affair in robin's egg blue. Despite this unvarying costume she was as chic as any of the girls who model today for the fashion magazines….It was surprising to see a coiffure so neat on a noggin so stormy."[87] The moonstruck Hecht, all of seventeen when he met her, said he forgave what he called Anderson's "chastity" because of her genius, but that so-called chastity was more likely an indifference to the male sex. Among her long-term lovers were Jane Heap, whom Anderson hired as a coeditor of the *Little Review*; opera soprano Georgette LaBlanc; and Dorothy Caruso, widow of the famous operatic tenor Enrico Caruso.[88] Hecht's contemporary novelist, Sherwood Anderson, extoled Margaret Anderson's cohesive function in the artists' social circles: "You gave a lot of queer isolated people a quick and sudden sense of each other. Something started. You walked about, being personally beautiful.… You talked with a quick rush of words.…You got us all together."[89]

In the first of three autobiographies, Anderson explained her inspiration for establishing the *Little Review* in the same playful manner she would frequently employ in her editorials and articles:

> *I had been curiously depressed all day. In the night I wakened. First precise thought: I know why I'm depressed—nothing inspired is going on. Second: I demand that life be inspired every moment. Third: the only way to guarantee this is to have inspired conversation every moment. Fourth: most people never get so far as conversation; they haven't the stamina, and there is no time. Fifth: if I had a magazine I could spend my time filling it up with the best conversation the world has to offer. Sixth: marvelous idea— salvation. Seventh: decision to do it. Deep sleep.*[90]

Highbrow from the outset, the *Little Review*'s inaugural issue featured articles on Nietzsche, psychoanalysis and Bergsonism. In the same issue, Anderson declared that the *Little Review* was not associated with "any organization, society, company, cult or movement"; instead, the journal embodied "the personal enterprise of [its] editor."[91] The journal tended toward the avant-garde and published some of the most influential new authors and artists of the era, such as Hart Crane, Ernest Hemingway, Ezra Pound, T.S. Eliot, Jean Cocteau, Marcel Duchamp, Gertrude Stein, Sherwood Anderson, Ben Hecht and Carl Sandberg.

Asserting its independence and progressivism, the *Little Review* unabashedly declared on its masthead that it would brook "no compromise with the public taste." And it never did. The *Little Review* would dabble in the many controversial "isms" of the early modernist era, including futurism, anarchism, cubism, expressionism, Dadaism, feminism and imagism. The journal was self-consciously aimed at the country's highest intellectual elite and became the bellwether of the avant-garde in American letters. In March 1918, Anderson's *Little Review* began serializing James Joyce's *Ulysses*, for which Anderson was charged with and convicted of obscenity and fined $100. On her prosecution for publishing the book, Anderson quipped, "I looked forward to a jury of my peers, if such could be found. We would have declared Ulysses a masterpiece, and I would not be a criminal." Anderson's editorials calling on Americans to free themselves of social conventions frequently invited scrutiny by federal and state law enforcement, but all official efforts to intimidate or muzzle her were to no avail.[92]

There were times when the *Little Review* experienced economic instability. During one such episode, Anderson camped out for six months in a tent on a Lake Michigan beach, where her friends Ben Hecht, Sherwood Anderson and Max Bodenheim would visit her, pin poems to her tent and tell bawdy stories around a campfire on the beach.[93] National newspapers had a field day reporting on the eccentric but formidable magazine publisher from Chicago camping out on the North Shore's dunes, preparing steaks and potatoes for artist friends and reporters alike.[94] But even in the face of abject poverty and homelessness, Anderson was valiant, vivid and "always exquisite, as if emerging from a scented boudoir, not from a mildewed tent or a camp where frying bacon was scenting the atmosphere."[95] Floyd Dell, a friend for whom Anderson wrote book reviews early in her career at the *Friday Literary Review*, said of her exuberance:

Her views, as expressed in 1911, had been in fact austerely idealistic, matching her starry-eyed, unearthly young loveliness, which was just too saint-like. She wrote well, if more enthusiastically than anybody had ever written before in the whole history of book-reviewing; an editor could not argue with her, for she stared him down with young limpid blue eyes which knew better than all his crass cynical wisdom.[96]

By 1918, Anderson would move the operations of the *Little Review* to New York and still later to Paris. There, the imperious Gertrude Stein called Anderson "a hysteric, pure and simple," likely protecting her turf and intimating her view that Paris was not big enough for both women, and it probably wasn't. The *Little Review* ceased publication in 1929, a victim of the Great Depression. The same year, the forty-two-year-old Anderson wrote an autobiography, *My Thirty Years' War*, which still remains one of the most charming and amusing autobiographies by an American. It has been reprinted several times and was supplemented by two additional volumes in 1951 and 1969. Margaret Anderson continued to live in France until the German occupation in 1939. She died in 1973.

FROM FAIR CONCESSION STANDS TO ARTIST STUDIOS: THE 57ᵀᴴ STREET ARTIST COLONY

If Margaret Anderson was not toiling away at her office in the Fine Arts Building, it was quite likely she could be found carousing with a group of intellectual bohemians in the Hyde Park neighborhood six miles south. There, Anderson and others from the Fine Arts Building colony took succor in a small collection of ramshackle buildings that housed a group of writers, artists, performers and bohemian hangers-on for the better part of six decades.[97] These ramshackle buildings had a previous function: they housed a group of souvenir and concession shops at the northwest entrance to the World's Columbian Exposition.

These L-shaped buildings lined both north and south sides of Fifty-Seventh Street from the Illinois Central Railroad viaduct on the west to Stoney Island Avenue on the east. They then ran for a few hundred feet north and south on the west side of Stoney Island. Together with the old Palace of Fine Arts (now the Museum of Science and Industry), La Rabida Children's Hospital and the Iowa State Building, these concession

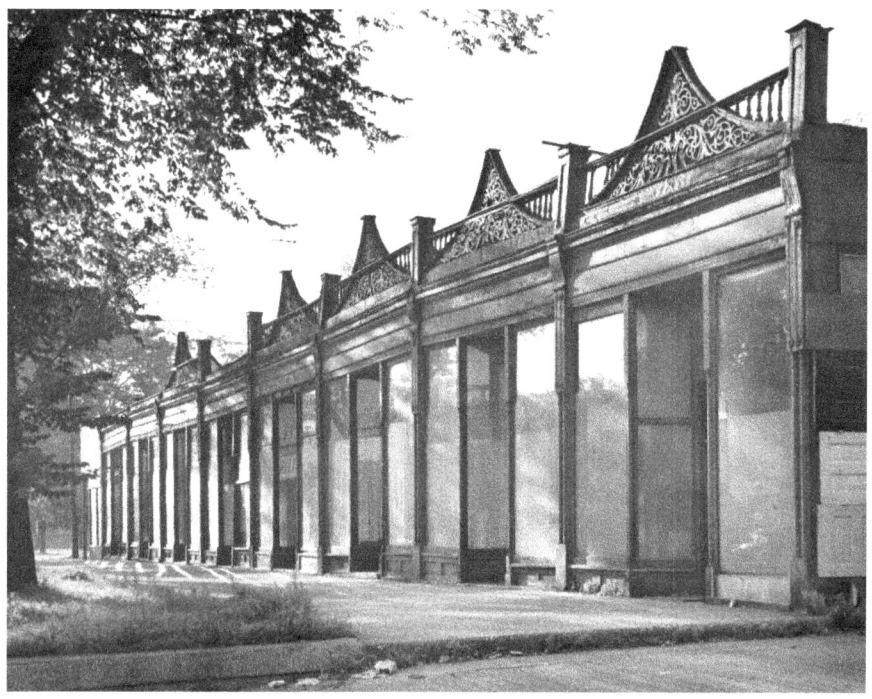

57th Street Artist Studios. *Cervin Robinson (1963), Historic American Buildings Survey. U.S. Department of the Interior.*

buildings were the only structures to survive the fires that destroyed the Columbian Exposition fairgrounds in 1894.

The concession buildings were designed by Chicago architect George Beaumont on behalf of Peyton Chandler and erected in 1891–92 in anticipation of the Columbian Exposition. Technically, they were not located within the fairgrounds proper but were across the street from the northwest reentrance to the grounds. Exposition maps do not show East Fifty-Seventh Street, so it is quite possible that this section of Fifty-Seventh Street had not yet been developed by 1893.[98] The buildings comprised a series of uniform, rather flimsy, single-story frame units featuring large plate-glass windows and crowned with decorative pagoda-like fretwork and balustrades running in between these gable-like ornaments. Each unit was eighteen feet wide and sixty feet deep.[99] They rested on wooden foundations and were constructed of wood and glass walls in the front and clapboard on the sides and rear. They had a door at the center of the storefront and a door in the rear of the unit opening to a common backyard, in which was located the privy.

Sixty years after they were erected, the concession buildings were described as

> *flimsy in the extreme, though they stand today largely unchanged and are housing artists still. Each one consisted of a single large storeroom with display windows at the street front and few windows elsewhere. Temporary partitions were erected though they fell far short of reaching high ceilings. Originally, decorated curtains could be hung in the windows to afford some degree of privacy and a capital chance for self-expression. Little could be done about the plumbing which consisted of one iron sink per building. As in the case of all Bohemians, the crowning glory of this one was its cheapness.*[100]

Originally, the buildings were not fitted with electricity, heat or gas, and the rent per unit at the turn of the century was about $12 a month ($340 in today's dollars).[101]

The first artist to move into the little collection of rickety concession buildings was apparently Bror Nordfelt, a painter and instructor at the Art Institute.[102] He created a studio in one of the concession buildings in 1900.[103] A neighboring unit was occupied by his friend, University of Chicago economist Thorstein Veblen, who became internationally famous as a pioneer on the economic theory of conspicuous consumption. His book *The Theory of the Leisure Class* was published in 1899 and influenced academics in several fields for decades.

Painter Charles Francis Browne, brother-in-law of Lorado Taft and Hamlin Garland, left his studio in the Fine Arts Building and retreated to a studio in the Fifty-Seventh Street complex around 1910 after his bored and restless wife, Turbia—understandably called "Turbulence" by the family—engaged in a lurid affair with a virile Scots Irish Chicago lawyer, followed by a quick divorce from the emotionally broken artist.[104] Other painters who located their studios at the artist colony on Fifty-Seventh Street under less dramatic circumstances included Emil Armin, Frederic Milton Grant, Fred Biesel, Beatrice Levy, Gertrude Abercrombie and Walter Sargent, professor of art at the University of Chicago.

The literary set arrived at the 57th Street Artist Colony by 1913, when journalist, novelist and literary critic Floyd Dell and his wife, Margery Currey, an early Chicago feminist, moved into two adjacent studios to foster an experiment with free love and an open marriage.[105] Their open marriage did not last long, but in the meantime, they hosted weekly salons,

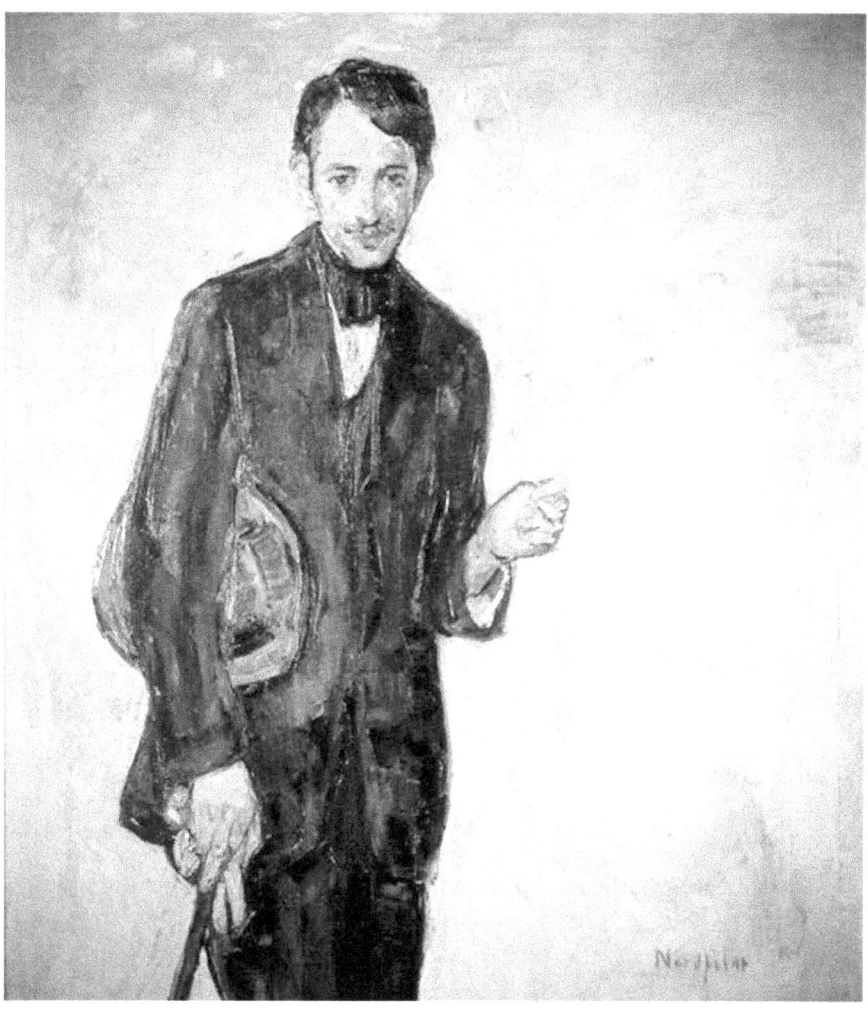

Portrait of Floyd Dell by Bror Julius Olsson Nordfeldt, circa 1913. *Special Collections Reading Room, Newberry Library.*

inviting Chicago literary lions Margaret Anderson, Carl Sandberg, Ben Hecht, Edgar Lee Masters, Theodore Dreiser, Sherwood Anderson, Harriet Monroe and members of the nearby university's intelligentsia.[106] Dell described his atelier, such as it was, as an ice-cold studio with "one book case and nine Fels-naphtha soap boxes full of books…a typewriter stand, a fireless cooker…and a couch with a mattress and a blanket."[107] In a few years, Dell would abandon the colony and move to New York's Greenwich Village, followed shortly thereafter by Hecht, Margaret Anderson and Sherwood Anderson.

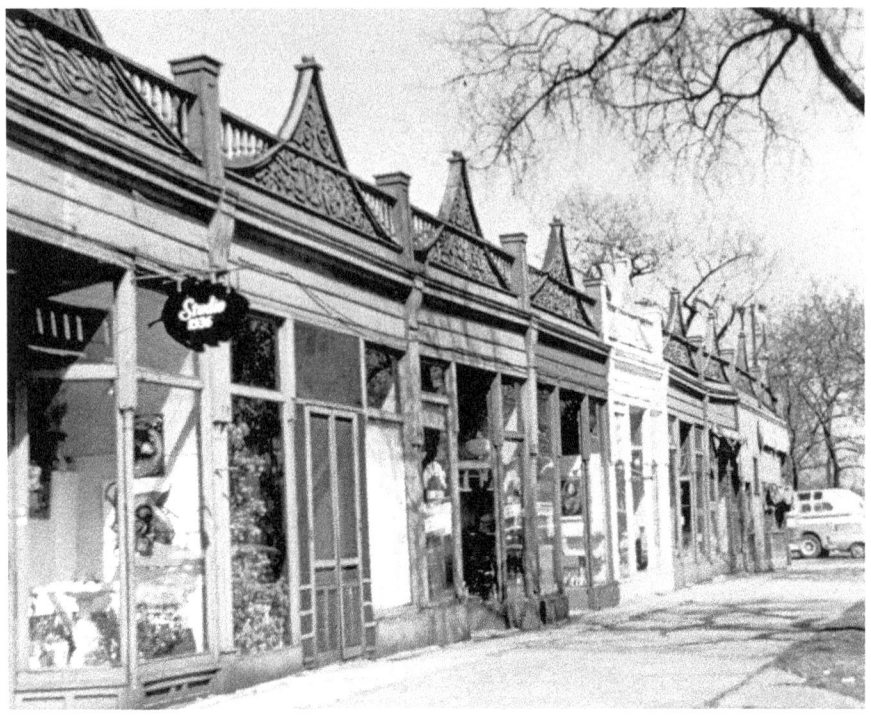

57th Street Artist Studios. *Photographer unknown, University of Chicago Photographic Archive, Special Collections Research Center, apf2-03965.*

Over the years, novelists Robert Herrick and Richard Wright; poets Margaret Walker, Langston Hughes and Gwendolyn Brooks; artist Charles Sebree; and poet and dramatist William Vaughn Moody were also active in the 57th Street Artist Colony. The colony was also home to a unique theatrical laboratory of sorts, where one-act plays were tested before its membership of more than one hundred playwrights and actors prior to being performed in front of the general public.[108] Every month, three or four plays written by the organization's members were tested and, if successful, offered to commercial theatrical managers. The stage measured only seventeen feet by fifteen feet, and the so-called auditorium contained seating for ninety.

The 57th Street Artist Colony was also a magnet for dancers. In 1927, Katherine Dunham, an innovative African American dancer, opened a dance studio in one of the old concession buildings after she was informed that other tenants in a Michigan Avenue building where she previously had a studio were "uncomfortable seeing negroes entering and leaving the building."[109] Dunham combined the study of classical ballet with African, Caribbean and Indonesian dance techniques. At the same time, she studied anthropology at the University of Chicago a few blocks away. She would be honored as a recipient at the Kennedy Center Awards in 1983 and received a National Medal of Arts in 1989. Previously, Dunham's brother Albert had organized the Cube Theater at the artist colony, where interracial theatrical productions were performed.

The artist colony at Fifty-Seventh Street would later spawn the Hyde Park Art Center (in 1939), which had its offices in the complex for several years, and the still-active 57th Street Art Fair in 1948, the oldest art fair in the Midwest. The artist colony continued to be a draw for artists, bohemians and art-related enterprises until the well-worn, ramshackle buildings were demolished in 1963 in the name of urban renewal.

LORADO TAFT AND THE MIDWAY STUDIOS

In 1906, Lorado Taft called it quits at the Fine Arts Building. He felt that the rent was too high and there was not enough room to work on the monumental sculptures for which he would become famous. He decamped to a Victorian house and red brick barn at Sixtieth Street on the south side of the old Midway Plaisance of the World's Columbian Exposition, across from the University of Chicago quadrangles. With the help of architect/ acrobat Irving Pond, Taft's atelier would later incorporate two additional frame buildings, thus forming thirteen rambling studios in what became the sculpture capitol of America.[110]

Between the 1893 World's Fair and his death in 1936, Lorado Taft became the most famous and distinguished artist in the Midwest and one of the most well-known sculptors in the United States.[111] Taft was born in Elmwood, Illinois, in 1860. He received a bachelor's degree in 1879 and a master's degree in 1880 from the University of Illinois at Champaign-Urbana. In 1880, Taft traveled to Paris, where he would spend the next three years studying sculpture at the École National Supérieure des Beaux-Arts. While in Paris, Taft twice exhibited his work at the Paris Solon. "Like all artists who emerged from the tradition-bound atmosphere of the Beaux-Arts, he was primarily a clay modeler whose sculptures were fluent and detailed, with lofty ideas and content based on a kind of literary symbolism."[112]

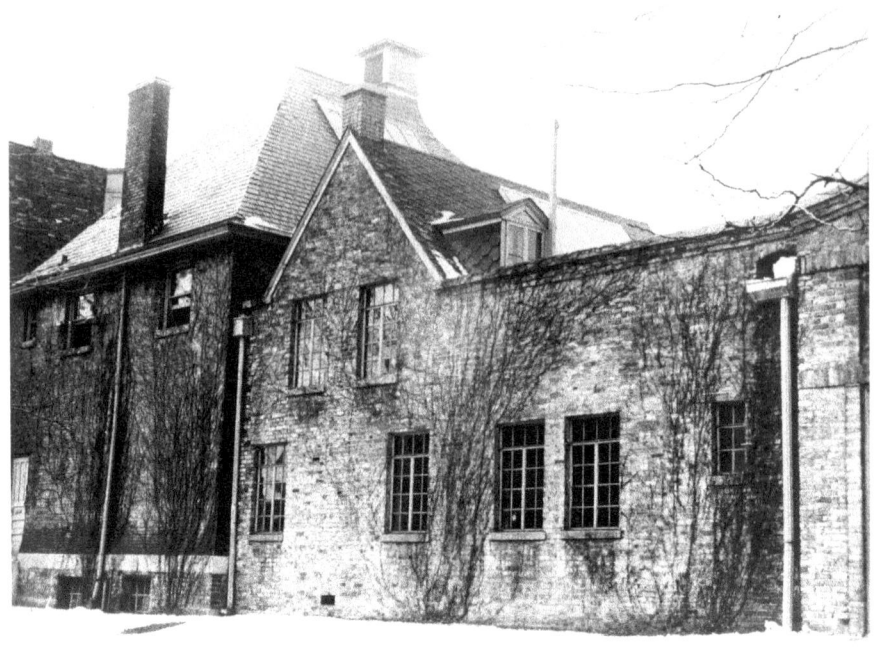

Midway Studios, exterior. *Photographer unknown, University of Chicago Photographic Archive, Special Collections Research Center, apf2-05137.*

In 1886, Taft opened a studio on State Street and founded the Department of Sculpture at the Art Institute, where he would remain a much-admired instructor until 1929. He executed several large sculptures for the World's Columbian Exposition in 1893, as well as Civil War memorials and other monumental statues and fountains scattered throughout the United States. Among these are the Columbus Fountain in front of Daniel Burnham's Union Station in Washington, D.C., a monument ordered by congressional fiat. In a competition joined by more than twenty of the nation's most distinguished sculptors, Taft was awarded the Columbus Fountain commission prize of $20,000 (about $470,000 in today's dollars). Three days of planned celebrations marked the dedication ceremony in June 1912. At the time, Taft's cousin, President William Howard Taft, was campaigning unsuccessfully for reelection against Theodore Roosevelt and Woodrow Wilson.

Taft moved his studio from State Street to the tenth floor of the Fine Arts Building in 1898, where his intimate friends Oliver Dennett Grover, Ralph Clarkson and Charles Francis Browne also opened studios. Taft became a member of the Little Room and the Cliff Dwellers Club. Over time, he would be invited to become a member of the country's most august art associations, including the National Academy of Design, the National Institute of Arts and Letters, the American Academy of Arts and Letters, the National Sculpture Society and, as an honorary member, the American Institute of Architects. After the death of Augustus Saint-Gaudens in 1907, Lorado Taft became the indisputable dean of American sculptors.

When Taft moved his studio to the Midway Plaisance in 1906, a brisk ten-minute walk from the 57th Street Artist Colony, he then had more than sufficient space to work on the enormous sculptures he favored. "Here, in thirteen rambling studios connected cell by cell like the chambered nautilus, Taft and a series of apprentices and students worked on the magnificent sculptures which were to be Lorado Taft's comment in concrete and stone on life, time and eternity."[113] At the center of the Midway Studios complex was a large court with very high ceilings lit by numerous skylights. The court featured a fireplace, a fountain, a stage for plays and a marble cutting room.

> On one end of the court was taken up by the original plaster cast of Taft's bronze group, Great Lakes, which stands today on the south side of the Art Institute. Beneath the huge figures of the five lakes was a little kitchen which Taft called "the only submarine kitchen in Chicago" where the noonday meal for the twenty-five or so apprentices, students and visiting artist friends was prepared.... The Midway Studio was an idyllic spot, and young men and women from all over the Midwest came there to work, while studying at the Art Institute.[114]

Taft's most dramatic monumental sculpture, and probably his greatest accomplishment, is the majestic *Fountain of Time*, much of which he would sculpt at the Midway Studios a few blocks away. Taft sited the fountain at the westernmost end of the Midway Plaisance, abutting the eastern edge of Washington Park. It was originally intended by its sculptor to be part of a larger beautification plan that would posit the *Fountain of Time* at the west of end of the Midway, an equally monumental *Fountain of Creation* at the east end, abutting Jackson Park, with several smaller statues lining both sides of the Plaisance in between.[115] In the end, only the *Fountain of Time* would be built.

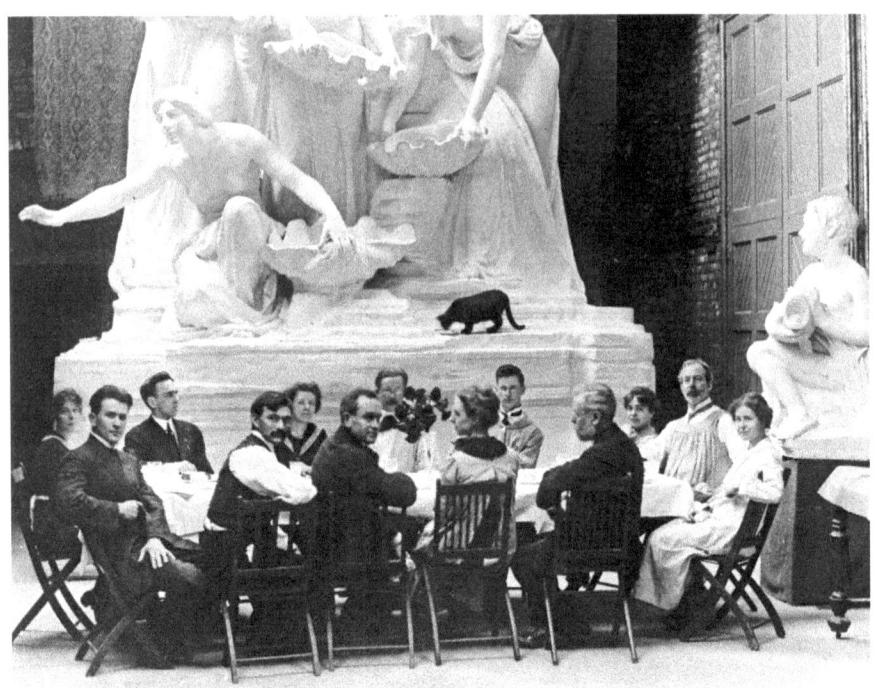

Lorado Taft and guests dining at Midway Studios in front of a plaster model of Taft's *Fountain of the Great Lakes*, circa 1907. Among those pictured are writer Henry Blake Fuller and sculptress Nellie Verne Walker. *Photographer unknown, University of Chicago Photographic Archive, Special Collections Research Center, apf1-08072.*

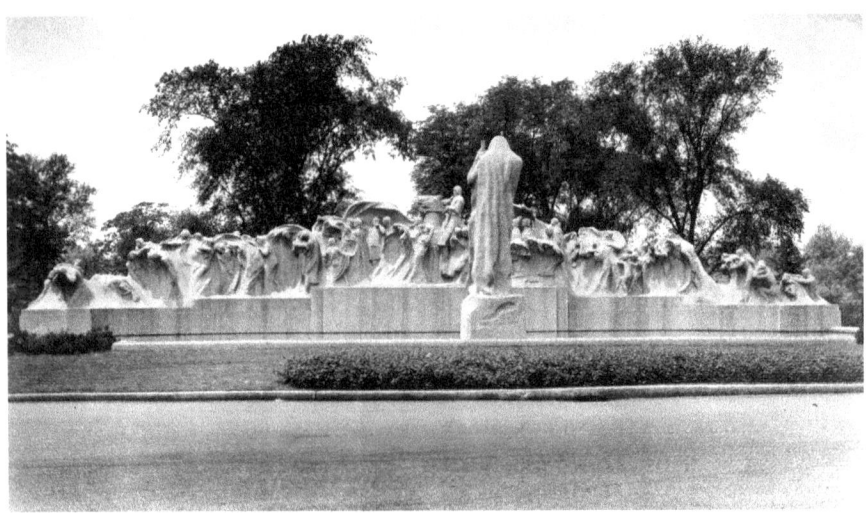

Lorado Taft's *Fountain of Time*, circa 1922. *Photographer unknown, University of Chicago Photographic Archive, Special Collections Research Center, apf1-08110.*

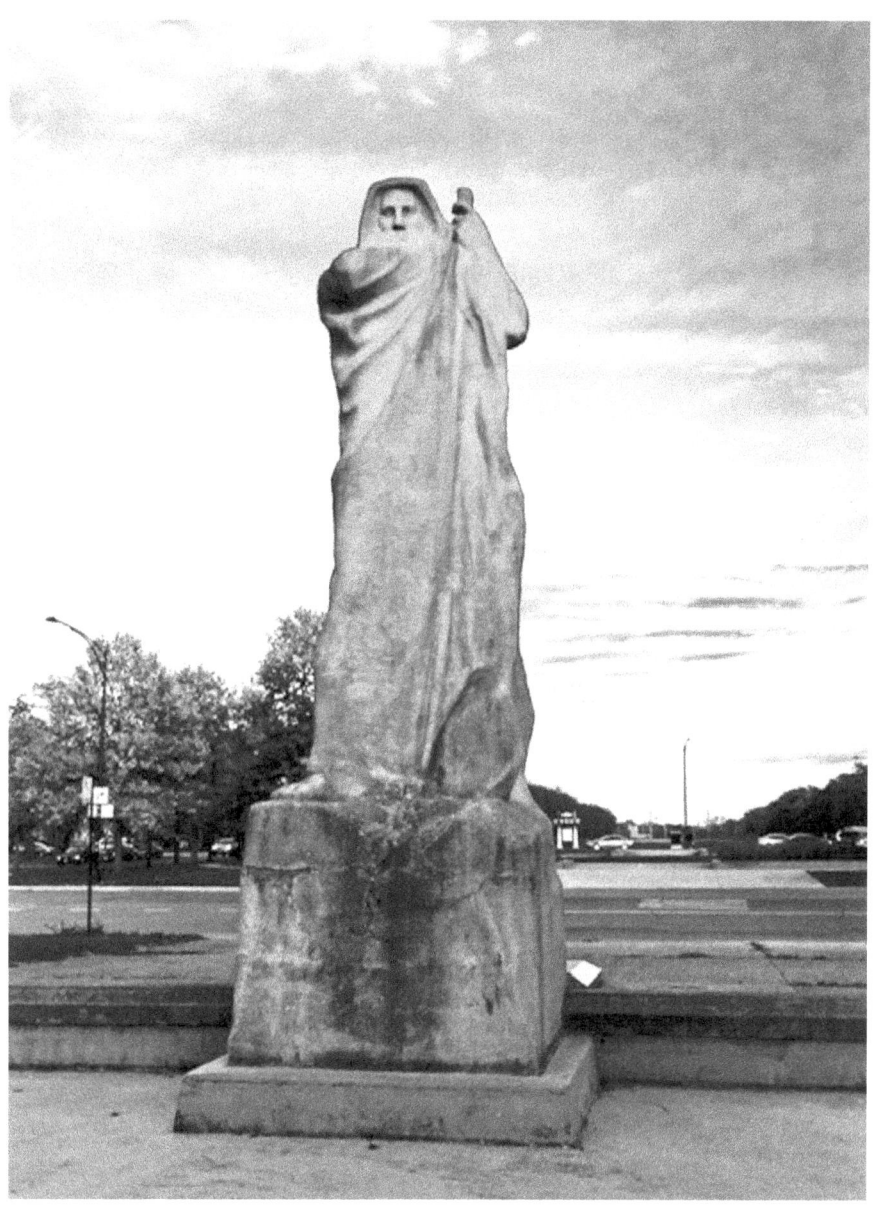

Sculpture of Father Time, part of the *Fountain of Time* by Lorado Taft in 1922. *K.M. Stolte (2018).*

The inspiration for the sculpture was based on the work of English poet Henry Austin Dobson: "Time goes, you say? Ah no, / Alas, time stays. We go." Taft himself provided further explanation of his conception with sweeping, romantic and philosophical sentiment:

> *The words* [of the Dobson couplet] *brought before me a picture which fancy speedily transformed into a colossal work of sculpture. I saw the mighty crag-like figure of Time, mantled like one of* [painter John] *Sargent's prophets, leaning upon his staff, his chin upon his hand, and watching with cynical, inscrutable gaze the endless march of humanity—a majestic relief of marble, I saw it, swinging in a wide circle around the form of the lone sentinel and made up of the shapes of hurrying men and women and children in endless procession, ever impelled by the winds of destiny in the inexorable lock-step of the ages. Theirs the "fateful forward movement" which has not ceased since time began. But in that crowded concourse how few detach themselves from the grayness of the dusky caravan, how few there are who even lift their heads. Here an over-taxed body falls—and a place is vacant for a moment, there a strong man turns to the silent shrouded reviewer and with lifted arms utters the cry of the old-time gladiators: "Hail Caesar, we who go to our death salute thee"—and presses forward.*[116]

Taft originally conceived of the colossal sculpture in 1909, but it was not completed until 1922, when it was unveiled during a large dedication ceremony. It was largely funded by the Ferguson Fund, a trust created by lumber baron Benjamin Ferguson in 1905 for the promotion and encouragement of public statuary.[117] The work, composed of concrete, measures almost 127 feet in width and at its vertical peak, depicting a medieval warrior on horseback, about 24 feet. There are one hundred figures in the sculpture, one of which visually represents Lorado Taft himself.

After Taft moved his studio to Hyde Park in 1906, Chicago's most distinguished sculptress at the time, Nellie Walker, joined him there. Occasionally, Walker assisted Taft on his monumental commissions, along with Taft's small army of apprentice-artists and students. Like her mentor, Walker previously maintained a studio at the Fine Arts Building and was a member of the Little Room. About the same time, both Taft and Walker would become founding members of another artist colony set in the country about one hundred miles west of Chicago called the Eagle's Nest Camp.

The stern, hooded figure of Father Time would ultimately take Lorado Taft at his studio/home in 1936, aged seventy-six. Nellie Walker lived to the age of ninety-eight, dying in 1973. The Midway Studios was placed in the National Register of Historic Places in 1966 and designated a Chicago Historical Landmark in 1993. It is presently home to the University of Chicago's visual arts and creative writing program and still contains artist studios for use by students and faculty.

5

Summering Away

The Bucolic Artist Colonies

One of the very first artist colonies anywhere was established at Barbizon, near the Fontainebleau Forest in north-central France. Around 1830, French and English painters began congregating there in order to draw inspiration from the beautiful natural surroundings, usually during the summers, although some settled there year-round. The Barbizon colony would be active until about 1870.

A few years after the World's Columbian Exposition, some Chicago artists and writers, especially the relatively successful ones, pined for spending summers away from the city, where the heat and humidity (and no doubt air pollution resulting from its factories, foundries and steel mills) were oppressive and unpleasant. They were determined to have their own idyllic "Barbizon," where they could breathe fresh air and create their art inspired by nature, free from the noise and dreariness of city streets.

Around the turn of the twentieth century, one set of artists and writers headed west and established an artist colony on thirteen acres perched over the east bank of the Rock River about 100 miles from Chicago. A second group headed east a few years later and formed an art colony on the banks of the Kalamazoo River near Saugatuck, Michigan, located about 140 miles from the city. Both artist colonies became a magnet for painters, sculptors and, to a lesser extent, writers. Both still exist in one form or another, albeit now under the formal aegis of institutions of secondary education.

THE EAGLE'S NEST CAMP ARTIST COLONY

In 1843, Margaret Fuller, a pioneer female journalist and early feminist activist, visited a Native American village on the banks of the Rock River near where the tiny town of Oregon, Illinois, would later be settled. She wrote of the natural beauty of the place, which she referred to as the Eagle's Nest, probably the name derived from the local Native American tribe.[118] Fuller concluded, "I do believe that Florence and Rome are mere suburbs compared to this capital of Nature's art."[119] Fifty-five years later, Wallace Heckman, the owner of the land Fuller described, offered to lease thirteen acres to a group of artists and writers for use as a summer camp for them and their families. In 1898, Heckman, a Chicago attorney and patron of the arts, signed the lease, which required the annual payment of one dollar and a commitment by each artist and writer to give a public lecture or demonstration to the nearby community's residents each year.[120]

The founding members of the Eagle's Nest Camp artist colony were artists Lorado Taft, Oliver Dennett Grover, Ralph Clarkson, Charles Francis Browne and Nellie Walker; novelists Henry Blake Fuller and Hamlin Garland; poet and editor Horace Spencer Fiske; University of Chicago administrator James Spencer Dickerson; composer/musician Clarence Dickerson; and architect brothers Irving and Allen Pond.[121] Given its core membership, the Eagle's Nest Camp could easily be viewed as the Little Room displaced to the beautiful countryside of rural Illinois for the summer months.[122]

The Eagle's Nest colonists spent June through October at the camp.[123] In the early years, they each paid dues of three dollars a week, which was earmarked for food, drink and compensation for a cook.[124] The first summer, 1898, the colonists resided in tents and set up a rudimentary camp kitchen and dining area comprising a low-lying building set close to the edge of the high river bluff and covered by a tent fly stretched between trees, below which were tables and benches.[125] Three years later, the Eagle's Nest colonists, tired of the bugs and wet conditions when it stormed, built a permanent structure of fieldstone that became known as the Camp House, to be used as a kitchen, dining hall and meeting space.[126] The building was dedicated during a party at which the colonists and their families came to dinner in fancy costumes.

The big room glowed with candle-light and fire-light as the procession wound in and out the doors and round and round the tables. There were shouts of laughter when Mr. Clarkson led a cakewalk, when Mr. I.K. Pond walked on his hands, or lifted the little red devils (now Mrs. H.B.

Fuller…and Mr. W.P. Dickerson) who had led the procession, up to sit at either end of the high mantel, where they stayed throughout the evening until a Virginia Reel brought the party to a close.[127]

Eventually, the artists, writers and hangers-on built permanent structures for their families' housing and dispensed altogether with the leaky tents. As the years went by, the colonists expanded and enhanced their cottages with fireplaces, screened porches, small kitchens, bedrooms and even bathrooms.[128] Taft used as his studio a wooden converted barn on the property. It had the advantage of a sloping roof with large skylights that allowed for large sculptures.[129]

In 1904, Harriet Monroe, a frequent guest of the Eagle's Nest Camp, published a six-page article (with eleven photographs) in *House Beautiful* describing the camp, the various public buildings and the artist cottages that had been built by that point.[130] Taft's cottage, the largest, was a handsome seven-room structure built of yellow limestone and roofed with red Spanish colonial tiles. Ralph Clarkson built a small wooden cottage/studio about one hundred feet north of Taft's. It featured a snug living room with a large fireplace, two sleeping chambers and a graceful veranda overlooking the Rock River. Clarkson painted several portraits in the studio, including those of Chicago mayor Carter Harrison and University of Chicago president Henry Pratt Judson.[131]

Oliver Dennett Grover built his small cottage in 1902. It featured stucco exterior walls, a shingled roof and a grand stone fireplace. Charles Francis Bowne's spacious stone cottage was the only one to have a second floor. Hamlin Garland, the alpha male of the group, whose literary subject matter was typically hardened western frontier settlers and Native Americans, opted out of the safety and security of a well-built cottage, choosing instead to spend his nights in a large canvas tepee located at the summit of the cliff overlooking the river. Monroe describes Garland's tepee as stuffed with "Navajo blankets, old baskets and other Indian treasures, and offers guests perhaps the most picturesque interior at Eagle's Nest."[132]

Most of the cottages and other buildings no longer exist. The most notable relic of the artist colony is Lorado Taft's colossal sculpture of a Native American, thought to be of Chief Black Hawk, which dominated the camp. Taft conceived of the statue in 1908 and completed it in 1911. Apparently, Taft's former brother-in-law Charles Francis Browne, draped in a blanket, acted as the model for the sculpture.[133] Cast in concrete, the statue rises to a height of almost sixty feet (with pedestal) on the banks of the Rock River.

Its gaze is affixed in thoughtful and dignified solace upon the natural beauty of the surrounding area, a site the Native American population had been chased out of by the federal government within the memories of Taft and his fellow Eagle's Nest campers. It is said to be the second-largest monolithic statue made of concrete in the United States.

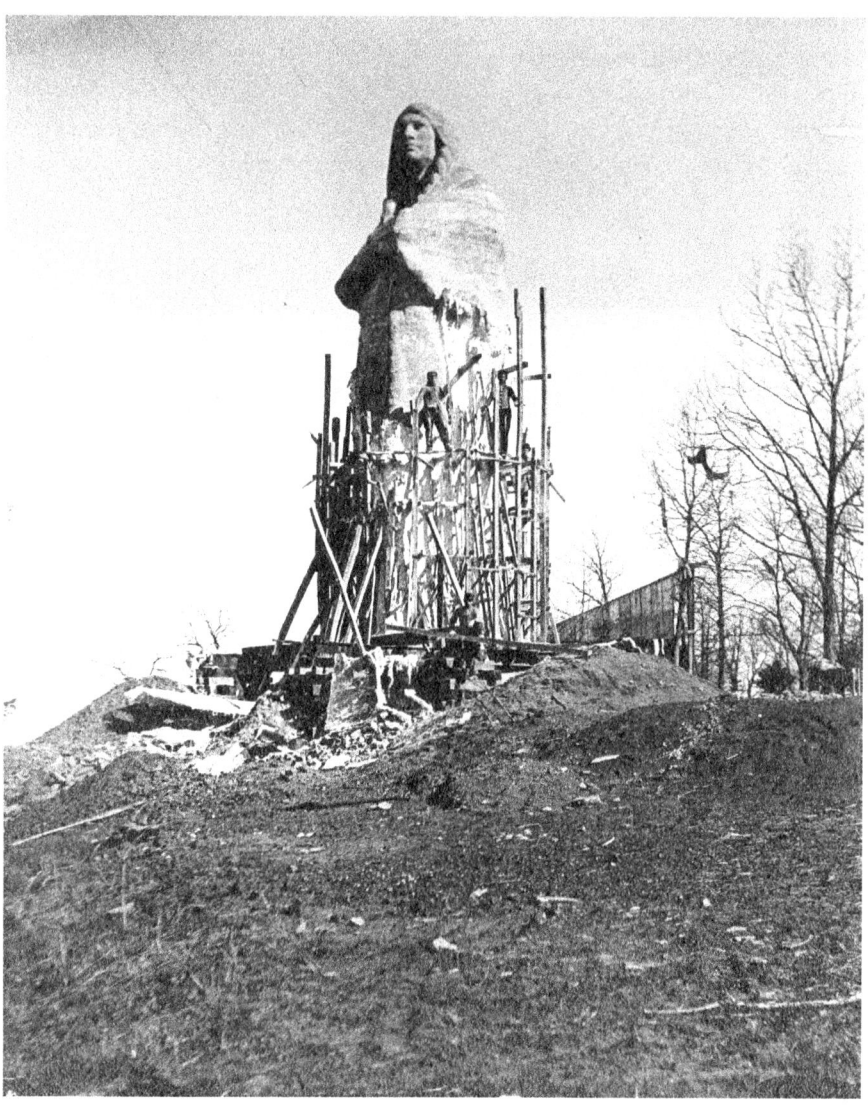

Lorado Taft's colossal sculpture of Chief Black Hawk under construction, circa 1911. *Photographer unknown, University of Illinois Archives, Lorado Taft Papers, Box 30, No. 17, Print No. 5.*

The spirited high jinks of the Eagle's Nest Camp residents made the camp a place of revelry when the artists were not occupied with more highbrow cultural endeavors. "There was activity everywhere. Walking through the camp, you might see Mr. Browne trudging along the edge of the bluff, whistling or singing, carrying his easel, his paint box and the picture he had just finished; you might come across Mr. Grover on the spring road soberly smoking his pipe and working on a large canvas."[134] The company apparently went in for dances and processions of any kind. Lorado Taft and his wife, Ada, had a supply of ancient Greek costumes from a previous pageant at the Art Institute, and the colonists would don the costumes and frolic in and out of the trees along the bluff, singing praises to Pan and Bacchus.[135] Other times, the group conducted processions dressed as gypsies or cowboys and Indians.

The most memorable procession was to welcome the world-renowned Egyptologist James Breasted, founder of the Oriental Institute at the University of Chicago. On that occasion, Breasted "was met by the white-shrouded figure of a priestess, who silently led the way through the forest. Before the camp gate was reached, the distinguished academic and his guide solemnly passed twenty white-shrouded, seated figures on other side of the road, supposed to represent the stone Colossi of Memnon," each with a candle burning between his or her feet to light the way.[136] (The Colossi of Memnon are a pair of stone statutes, sixty feet high, of Amenhotep, an Egyptian pharaoh who ruled in the fourteenth century BC.) The next day, Dr. Breasted joined the colonists dressed as an Egyptian slave driver in a full-dress procession of "ancient Egyptians" along the bluff while a flutist played selections from *Aïda*. The procession terminated at the next-door home of the artist colony's landlord, Wallace Heckman, where Breasted made an impressive speech in Arabic and offered Heckman two manacled "slaves" (bound with the chains from the porch swing). The colonists ceremoniously paid their annual one-dollar rent—"eighty-nine pennies, two slugs and some postage."[137]

Almost as a testament to the art colony's penchant for processions, the 1902 sculpture *Funeral Procession*, a collaborative effort executed by Lorado Taft and six of his students at the colony, stood, and continues to stand, near Taft's Eagle's Nest cottage and studio. The sculpture features six life-sized hooded mourners bearing a coffin on their shoulders. According to legend, Taft's students cast the finished sculpture while he was away in Europe, and Taft is said to have disapproved of this unassigned student work for obscure reasons. Perhaps he did not appreciate a funeral procession permanently looming outside his cottage door.[138]

The last of the original Eagle's Nest Camp's colonists died in 1942; accordingly, the lease to the Eagle's Nest Camp property was terminated. In 1951, land that incorporated the Eagle's Nest Camp was conveyed to what is now Northern Illinois University at DeKalb, Illinois. The site, renamed the Lorado Taft Field Campus, is used as a year-round center for conducting natural science classes in an outdoor setting. Some of the artist cottages, including Lorado Taft's handsome cottage, and the Camp House have been restored and are currently used by the NIU program.

THE OX-BOW ARTIST COLONY

Deep in the Lake Michigan woods and dunes, nestled along the banks of the Kalamazoo River near the hamlet of Saugatuck, Michigan, is a camp of rustic cottages, dormitories and art studios. It was established in 1910 as a summer school for artists and art students by two instructors from the Art Institute and has operated as an artist colony ever since. The bucolic camp provides an inspiring setting to paint, sketch or sculpt.

Ox-Bow, originally called the Summer School of Painting, was founded as a seasonal respite for artists by Frederick Frary Fursman and Walter Marshall Clute after they visited the area in the summer of 1910. Fursman was born in the small town of El Paso, Illinois, in 1874. After a ten-year stint in business as a clerk, Fursman attended the Art Institute for several years, beginning in 1901. There, he studied with visiting professor Gari Melchers, an internationally known naturalist painter; John Vanderpoel; and Karl Albert Buehr. In 1906, Fursman traveled to Paris, where he studied at the Académie de la Grande Chaumière and the Académie Julian.

As early as 1902, Fursman began exhibiting his paintings at the Art Institute. In 1909, following his return from Europe, the Art Institute organized an exhibition of twenty-nine of his canvasses, a remarkable achievement for someone at that stage of his career. He also exhibited his work at the Pennsylvania Academy of Fine Arts. Fursman's paintings generally reflected a loose impressionist style with strikingly vibrant and vivid colors. They often featured beautiful young women in lovely outdoor settings. In 1910, Fursman became an instructor at the Art Institute.

Walter Marshall Clute was born in Schenectady, New York, in 1870 and studied under Kenyon Cox at the Art Students League in New York City as well as at the École des Beaux-Arts in Paris. In the mid-1890s, Clute began working as a newspaper illustrator in Buffalo, New York. In 1898, Clute traveled to Chicago, where he worked as an illustrator for the *Chicago Daily News*. That same year, the *Daily News* sent Clute to Cuba to cover the Spanish-American War. When he returned to Chicago, he was invited to become an instructor of illustration at the Art Institute. The following year, the Institute exhibited many of Clute's Cuban war illustrations, together with those of fellow illustrator John T. McCutcheon. About the same time, Clute was elected president of the Palette and Chisel Club, where he exhibited some of his works. Clute became a regular exhibitor at the Art Institute's annual American Art Exhibition and Chicago and Vicinity Exhibition. Clute was the first director of Ox-Bow.

Initially, Fursman and Clute began teaching summer painting courses at the Brandle Farm on the east bank of the Kalamazoo River about a mile upstream from the art colony's present location. In 1912 and 1913, they

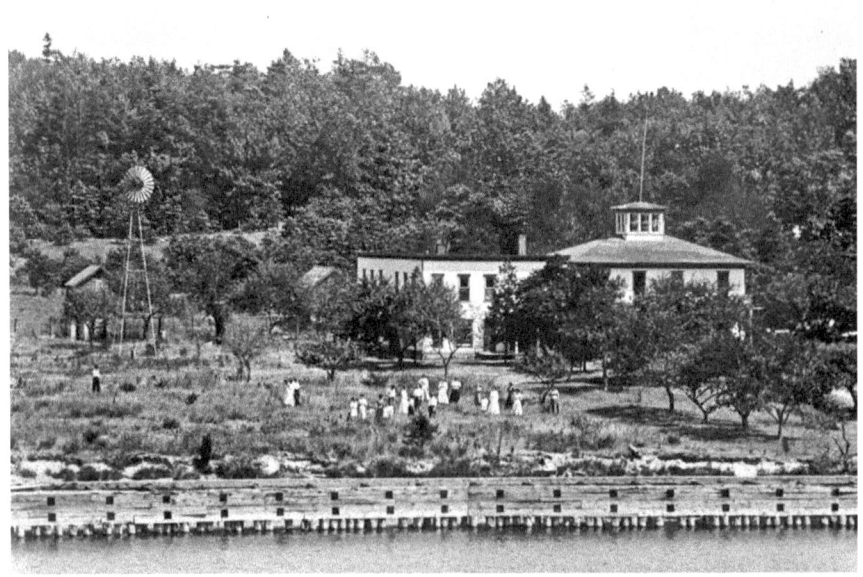

Ox-Bow Summer School, c. 1915. *Photographer unknown,* Holland (Michigan) Sentinel.

moved their classes to the nearby Park House, a small inn.[139] The following year, the colony again moved its operations to the twenty-room Riverside Hotel, which was soon thereafter renamed the Ox-Bow Inn for the ox-bow shaped bend of the Kalamazoo River at that location.[140] The area is located near the eastern shore of Lake Michigan, where Fursman and the colony's instructors and students held festive picnics.

In time, the group built numerous makeshift studios, tiny rudimentary cottages and other service buildings. Painting courses were held outdoors. In 1915, Clute prematurely died of a heart attack at age forty-five, and Fursman became the art colony's director, a position he held for thirty years. That same year, Albert Henry Krehbiel, another instructor at the Art Institute and a distinguished impressionist painter, joined the faculty of the Ox-Bow school. Krehbiel's works were displayed in more than thirty exhibitions at the Art Institute between 1906 and 1939, and he was given a one-man show there in 1922. Thomas Tallmadge, renowned Chicago architect and adherent of Frank Lloyd Wright's prairie school, also joined the faculty in 1915. (Tallmadge would later bequeath Ox-Bow 110 acres adjacent to the art colony upon his death.)

Francis Chapin, a popular Art Institute instructor and prolific Chicago painter, began teaching at Ox-Bow in 1934, becoming the school's director after Fursman's tenure in the early 1940s. Over the years, several other established artists associated with the Art Institute taught summer courses at the Ox-Bow artist colony, including Edgar Rupprecht, John Warner Norton and Frederic Milton Grant.

Fursman would continue teaching at Ox-Bow each summer until his death in 1943. Although it started as a school for painting and drawing, as the years passed, Ox-Bow came to offer programs in ceramics, glass, papermaking, printmaking and metalcraft.[141] As many as four hundred students annually would take instruction at Ox-Bow, and the faculty grew to a total of more than sixty.[142] In 1987, the Art Institute assumed responsibility for the summer school's academic program and formalized its stewardship relationship with Ox-Bow in a sponsorship agreement in 1995.[143]

6

Towertown

Chicago's Left Bank

Chicago's very first settlers built their homes and farms on land north of the Chicago River, in what is now referred to as the Near North neighborhood. Jean Baptiste du Sable and John Kinzie had erected their humble cabins north of the river before 1805. From 1830 on, Chicago's commercial and industrial interests were consolidated in the area south of the river in the so-called Loop. Both before and after the Great Fire of 1871, the Near North Side neighborhood was largely a well-to-do residential district. Much of Chicago's earliest wealth was poured into the fashionable mansions and row houses that once lined Ohio, Ontario, Erie, Huron, Rush, Cass, State, Dearborn and LaSalle Streets. These homes were occupied by families bearing such distinguished and respectable names as McCormick, Ogden, Wentworth, Medill, Field, Blatchford, Tree and Nickerson. A handful of these homes still survive.

As the city prospered and grew, commercial interests began invading the tranquil and rarefied neighborhood immediately north of the Chicago River. This northward encroachment of commerce and its attendant ills (increased traffic, noise, crowding and air pollution) ultimately had the effect of pushing Chicago's wealthy south to Prairie Avenue and north to what is now called the Gold Coast. The void this sociological phenomenon created was quickly filled by slum conditions in large swaths of the Near North Side neighborhood. Over time, once-fashionable mansions were subdivided into multi-unit tenements. Rooming houses and apartment buildings were erected, each increasingly shabbier than its predecessors.

Relentless development along the banks of the Chicago River had a hand in this social transformation. Greater industrialization on the river attracted immigrants newly arrived from Europe.

Great industries have sprung up along the river, and peoples speaking foreign tongues have come to labor in them. The slum has offered these alien peoples a place to live cheaply and to themselves; and wave upon wave of immigrants has swept over the area—Irish, Swedish, German, Italian, Persian, Greek, and Negro—forming colonies, staying for a while, then giving way to others.[144]

On once-charming streets where the children of McCormicks and Medills played now sprang up pawnshops, secondhand stores and small flophouses. In the windows of former gleaming mansions appeared neatly lettered cards reading "Furnished Rooms Available." By 1915, Clark Street had become the bustling, sleezy Rialto of the slum, where small transient hotels, cabarets and nightclubs, gambling halls, cheap dance halls, rudimentary cinemas and dingy restaurants and taverns operated day and night.[145]

Writing about this area in 1929, sociologist Harvey Zorbaugh noted, "In the slum, but not of it, is 'Towertown.' South of Chicago Avenue, along east Erie, Ohio, Huron and Superior Streets is a considerable colony of artists and of would-be artists."[146] Viewed a little more broadly, Towertown was a haven of artists, musicians, dancers, architects, poets, novelists, art students, dilettantes, would-be artists and other imposters, poor bohemians, rich bohemians, radicals and assorted kindred spirits and hangers-on. Collectively, these residents formed Chicago's largest and most heterogenous artist colony. The name *Towertown* derived from the nearby famous municipal Water Tower, located at the intersection of Michigan Avenue and Pierson Street, that survived the Great Fire of 1871.

Attracted by Towertown's low rents, artists and other creative types began taking up residence in subdivided mansions, shabby rooming houses, attics and basements throughout the district beginning before World War I. Some of the more ambitious artists converted coach houses, barns and stables into large, airy studios. By 1920, Chicago had a new "Left Bank" district, so to speak, of considerable size, diversity and allure.

The boundaries of Towertown were never precise but were generally regarded to be north of Grand Avenue, south of Chicago Avenue, west of Michigan Avenue and east of LaSalle Street. Smack in the middle of this teeming, bustling hive of creative types stood the dignified Tree Studios,

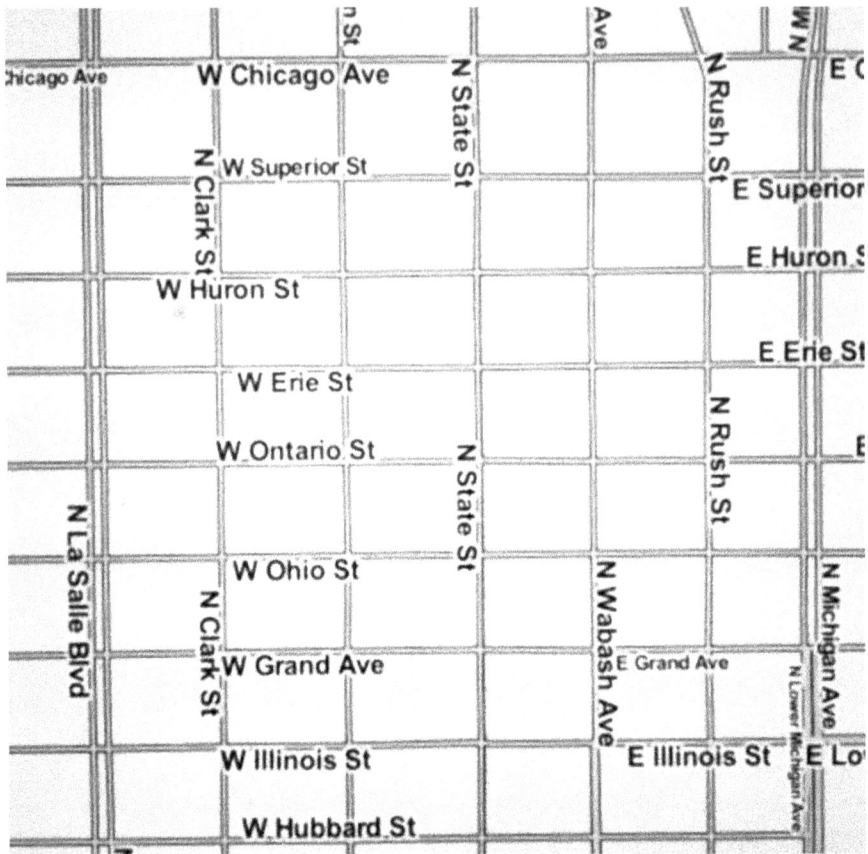

Map of Towertown. *Chicago Public Library.*

the granddaddy of all artist colonies and home to the equally dignified members of the old guard: Oliver Dennett Grover, Ralph Clarkson, Karl Albert Buehr, Walter Marshall Clute and Pauline Palmer.

Among the hundreds of creative types who moved into the artist warrens of the Towertown district, some had maintained studios or worked for arts-related institutions that had offices at the Fine Arts Building. Painters Grover and Clarkson have already been mentioned. Harriet Monroe moved the operations of *Poetry* magazine to the very heart of Towertown at her residence/salon on North Cass Street (now Wabash Avenue). Other small progressive periodicals that took root in Towertown include *Youth Magazine*, the *Wave*, the *Dil Pickler* and the *Dil Pickle Can.*[147] In 1915–16, Sherwood Anderson wrote his classic group of tales, *Winesburg, Ohio*, while living in a Wabash Avenue boardinghouse that he called "the little brother of the arts."

His close friend Ben Hecht, reporter for the *Daily News* and author of *Eric Dorn* and *A Thousand and One Afternoons in Chicago*, was one of Towertown's better known celebrities.[148] So, too, was another close friend, Maxwell Bodenheim, whose first writings were introduced by Harriet Moore's *Poetry* magazine and whose novels and books of poetry would make him nationally famous in the 1920s.

Other writers who would become nationally and even internationally famous were fixtures in Towertown. Nobel-winning novelist Ernest Hemingway lived briefly in the artist enclave after World War I.[149] Poet/playwright Edna St. Vincent Millay and playwright/novelist Edna Ferber, both of whom would later win Pulitzer Prizes and become important members of the national literary set and Hollywood contributors, spent formative years in the district.[150] And, of course, there was Carl Sandburg, another Pulitzer Prize winner.

Among the newer generation of painters, illustrators and sculptors who came of age in the first two decades of the twentieth century and took up residence in the Tree Studios or converted Towertown coach houses, barns and stables were painters/illustrators Frederic Milton Grant, Macena Barton, Peter Diem, Ruth Van Sickle Ford, Rowena Fry, Edgar Miller, Anthony Angarola, Boris Anisfeld, Rudolph Weisenborn and Indiana Gyberson; and sculptors John Storrs, Albin Polasek and Stanislas Szukalski. The last listed cut quite a figure in the neighborhood. An immigrant from Poland, Szukalski has been described as temperamental, full of genius and rage: "a friend of Ben Hecht and Max Bodenheim who delighted in bating the prim and successful and was not above smashing his own work with his cane when he did not like the way it was displayed at the Art Institute. He wore his thick black hair like a girl's, crowned it with a left-bankish tam, and let his ill-fitting clothes hang from his spare frame."[151]

Szukalski arrived, age eighteen, in Chicago in 1913, attended the Art Institute and "galvanized the city's art world."[152] He was honored with two one-man shows by the Art Institute in 1916 and 1917, an almost unheard-of achievement for someone at that phase of his career. Ben Hecht described Szukalski as starving, muscular, aristocratic and disdainful of lesser beings than himself.[153] Together with Rudolph Weisenborn and Edgar Miller, Szukalski would become a leader of the forces of modern and avant-garde art in Chicago and would delight in clashing with the Triumvirate (Messrs. Taft, Grover and Clarkson) and other traditionalists.

Progressive architects also established themselves in Towertown. As already noted, Andrew Rebori and his wife had leased one of the larger suites in the Ontario Annex of the Tree Studios in 1913. Dwight Perkins, who is best known for his designs in the arts and crafts and prairie school vernaculars, and his partners erected a modest office building for themselves a few hundred feet west of the Water Tower in 1917. This much-beloved building has been protected as a Chicago Historical Landmark since 1993.

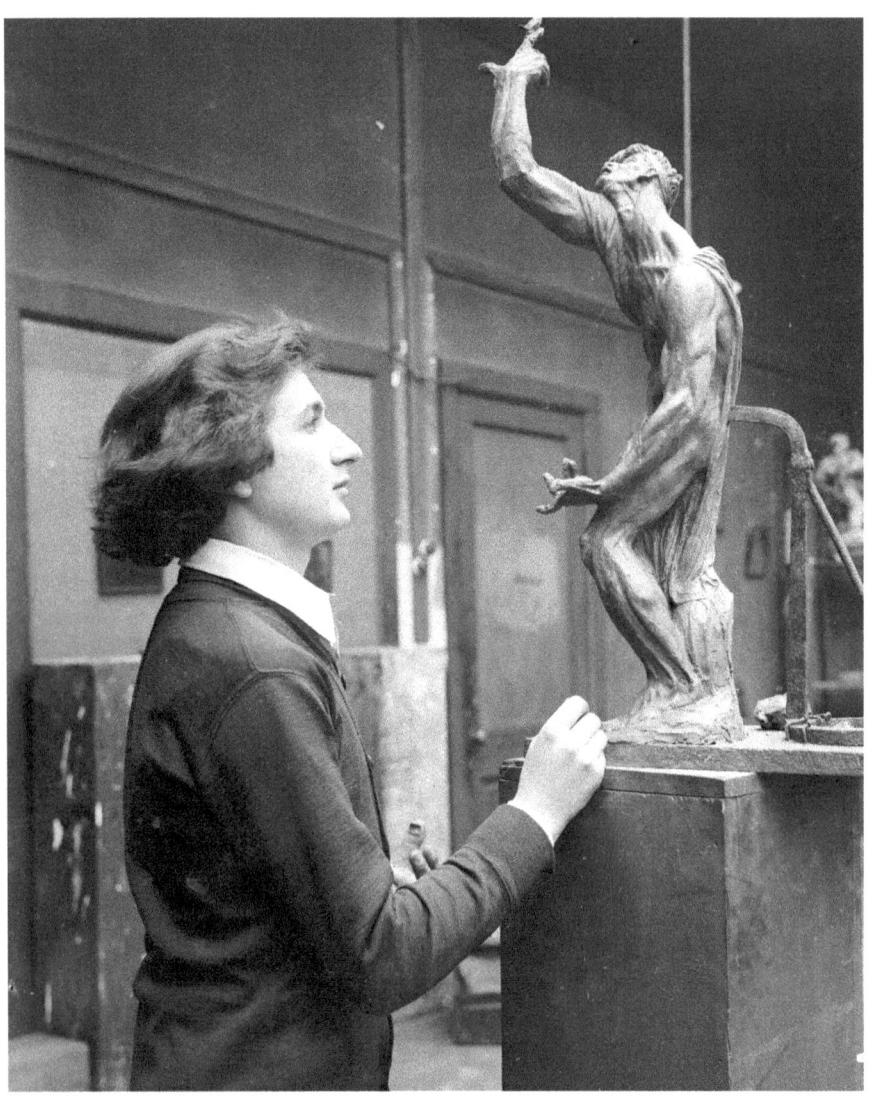

Stanislas Szukalski in his Towertown atelier. Chicago Daily News *(1914)*, *Chicago History Museum, DN-0063787.*

TOWERTOWN ARTISTS' STUDIOS

While most artists, writers and creative types in Towertown lived and worked in small individual apartments or studios within converted mansions and rooming houses scattered throughout the district, there were a few notable larger studio buildings that catered almost exclusively to artists. One was the former mansion of U.S. Senator Charles Farwell, located at 116–120 East Pierson Street, which had originally been built in the 1880s. Chicago architect Bertrand Goldberg, who designed the world-famous Marina City complex on the Chicago River in the late 1960s, shared a studio in the Farwell Mansion in the early 1930s with painter/muralist Edward Millman. In an oral history, Goldberg explained that the huge Farwell Mansion and its rear coach house and stables functioned essentially as an inexpensive commune containing studios for forty to fifty artists.[154]

The Three Arts Club was conceived at a meeting of prominent Chicagoans, including Jane Addams, in 1911, with the express purpose of providing safe and affordable housing and work space for young women aspiring to be artists. The driving forces behind the club were Gwethalyn Jones, Lolita Armour and Mary Aldis.[155] Jones's father donated the land and the funds necessary to construct the building.[156] The structure, designed by

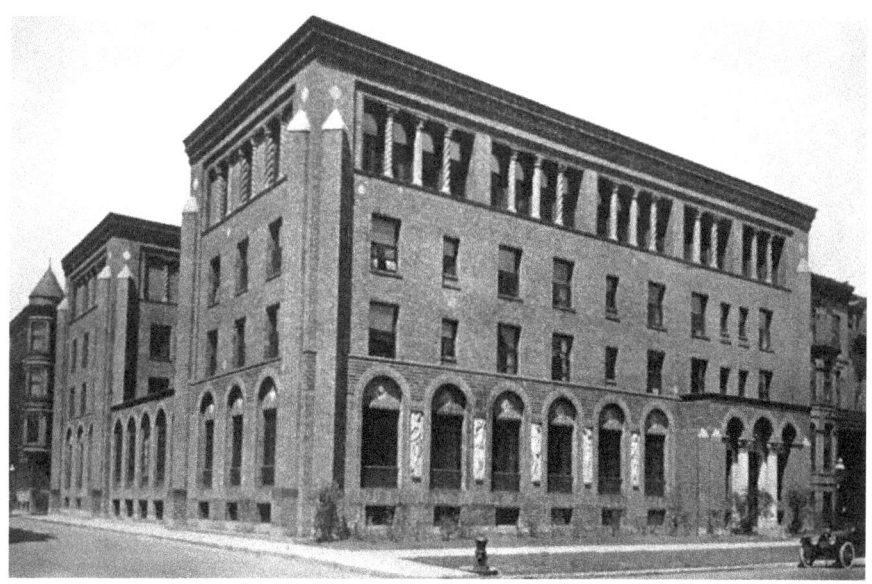

Three Arts Club of Chicago, eastern and southern façades. Brickbuilder *XXIV, no. 8, Plate 112 (August 1915).*

Holabird & Roche to resemble a Tuscan-style villa, was actually built slightly outside the boundaries of the Towertown artist colony at the intersection of Dearborn and Goethe Streets and was intended to offer an affordable alternative to the naughty temptations of Towertown.[157]

The club's name refers to the three arts of painting, music and theater that the resident artists were expected to pursue.[158] Similar Three Arts clubs were established in New York, London and Paris. The club was instrumental in attracting female artists to Chicago to develop their careers.

The four-story, red brick building is U-shaped and features a Byzantine-style entrance with mosaics. On the front façade at the first floor are three stone friezes representing the three arts. Besides 110 dormitory-like resident rooms arranged around a central courtyard, the facility also offered a large communal dining room, two large comfortable common living rooms (one with a stage for performances), a library, an enclosed porch/tearoom and several reception and recital rooms on the first floor. The large open-air courtyard could be used for outdoor meals and events. The Three Arts Club operated as a women's-only arts enclave until 2004. It has been estimated

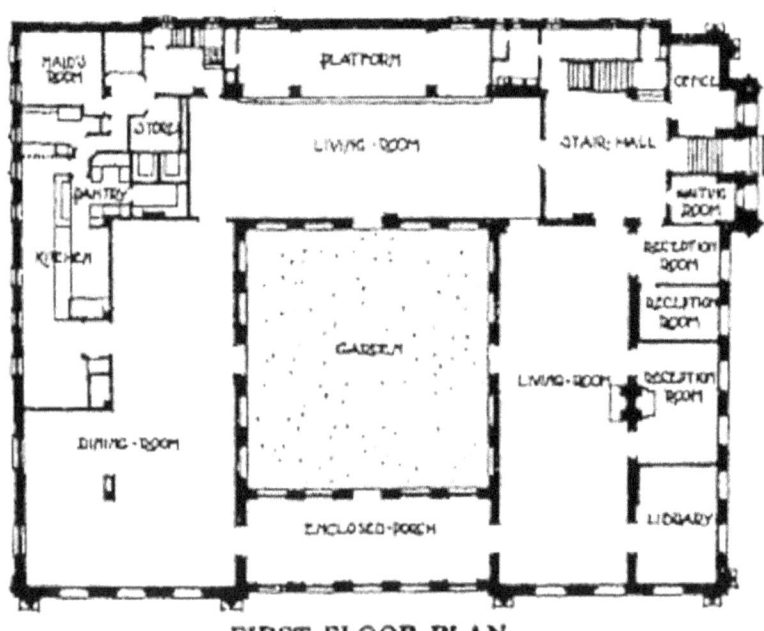

FIRST FLOOR PLAN

Three Arts Club, first floor diagram, Holabird & Roche, 1914. Brickbuilder *XXIV, no. 8, Plate 113 (August 1915).*

that more than thirteen thousand female artists and art students resided in the building during its ninety years of operation.[159] The building was designated a Chicago Historical Landmark in 1981.

One of the more exclusive artist studio buildings of Towertown that became something of a highbrow cultural mecca was the charming Italian Court Building, located at the southeast corner of Michigan Avenue and Ontario Street (619 North Michigan), about halfway between the Chicago River and Chicago Avenue. Real estate developers Chester and Raymond Cook engaged Chicago architect Robert DeGolyer to convert two existing brick walkup apartment buildings with a courtyard into a discrete, tasteful European-style shopping court and artist enclave.[160] The remodeling was completed by 1920. Its main attraction was the interior ground-floor courtyard enveloped within a structure containing three floors of artist studios, shops and offices. The courtyard featured a lovely Greek fountain and was paved with flagstone.

The building was fully rented long before construction was complete.[161] Among its first tenants was Le Petite Bazar, an antiques shop and tearoom regularly patronized by ladies listed in Chicago's Blue Book. Nearby on the second floor was a female haberdashery owned by William Castberg, who moved there from the Loop to be closer to his wealthy clientele living on the Gold Coast.[162] The commercial anchor of the building, and by far its best-known business, was Harriet Moody's Le Petite Gourmet, an elegant bistro that generations of Chicagoans would patronize for almost fifty years.

Moody, the widow of poet and dramatist William Vaughn Moody, had been one of the city's premier caterers since the early 1890s when she founded the Home Delicacies Association. Among her clients were Marshall Field's restaurant and the food service department of George Pullman's railroad services company.[163] Along with her friend Bertha Honore Palmer (wife of Potter Palmer, Chicago's richest man), Moody was one of the "lady managers" of the World's Columbian Exposition.[164] By 1899, Moody's catering business had fifty employees, and in 1911, she established a branch of Home Delicacies Association in London, which supplied Selfridge's Department Store.

Moody periodically sponsored "poetry nights" at her Italian Court restaurant, which she called "Le Petits Jeux Floraux." On such nights, diners paid one dollar to hear Chicago poets recite their verses; the money went to the poet.[165] Le Petit Gourmet was a favorite haunt of poets Vachel Lindsey, Edgar Lee Masters, Robert Frost, Max Bodenheim and Carl Sandburg.[166]

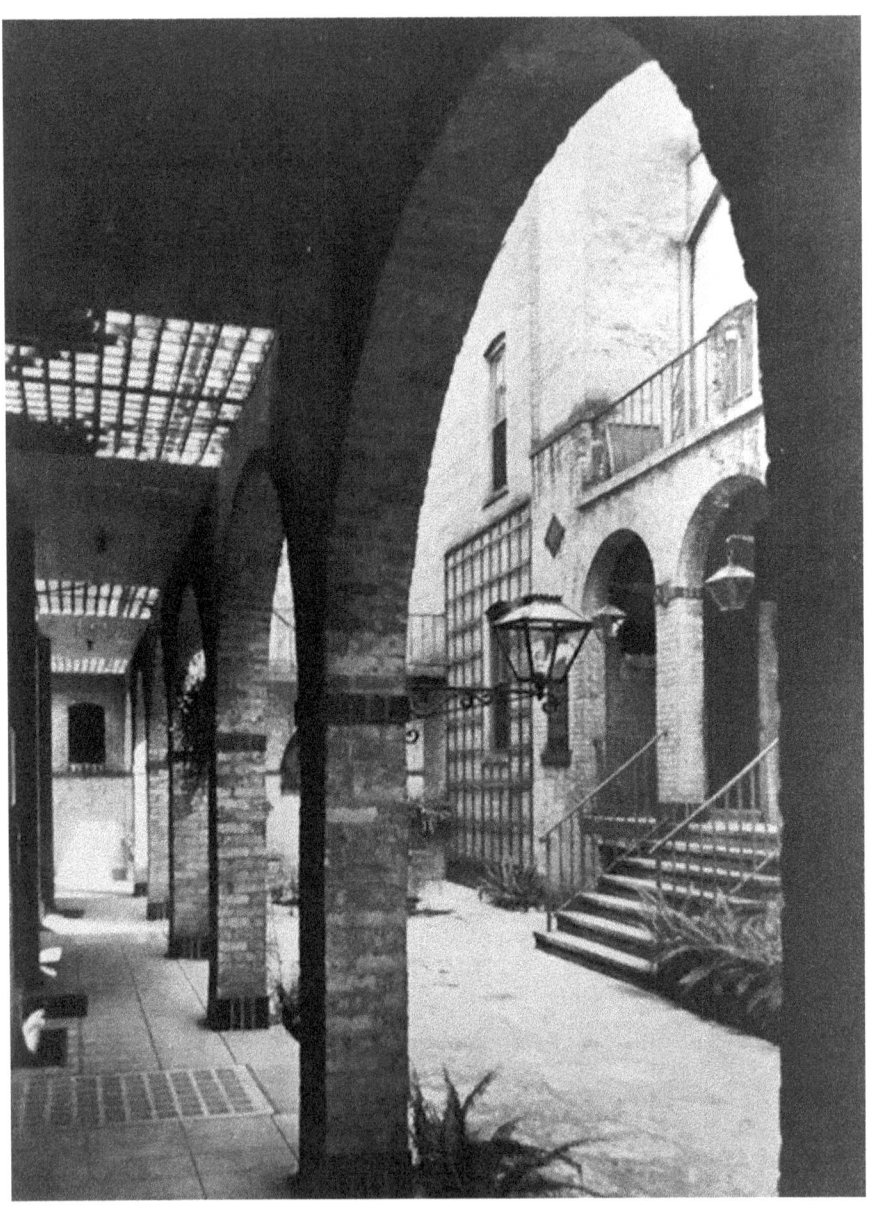

The Italian Court Building, courtyard, Raymond Trowbridge, 1922. Western Architect *XXXIX, No. 12 (Dec. 1930), frontispiece.*

Apart from commercial tenants, the Italian Court also contained several sought-after artist studios on its second and third floors surrounding the central courtyard. Among the fortunate artists to live and work at the Italian Court were painters Frederic Milton Grant, Julio de Diego, James Sessions, Lily Mark Tolpo and English-born Baroness Violet Beatrice Wenner, who painted portraits of Kaiser Wilhelm of Germany, Emperor Franz Josef of Austria and Presidents Calvin Coolidge and Herbert Hoover. Photographers Wynn Richards and Elizabeth Frear opened a studio in the building in the early 1920s.

THE BOHEMIAN MILIEU OF TOWERTOWN

The poets who lunched at Le Petit Gourmet and the artists who lived and toiled at the Italian Court Building were experiencing the hoi polloi of Towertown. Strolling a block or two west of Michigan Avenue, one would find tucked away in the district's dilapidated buildings less distinguished albeit quaint bistros and diners, musty antique shops, interesting bookstalls, small coffeehouses and so-called tearooms, art shops, art galleries, little theaters, converted old stables and garrets with flowerboxes and curious alley dwellings.[167]

Towertown was the Chicago equivalent of Paris's Latin Quarter, although less picturesque. There, young women repudiated and escaped the Edwardian social strictures imposed on them elsewhere. "In 1917 came war, high wages, prohibition (sic),[168] and a transition on the Near North Side. The girls in the neighborhood rose up in arms against the old landladies. They demanded to live their own lives and many of them established studios in the neighborhood."[169] Towertown was an oasis of racial, ethnic, cultural and sexual diversity where individual freedom reigned supreme and respect for the law was undermined by the antics of mob bosses, gangs and pliant residents. To be "different" here was not a handicap, it was an asset.

The district was a more or less accepting haven to, or more frequently the clandestine nocturnal destination for, male and female homosexuals and bisexuals.[170] It was a place where married and unmarried men and women sought to satisfy their more prurient interests and desires in unattached relationships. It was a magnet for bohemian types, rich and poor alike; for socialists and anarchists; and for the full spectrum of society's misfits. And no place in the nation was more welcoming to this panoply of liberated souls than the Dil Pickle Club.

The Dil Pickle was founded by John "Jack" Archibald Jones, the king of Chicago's hobohemians. Jones was a former miner, itinerant laborer and labor organizer with an enormous imagination. He established the Dil Pickle Club in 1914 primarily as a venue for speeches, discussions and events involving labor leaders. It quickly morphed into a social club and cultural center of sorts for the city's bohemian set, artists, writers and progressive intelligentsia.

The Dil Pickle was accessed from a small service alleyway quaintly named "Tooker Alley" off Dearborn Street across from Washington Square. This park, the second oldest in Chicago, was popularly referred to as Bughouse Square, and on weekends and weekday evenings leading "soap-boxers" harangued attentive crowds that numbered in the hundreds and, at times, the thousands. On the door to the club was painted a cautionary notice: "Step High, Stoop Low, Leave Your Dignity Outside."

> *Here for some sixteen years an enterprising oddball named Jack Jones emceed the hottest debates and most outrageous lectures in town: on politics, poetry, economics, sex, art, philosophy, psychoanalysis, science, history, and a thousand other topics....Jones considered himself an "industrial anarchist," but he kept his forum open to anyone who was a "nut about anything." The Pickle's roster of speakers...is a who's who of the outstanding revolutionaries, poets, writers, artists, eccentrics, and other creative intellectuals of the time.*[171]

During Prohibition, the Dil Pickle became a scarcely disguised speakeasy, drawing an even wider array of Chicagoans and visitors to the city. On Saturday nights, amateur performers enacted one-act plays written by Eugene O'Neill and Theodore Dreiser or some unknown Chicago playwright. It hosted musical performances, including light opera and jazz dances, poetry readings and masquerade balls. "In such an atmosphere a girl becomes sophisticated. She discusses Freud, Nietzsche and other writers whom she has never read, but whom she has learned to quote smatteringly."[172]

The Dil Pickle Club managed to survive Prohibition, although it had been raided several times—some say the club had itself raided to gain publicity—and weathered five years of deep economic depression. The Dil Pickle finally closed in 1934, not because of severe economic

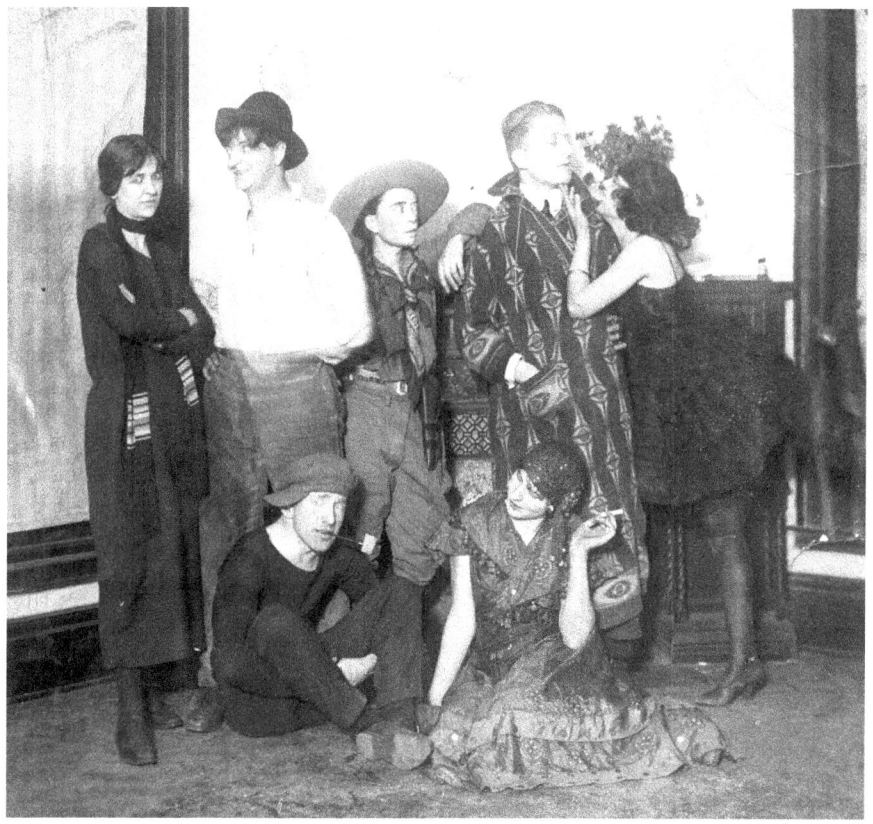

Holiday Costume Ball, Dil Pickle Club, December 21, 1921; *clockwise from top left*: Mina Bodenheim, Jack Jones, Ann Mitchell, Maxwell Bodenheim, Lillian Collier, Esther Loeb and Jerry (last name unknown). *Dil Pickle Club Records, Newberry Library Special Collections.*

circumstances, which it certainly would have otherwise continued to overcome. Reportedly, the Chicago police, corrupt and compromised in the 1920s and '30s, shuttered the club's doors because Jack Jones, the principled oddball, refused to pay protection money to the mob.

Other Towertown so-called tearooms and hangouts included the Wind Blew Inn, Gold Coast House of Correction, Lower Depths, Green Mask, Seven Arts, Little Gray Cottage, Pizen Pub and Riccardo's Restaurant.[173] Each of these establishments catered to artists, poets, novelists, bohemians and hangers-on. Several of them attempted to imitate in some fashion the antics of the Dil Pickle, including featuring lectures, little skits, poetry readings and other performances.[174] The whimsically named Wind Blew Inn was relatively short-lived but made sensational news nationwide for several months in 1921–22 and gave rise to one of Chicago's legendary epigrams. Riccardo's opened in the twilight years of Towertown's epoch as an artist colony but remained a cultural epicenter of the Near North Side for sixty years. But both contribute to an understanding of the high jinks of Towertown.

In 1920, a scintillating, bob-haired nineteen-year-old flapper named Lillian Collier[175] blew into Towertown from New York City and, it is reported, soon became the darling of the poets and artists who congregated at the Dil Pickle Club.[176] In 1921, Collier opened her own "tearoom" at the northwest corner of Michigan Avenue and Ohio Street, adopting the jocular name Wind Blew Inn. (A block away and a generation earlier, an impoverished teenaged Isadora Duncan introduced her neighbors to a new, exotic form of dancing, to their bemusement and derision.[177]) It was not long before neighbors complained of the "syncopated blues" music that emanated from

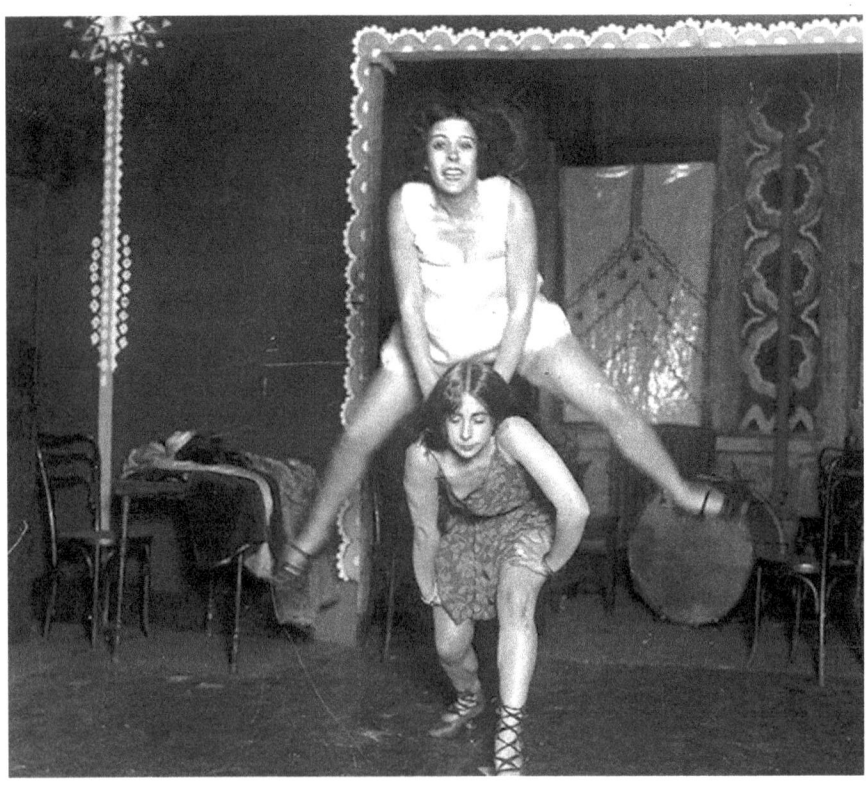

Lillian Collier (*top*) and May Charlotte Gilcrest (*bottom*) leapfrogging, possibly at the Dil Pickle Club. Collier and Gilcrest were Chicago's most notorious flappers during the early 1920s. *Photographer unknown, Dil Pickle Club Records, Newberry Library Special Collections (c. 1921).*

the place. The tearoom's atmospherics included nude Greek statues, strange modern paintings and lighting by candles.

Rumors flew throughout Towertown that the Wind Blew Inn hosted wild "petting parties," where young people engaged in "snugglepupping."[178] A cup of "tea" cost seventy-five cents, which is just short of ten dollars in today's money. A pet goose named Mouldy, which Collier dyed green, was allowed to roam about at will throughout the tearoom. Its disappearance one night in November 1921 resulted in a dragnet by Chicago police and news reports as far away as Lincoln, Nebraska, and Buffalo, New York.[179] A former waitress described the atmospherics of the Wind Blew Inn in a 1922 article:

> *One entering the place for the first time will do so gropingly. His eyes will be unaccustomed to the dim semi-darkness. Inside he will find a collection of little rough wooden tables, each covered with a red bandana handkerchief. On each table is a solitary sputtering candle. On the walls are ultra-modern and "futuristic" art. Scattered about the tables are couples and little groups, heads close together, conversing in low tones and eying the other inmates with curious glances from time to time....As the evening ages the place becomes lively. Soon it is thronged to overflowing. Outside are the automobiles of "slummers," for Chicago society is discovering Chicago's "quarter." Many of the guests are young and very young men of the type F. Scott Fitzgerald might characterize as "slickers," corresponding roughly to the "flapper."[180]*

On February 11, 1922, the Chicago police raided the place; syndicated newspaper articles published throughout the United States reported that "the police blew in to the Wind Blew Inn." The police arrested Collier, her "aid" Virginia Harrison and all thirty-eight patrons in the tearoom and hauled them into court. The judge dismissed the charges against the tearoom's patrons, continued the case against Collier and Harrison and assigned a date in March for a trial. In the interim, Collier was forced to cover the nude statues in her tearoom with overalls.

At the ensuing trial, the police testified that they had seen "couples, lit only by candles and surrounded by weird art, cuddling and holding hands."[181] They also intimated that a cup of tea that cost seventy-five cents had to contain more than just tea. When Collier took the stand, she was reported in scores of the nation's newspapers to have declared, "There is no snugglepupping at the Wind Blew Inn!" She also claimed that the strongest drink the inn served was hot chocolate. The judge asked Collier and Harrison

Girls Sentenced to Read Fairy Tales to Smother Bohemian Fancies

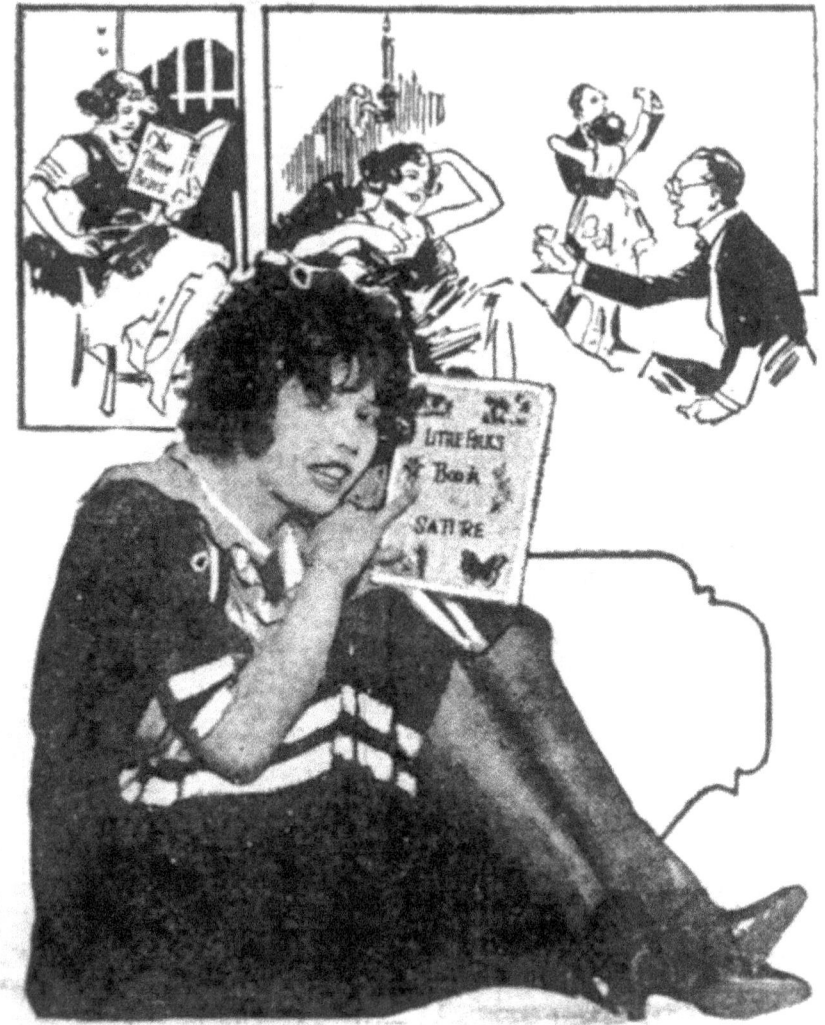

MISS LILLIAN COLLIER

Regaining her lost childhood; the trial judge's sentence of Lillian Collier to read a book of fairy tales was satirized by scores of newspapers throughout the United States. Buffalo Times, *March 28, 1922*.

if they had ever read *Little Women*, *Flaxie Frizzle* or Hans Christian Andersen's tales. Upon the two flappers' denial that they had read such books, the judge sentenced Collier and Harrison to read a book of fairy tales, stating that "all that's the matter with you is that you have a false value of things of life in general. Start on the fairy tales right away."[182]

A month later, the Wind Blew Inn burned to the ground. Whether the fire was started by "puritan arsonists," as Collier believed, or by Virginia Harrison, as the Chicago police believed, or by one of the candles used to give the place "atmosphere," is a question for the ages. Lillian Collier later wrote under the assumed name Nellise Child[183] several plays, at least one of which was performed on Broadway, as well as novels and mysteries in the 1930s, '40s and '50s.

Virginia Harrison's future was far less edifying. Following her marriage to a hoodlum named Francis James Ryan, she became the mastermind of a gang of five or six bandits who committed about a dozen armed robberies in California and New York.[184] Virginia's husband was slain during a robbery in New York in 1925, and most other members of the gang were indicted and jailed, except Virginia, whose only punishment appears to have been that the New York press revealed she possessed the "shapeliest wooden leg in America."[185]

By 1934, the bohemia of Towertown had begun to fade and many of the artists and writers who once populated its old alley dwellings and garrets had fled elsewhere, with the biggest names (Hecht, Anderson, Bodenheim, Ferber, Millay) heading to New York or Hollywood. It was in that year that Richard ("Ric") Riccardo (born Richard Novaretti in Italy) came a little late to the party and opened a small Italian bistro at the foot of Rush Street in the shadow of the new Wrigley Building that would keep the bohemian flame alive for the next sixty years. During much of that time, the bistro would grow in size, absorbing two additional adjacent buildings, and maintain a vibrant clientele that included most of the city's best writers and illustrators, painters, musicians and art patrons.[186] Called by many the "Montmartre of the Midwest," Riccardo's became the undisputed headquarters of Chicago's West Bank in the post-Depression period.

"Riccardo's is the only restaurant of its kind in the country, and Ric himself is the only one of his kind in the world. Some New Yorkers wanted him to come to New York and set up another Riccardo's there, but he turned them down."[187] At the time Ric opened his little bistro, he decorated it with several paintings by his own hand, including two female nudes mounted on the ceiling.[188] Customers liked the paintings and even bought some.[189] In

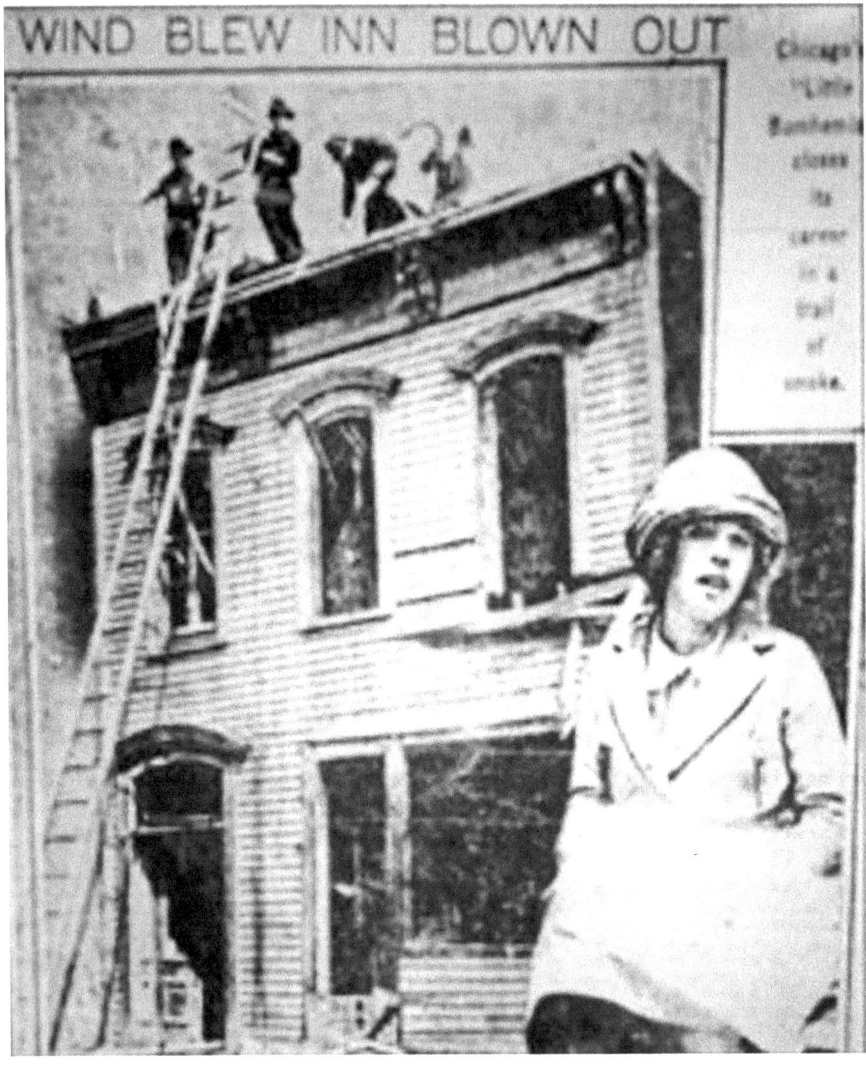

"Wind Blew Inn Blow Out," *Chicago Daily News (April 23, 1922). From the* Chicago Daily News.

time, he began displaying one painting by a different Towertown artist every month. Finally, he established a monthly exhibition of his own paintings and those of several local artists. This went on for decades.[190]

In the mid-1940s, Ric persuaded the seven best-known painters in Chicago to paint a large canvas (four feet by eight feet), each depicting one of the seven arts. These artists included Aaron Bohrod (architecture), identical twins Ivan and Malvin Albright (drama and sculpture), Rudolph

Weisenborn (literature), William Schwarz (music) and Vincent D'Agostino (painting), with Ric painting "dance."[191] Ivan Albright's painting of "drama" featured Ric depicted as Mephistopheles. Ric hung these seven paintings prominently behind Riccardo's always-busy bar, built in the shape of an artist's palette. There they delighted and enticed patrons for decades.

In its heyday, Riccardo's featured a bocce court in the basement, a private room called the Padded Cell and Ric's three Great Danes that roamed freely about the restaurant. Ric died in 1954 at age fifty-one, after which his son Ric Jr. managed the restaurant. Patrons then noticed that, one by one, the Lively Arts paintings began to disappear, replaced by large photographs of the paintings.[192] It was generally assumed that Ric Jr. sold the paintings to cover the costs associated with fast living and alimony payments to three wives.[193] These Chicago treasures, dispersed over the years but ultimately relocated and purchased by real estate mogul Samuel Persky, were publicly exhibited for the last time in 2002 in an intimate bar space at the Union League Club of Chicago.

Ric Jr. was found choked to death in 1977. Riccardo's continued under different owners until it closed in 1995. The last vestige of bohemia in the Near North Side and the dim spirit of old Towertown died with the closing of Ric's doors.

FREDERIC MILTON GRANT

One of the most successful painters who lived and worked in Towertown during the interwar period was Frederic Milton Grant. At various times between 1907 and 1947, Grant would occupy studios at the 57th Street Artist Colony, the Tree Studios, the Italian Court and other premises in Towertown, including a converted coach house studio behind the old Joseph Ryerson Mansion at 615 North Wabash. He also visited the artist colonies at the Eagle's Nest Camp and Ox-Bow during some summers. He was a member of both the Little Room that regularly met at the Fine Arts Building and the Cliff Dwellers Club. Accordingly, Grant probably had more connections with Chicago's many artist colonies than any other artist.

Grant was born in Sibley, Iowa, in 1886. He studied architecture at North Dakota State University in 1904–06.[194] Grant then moved to Chicago and attended the Art Institute of Chicago, studying under John Vanderpoel, Walter Marshall Clute and Frederick W. Freer.

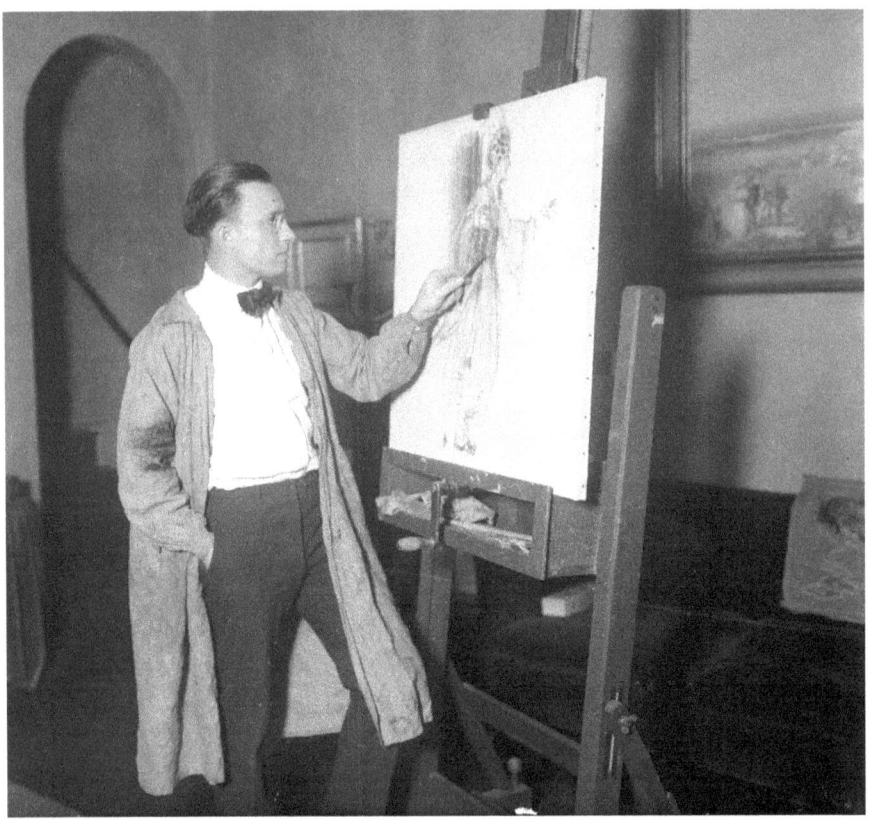

Frederic Milton Grant in his Tree Studios atelier. The painting on the wall to Grant's right, entitled *United States Mail*, was exhibited at the Art Institute and won the Joseph Eisendrath Prize in 1919. Chicago Daily News *(1921), Chicago History Museum, DN-0073018.*

He later studied under Alphonse Mucha, Jonas Lie, Richard Miller, William Merritt Chase and Henry Snell. In 1913, Grant attended the Académie Colarossi in Paris. Shortly afterward, he traveled to Venice, where he studied with Chase and was awarded the Chase School Prize for his painting *Noon*, which Chase found to be a unique and innovative interpretation of Venice. This was quite an achievement given that the Serene City had been subject to many thousands of paintings before Grant picked up his brush.[195] Grant returned to the United States at the beginning of World War I. Later that year, he again studied with Chase at Carmel-by-the-Sea and produced *The Sketch Class* from a unique perspective. It later won first prize at the Student Art League's exhibition at the Art Institute, and is now on display at the Union League Club.[196] Few, if any, Chicago painters had a training pedigree as impressive.

From 1907 to 1913, Grant engaged in commercial art, illustrating several books, short stories published in magazines and sheet music. When the United States entered the First World War in 1917, he enlisted as a chief petty officer in the navy and was stationed at the Great Lakes Naval Training Center, where he painted murals. But, for most of his career, Grant would primarily paint in oils, sometimes rendering a watercolor or gouache sketch of the prospective oil painting before he approached the canvas. His painting style reflected a more structured impressionist technique, and his paintings were known for their "jazz-mad riot of color,"[197] somewhat reminiscent of the work of the English painter Frank Brangwyn, whose work Grant must have known.

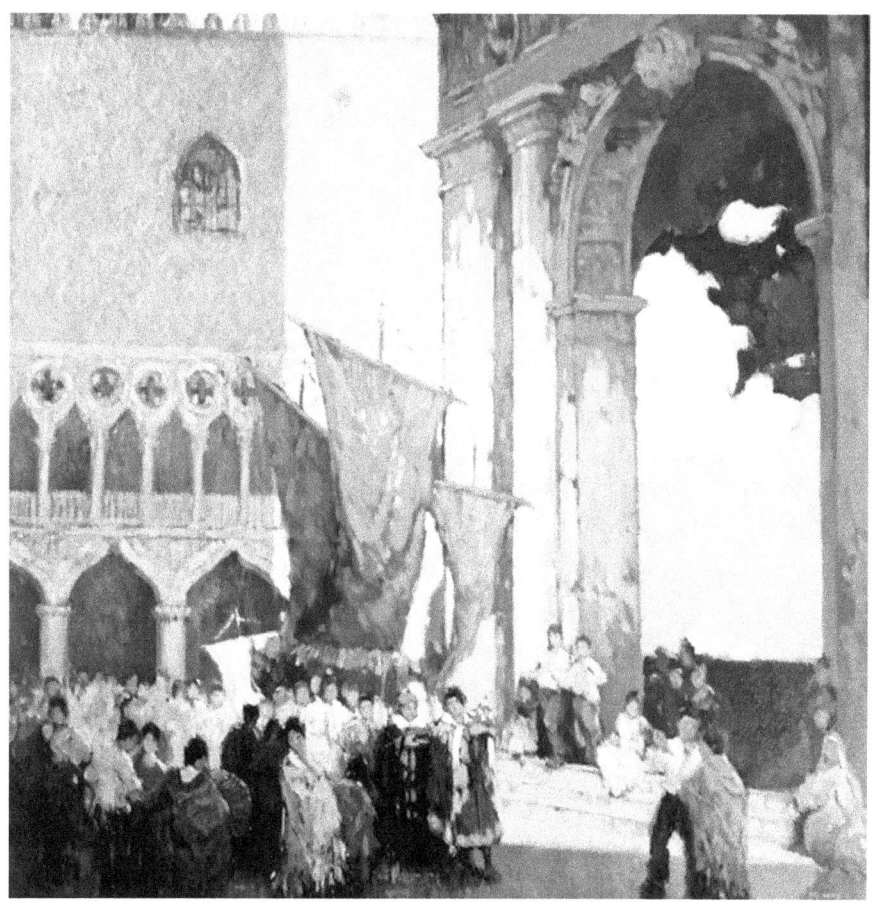

The Departure of Marco Polo by Frederic Milton Grant, exhibited at the Art Institute of Chicago in 1926. It won the Frank G. Logan Art Institute Prize. *K.M. Stolte (2018).*

Grant exhibited his paintings at the Art Institute of Chicago, National Academy of Design, Corcoran Gallery in Washington, D.C., Pennsylvania Academy of Fine Arts, Cincinnati Art Museum, Rhode Island School of Design, Chicago Arts Guild, Chicago Arts Club, Palm Beach Art Club, Detroit Museum of Art and Minneapolis Institute of Fine Art. He had a string of annual one-man shows at Anderson Galleries in the Congress Hotel and exhibited frequently at New York's Grand Central Gallery, Carson Pirie Scott's Gallery and other East Coast and Midwest galleries.

Between 1916 and 1927, Grant won almost every prize the Art Institute conferred at its two annual exhibitions, including the Logan Prize in 1926 for his painting *Departure of Marco Polo* (see accompanying image) and the William Randolph Hearst Prize the following year for *Thieves Market*. Frederic Grant enjoyed a solid reputation as one of the most popular and successful artists in Chicago between World War I and World War II. He was the darling of Chicago art critics, and the city's newspapers regularly featured photographs of his works on exhibition. Eleanor Jewett, conservative art critic for the *Chicago Tribune*, was particularly smitten with Grant's paintings. She wrote in 1931, "There is no more brilliant decorative painter living today than Frederic M. Grant."[198] Twenty years later, she wrote, "His work is infamous for its magnificent color and fine design. He is probably the greatest colorist Chicago has ever known."[199]

Grant was probably Chicago's most traveled painter. He visited Paris and Venice in 1913–14 and Naples, Capri, Rome and various other towns in Italy and France in 1922–24. He made a world tour in 1928, visiting Bali, Ceylon, China, Japan, Singapore and Africa. His paintings throughout the 1920s reflected subject matter of his European and Far East travels. Grant's European scenes depict small-town life in picturesque villages, sometimes with fanciful ruins as majestic backdrops. Especially noteworthy are his paintings of the Far East, particularly Bali and other Pacific islands, because American artists at the time had rarely visited and painted at such places. His Balinese and Ceylonese paintings depicted cultural and religious rites, dances and processions. One writer who witnessed Grant's exhibition of his Far East paintings had this to say: "Jewel-like in color, picturesque in composition, they breathe the very spirit of the Orient. The barbaric splendor of a festival in Bali, ox carts rumbling through the streets of Singapore, the eternal pageant of the harvest in Ceylon, all have inspired the artist to reproduce pictures that at once stimulate the mind and satisfy the eye."[200]

In 1933–34, Grant painted a series of about twenty very colorful paintings of the Century of Progress World's Fair that Chicago hosted forty years after the World's Columbian Exposition. C.J. Bulliet, Chicago's most astute art critic of the time, stated that of all the Chicago artists who painted scenes at the 1933 fair, Grant "was the one painter who got under the surface consistently. In a whole series of pictures, conveying the 'emotional content' of the Exposition along with the ocular."[201]

Regrettably, Grant admitted that he destroyed several of his Century of Progress paintings for unknown reasons.[202] Given that his Far East paintings have hardly ever resurfaced in galleries or auctions over the past seventy-

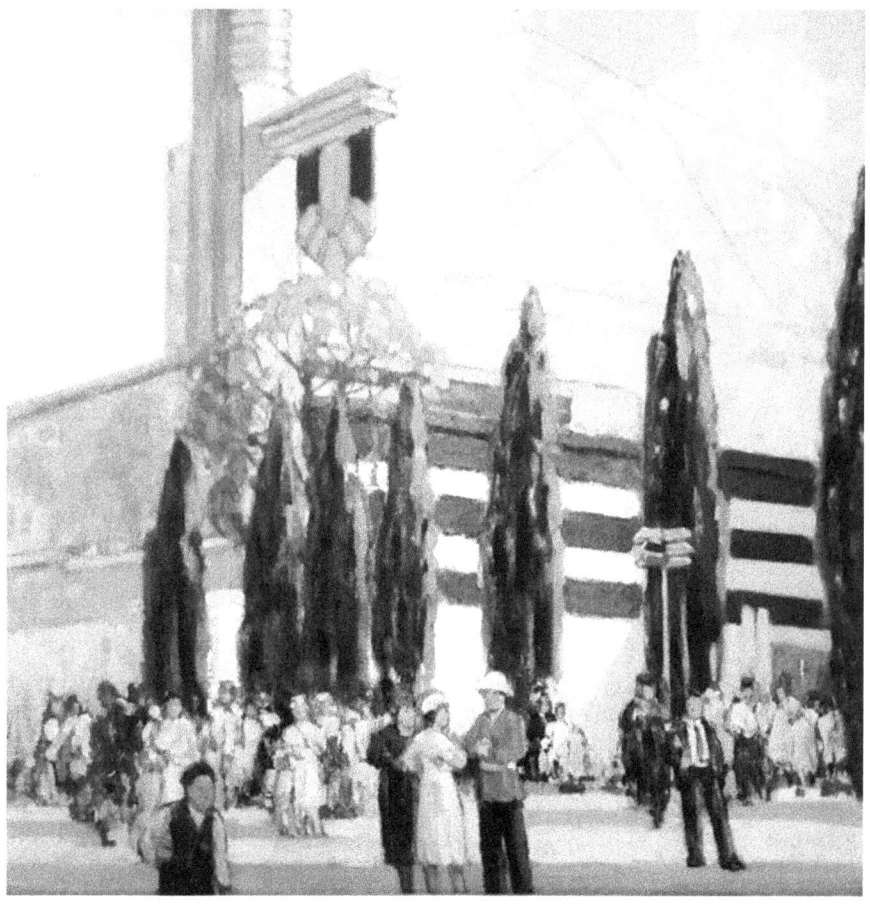

Morning at the Chicago World's Fair by Frederic Milton Grant, exhibited at Anderson Galleries, Chicago, in 1933–34. *K.M. Stolte (2018).*

five years, it may be possible that Grant destroyed some or most of those paintings as well. Fortunately, small watercolor or oil sketches of Grant's Far East paintings have occasionally hit the market and give a sense of what his large-scale Far East canvases looked like.

Throughout much of Grant's career, he reflected the conservative prejudices and sensibilities of many, if not most, Chicago painters and art patrons concerning the modernist movement that started in Europe

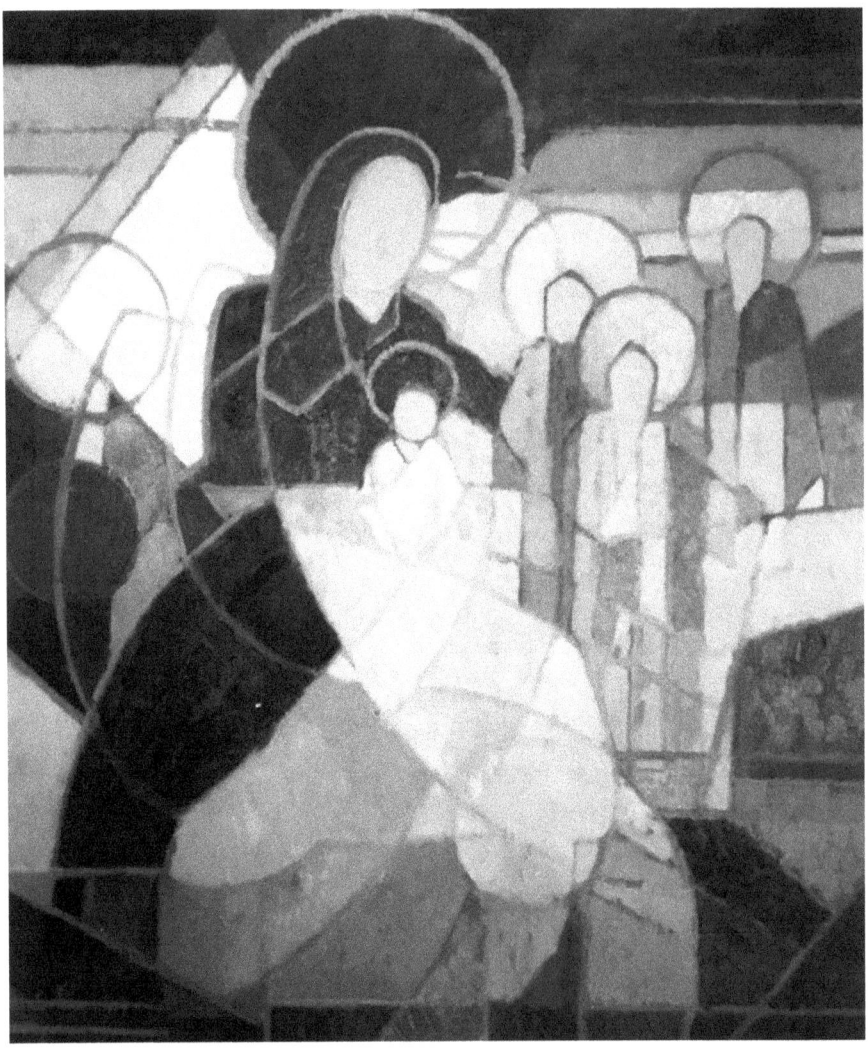

Madonna and Child with Three Wise Men by Frederic Milton Grant, circa 1948. *K.M. Stolte (2018).*

and moved to America with the Armory Show of 1913. In terms of subject matter and style, his modified impressionistic technique and decorative vernacular remained popular with Chicago art patrons until the mid-1930s. At about that time, however, the public's interest in Grant's decorative paintings started to diminish. In response, Grant shifted toward painting highly colorful modernist abstract works. Among the abstract paintings Grant executed in the 1940s and 1950s is a series of what he called "musical transcriptions," in which the artist attempted to convey in paint what he heard in musical scores by composers such as Bach, Brahms, Debussy, Elgar, Mussorgsky, Sibelius and Richard Strauss.[203] (Grant began composing musical scores and songs starting at age nine and became an accomplished pianist.[204])

He also painted other works in a modernist, abstract vein, such as two paintings depicting the Madonna with child and the three wise men. Of the differing styles reflected in the paintings of his earlier career and his later abstract works, Grant said, "The paintings I made before this experiment [his musical transcriptions] I felt were everyone's world. My musical paintings are my own world of imagination."[205] In 1948, Grant moved to Oakland, California, where he painted and taught until his death in 1959 at age seventy-two. By that time, Grant, like his friend Pauline Palmer, was largely forgotten in the city where he had found so much success earlier in his career.

MODERNISM INVADES CHICAGO: THE ARMORY SHOW OF 1913

Modernism came to Chicago in several stages. First came modernist architecture, of which Chicago was actually in the vanguard. Louis Sullivan, Frank Lloyd Wright, Charles Atwood, Walter Burley Griffin and Dwight Perkins broke the tethers that had previously bound American architects to European traditionalist schools of architectural design so exquisitely displayed by the World's Columbian Exposition in 1893. Modernist writers were next, with novelists Hamlin Garland, Theodore Dreiser and Henry Blake Fuller introducing realism in literature with its focus on the corrupting influence of urban life on the human soul, and poet Carl Sandberg disposing of meter as a guiding principal of verse. Although Chicago did not have any modern composers to speak of, by 1913, the Chicago Symphony Orchestra added such avant-garde composers as Gustav Mahler, Jean Sibelius, Richard Strauss and Arnold Schoenberg to its repertoire.

But when it came to the visual arts, Chicago would resist modernism long past the time that the avant-garde movement took hold elsewhere in the United States. And its recalcitrance was both dramatic and militant. Nowhere was this more evident than in Chicago's response to the Armory Show in the spring of 1913, officially referred to as the International Exhibition of Modern Art. This major exhibition was organized by artists Walter Pach, Arthur Dove, Arthur Davies and other New York–based artists to be on display at the Seventh Regiment Armory Building on Park Avenue in the winter of 1913.

The Armory Show in New York included 1,350 works, including oil paintings, watercolor paintings, etchings and engravings and sculptures. Included were avant-garde works by Paul Cezanne, Paul Gauguin, Vincent van Gogh, Henri Matisse, Pablo Picasso, Marcel Duchamp, André Derain, Juan Gris and Constantin Brâncuşi. When the Armory Show was sent to Chicago, it was pared down to consist of 634 of the most recent works of the European avant-garde artists.[206]

The cultural backdrop that existed in Chicago when the Armory Show arrived was significantly different than when the city hosted the World's Columbian Exposition twenty years before. Chicago was no longer the cultural backwater it had been at the time of the 1893 fair. In part because of the artist colonies and numerous art-promoting organizations that established themselves in and around Chicago in the interim, the city's art scene was quite productive and vibrant. But it was guided by certain conservative principles that would favor the control of Chicago's visual arts by artists and art patrons with a decidedly traditionalist bent.

By 1910 certain underlying assumptions about making and viewing art prevailed in Chicago, having been formulated and nurtured by local philanthropists who had founded and still governed the Art Institute. Self-righteous and civic-minded, these bourgeois patrons valued art for its social utility: they wanted to educate and elevate the masses to the finer things in life, in short, to support an art that was "good for the people." Inherent in that good was a theory of art which implied order and beauty along with a disciplined adherence to apparently infallible, universal laws—in other words, everything that nineteenth-century academic art had to offer. In the early teens, their ideals still prevailed, promulgated by the people they hired to run the Art Institute and its School and in general by their own power as leaders of the city's social and cultural elite. As long as they controlled the scene, art would be safe, comfortable, definable, controllable and morally correct.[207]

In that cultural environment, the "triumvirate" of Taft, Grover and Clarkson and artists like them wielded power over the committees that selected the works to be included in exhibitions and over the juries who chose works to be awarded prizes, which usually carried a monetary stipend. They also controlled the curriculum at the School of the Art Institute. Therefore, it was solidly academic artworks like their own that would be presented to the students and public and rewarded as exemplars of Chicago's culture. Chicago artists, mindful of these facts, conformed their works to the tastes of the traditionalist.

Into this cultural inertia of the Chicago art world burst the bombshell of the Armory Show. The show opened on March 24, 1913, at the Art Institute and offered the Chicago public its first, and for many years its last, comprehensive view of avant-garde art by postimpressionists, cubists, futurists and expressionists. The public was very curious about this new European art, and its reaction was intense. The opening reception set an attendance record, and the show attracted almost 190,000 visitors during its three-week run, by all measures an enormous attendance that more than doubled the number of visitors who viewed the show in New York. It is impossible to determine precisely what the general public thought about the avant-garde art they viewed at the Armory Show, but the reaction by the press and by the "traditional" artists was largely one of shock, disdain and ridicule.

The *Chicago Evening Post* referred to the Armory Show as "Barnumized art" and anticipated a big crowd "at the freak art exhibit."[208] A *Chicago Tribune* editorial cautioned: "The nudes pervert the ideal of physical perfection, obliterate the line which as heretofore distinguished the artistic from the lewd and obscene, and incite feelings of disgust and aversion."[209] Another article warned about the need for barring children from the show on moral grounds.[210] Yet another piece in the *Chicago Examiner* complained: "Our splendid Art Institute is being desecrated. This pollution is materialized in several portraits of the nude: portrayals that unite in an insult to the great self-respecting public of Chicago."[211]

William French, the director of the Art Institute, spoke for most of the traditionalist artists of Chicago when he gave his own appraisal of the artworks in the Armory Show: "The fraction of the Exhibition comprising the real modernists—the post-impressionists, cubists,

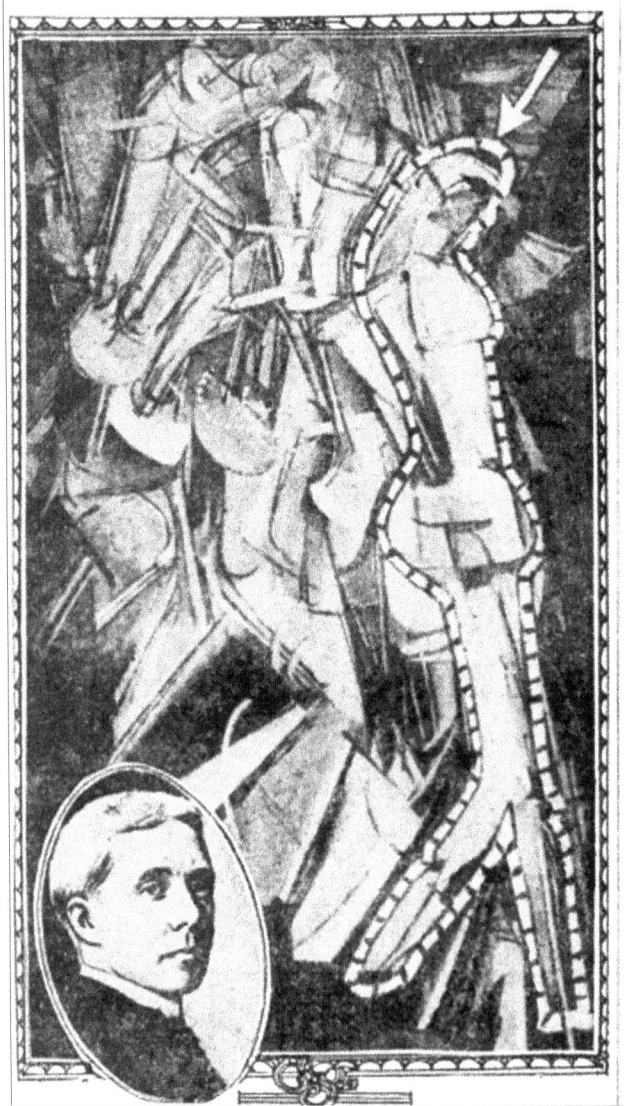

Here Is the Nude in a Woodyard

Simple as Fireworks, Says Eddy

Arthur J. Eddy's diagram of the futurist picture, "Nude Descending Stair," which some of the unenlightened have labeled, "A Storm in a Woodyard." "It's perfectly plain," said Mr. Eddy, as he outlined the figure of the lady (indicated by arrow). The ensemble is the way her appearance struck the artist, giving the impression of a kaleidoscope or moving pictures at high speed. A photographic illustration of the cubist idea might be obtained by leaving a camera's plate exposed while a figure walks—or tumbles—downstairs. Below is Mr. Eddy.

"Here Is the Nude in a Woodyard." *Chicago Tribune* (March 25, 1913). *Courtesy Chicago Public Library.*

134

pointillists, futurists—anything more fantastic it would be hard to conceive. Some of the works are mere unmeaning assemblages of forms, with gay color, conveying no idea whatever, but bearing such titles as 'Dance' or 'Souvenir'…a few, more logically, have no titles but merely numbers."[212] French called works in the Armory Show by Henri Matisse "a joke" and referred to Marcel Duchamp and Francis Picabia as "humbugs."[213]

A small minority of commentators praised the exhibition, or at least tried to keep an open mind.[214] Chicago attorney Arthur Jerome Eddy was sympathetic to the modernists and purchased the second-largest number of works at the show, both while it was in New York and then in Chicago. Eddy was a remarkable man who managed to get his portrait painted by Whistler and a bust of himself sculpted by Auguste Rodin, the first one Rodin did of an American, by the time he was thirty-five. He authored the first book on cubism and postimpressionism in English and the first biography of Whistler. Eddy also wrote a very interesting travelogue following a record-setting 2,900-mile, two-month automobile trip in the summer of 1901.[215]

In a diagram published in the *Chicago Tribune* that we would find amusing today, Eddy attempted to explain to the general public Marcel Duchamp's *Nude Descending a Staircase, No. 2*. Art critics Lena May McCauley, of the *Chicago Evening Post*, and Harriet Monroe, of the *Chicago Tribune*, were both refreshingly open-minded, receptive and sensitive to the works in the show.[216] Indeed, Monroe was prescient enough to quote a French art critic who claimed that "these first years of our century announce an efflorescence which will be one of the richest in the history of art."[217] And so it turned out.

On April 16, 1913, students at the Art Institute celebrated the close of the Armory Show with a mock trial of Henri Matisse (whom they called "Henri Hairmattress"), convicting him of artistic crimes. Initially, they intended to burn Matisse in effigy, but good taste prevailed, and they instead burned four copies of his paintings in effigy.[218] At about the same time, Manierre Dawson, the only Chicago artist—and one of only a handful in America—who painted pure abstracts at the time of the show, wrote in his diary: "I am feeling elated. I had thought of myself as an anomaly and had to defend myself, many times, as not crazy; and here now at the Art Institute many artists presented show these very inventive departures from the academies."[219]

One long-term residual effect the Armory Show left in its wake was an ever-increasing tension that arose between the ascendant academic traditionalists, who would continue to control Chicago's visual art scene for another decade or so, and a new generation of artists and art students, generally born in the earliest years of the twentieth century, who would one day vanquish the traditionalists and make modernism in Chicago commonplace.[220] Many of these artists would abandon Towertown and create by hand a series of new funky artist colonies in Chicago's Old Town neighborhood.

The Houses that Sol and Edgar Built

The Old Town Artist Colonies

The 1909 Burnham Plan of Chicago proposed a bridge linking Michigan Avenue south of the Chicago River with Pine Street north of the river. Similar plans went back to the 1890s. The City of Chicago finally erected the Michigan Avenue Bridge in 1920, and the city renamed Pine Street as North Michigan Avenue. Development of North Michigan began almost immediately following the opening of the bridge. In April 1921, the south tower of the Wrigley Building was completed; the north tower was built by 1924. Across Michigan Avenue to the east, construction of Tribune Tower was completed in 1925. The elegant Allerton and Drake Hotels were also constructed during this period. By 1927, North Michigan Avenue was well on its way to becoming the "Magnificent Mile," brimming with expensive, and even exclusive, retail shops, chic hotels and restaurants.

The commercial development that was transforming North Michigan Avenue into one of the nation's prime shopping districts began encroaching westward and northward into the heart of Towertown. As much of the eastern portion of Towertown became increasingly commercialized, the old mansions of yesteryear's elite, and the shabby apartment buildings, rooming houses and coach houses where many of the district's artists had lived and worked were torn down and replaced with commercial buildings. This encroaching development had the effect of increased rents for old buildings that were not demolished. In short, progress and economics were squeezing Chicago's artists and the bohemian set out of Towertown. So, they headed north to Old Town.

Old Town, originally called North Town until the nomenclature changed in the 1940s, had a similar history as Towertown. The neighborhood was originally settled by Germans and semiskilled workers of other European ethnicities. After the Great Fire of 1871 completely wiped out the neighborhood, new and old property owners built hastily constructed "fire shanties," usually at the back of the lots. [221] A few years later, they constructed permanent two- and three-story brick structures in popular architectural styles such as Queen Anne and Italianate while their families resided in the fire shanties. Later these fire shanties became stables and coach houses.[222]

Between 1875 and the 1910s, the part of Old Town we are concerned with was a fashionable district for Chicago's second-tier elite and upper middle class. In the 1910s and 1920s, the socioeconomic status of the neighborhood declined significantly, with German, Bohemian and eastern European immigrants constituting the primary ethnic makeup of the new resident pool. Many of the Victorian mansions and elegant three-flats in the area were subdivided and converted into boardinghouses and other multifamily dwellings, and some fell into disrepair.[223] The value of real estate in the neighborhood suffered a corresponding decline. Between the 1900 and 1920 censuses, there was a shift in tenancy, with a dramatic increase of renters and lodgers and a much denser population.[224]

Carl Street, renamed West Burton Place in 1936, was a single-block street running east–west between LaSalle Street and Wells Street, one block south of North Avenue. Its oldest homes were Victorian mansions built in the late 1870s and early 1880s. A little later, some three-flats were constructed on the block. The last structures built on the block were elegant three-flats constructed in 1892 and 1896.[225] The oldest and largest post-fire house was located at 16 Carl Street, on the south side of the street (later 155 Carl Street after the city altered the street numbering system at the turn of the century, and still later 155 West Burton Place after the street's name change in 1936). It was a large, three-story, red brick structure with a mansard roof built in 1877 by Charles Emmerich, owner of the largest pillow factory in the United States. In 1927, its then-owner, Antonia Radieske, widow of a former city official, sold the mansion to Saul "Sol" Kogen, a remarkable and energetic young man with a vision.[226]

WEST BURTON PLACE AND CARL STREET STUDIOS

Kogen's parents were Russian immigrants who fled the Czar's anti-Semitic policies and settled in Chicago in 1890.[227] By the time Sol was born in 1900 as their fifth child, the Kogens were prosperous owners of a shop that sold lacy accessories for fashionable ladies' clothing. At age eleven, Kogen was taking art lessons at Hull House, where Jane Addams taught him "to love everybody."[228] He later took summer and weekend courses at the School of the Art Institute but was expelled in 1917 after he led a rebellion of students against the school's management for its over-regimented teaching policies, which, in the students' view, took too much freedom out of art. In response, Jane Addams created studio space at Hull House for Kogen and four other students who had been expelled.[229]

Shortly after Sol graduated high school, Kogen's father retired from the family business, and Sol was tapped to take over the management of the shop. Within four years, Kogen expanded the business and opened three additional shops, one across from the Chicago Theater.[230] By 1925, Kogen

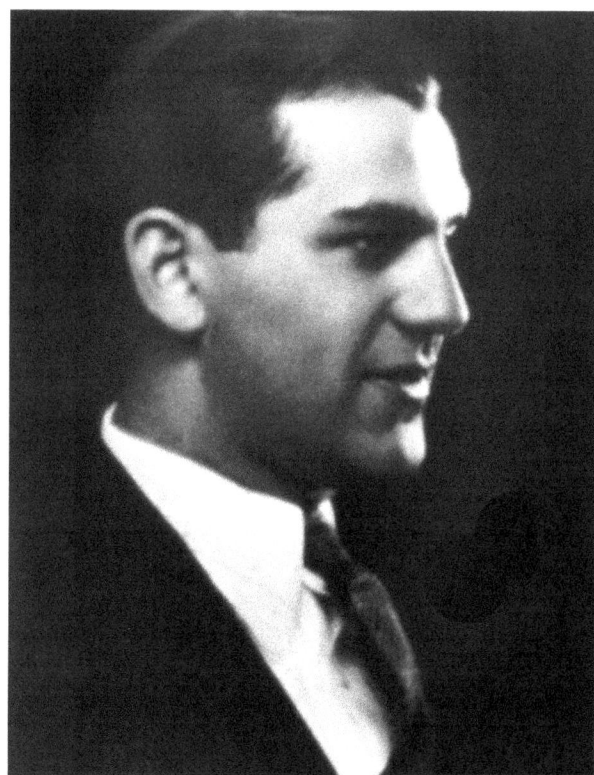

Sol Kogen, circa 1925.
Photographer unknown,
Edgar Miller Legacy.

139

believed he had made enough money to live comfortably the rest of his life, so he "retired" from the family business. Kogen left for Paris in 1925, lived in the Left Bank area of the city and studied art. Although he was surrounded by artists who had adopted avant-garde techniques, Kogen preferred the straightforward representational art so entrenched in the Chicago art scene.[231] During a tour in a Paris museum, a guide attempted to explain an abstract painting, to which Kogen replied, "If it has to be explained, it's no good."[232]

When Kogen returned to Chicago in the summer of 1927, he was unable to find digs with the charm and romantic ambiance he had experienced living among the artists in Paris, so he resolved to create his own poetic environment. Kogen dipped into his nest egg and purchased the old Emmerich Mansion on Carl Street, which sat on two and a half lots. Then he asked a multitalented former classmate from the Art Institute, Edgar Miller, to assist him in transforming the house into a haven for artists. For almost a decade, the two men designed and built a series of unique and enchanting artist studios in what one contemporary critic called "a modernistic duet."[233] Miller's friend Andrew Rebori was a "consulting architect" on the project, but he later complained that he was consulted "damn little."[234]

James Edgar Miller was born in 1899 in Idaho Falls, Idaho. In 1917, he moved to Chicago and attended the School of the Art Institute, where he met Kogen. After a while, he became disenchanted with the school, left and began taking art instruction at Hull House, like Kogen. In the early 1920s, Miller was hired as an apprentice by Chicago modernist sculptor Alphonso Iannelli, a prolific artist whose sculptural works in public spaces still inspire awe in those who view them. In 1913, Frank Lloyd Wright tapped Iannelli to create a large number of unique, streamline "sprite" sculptures, rendered in what would much later be referred to as the art deco style, for Wright's Midway Gardens, an entertainment and dining complex a few blocks east of Lorado Taft's Midway Studios (demolished in 1929). After a few years, Edgar Miller left Iannelli's studio and entered into a lifelong career as a freelance artist, working for publishers, advertising agencies, architects, hotels, churches, social clubs, universities, restaurants, local governments and, of course, himself. During the period Miller was living and working at the artist enclave on Carl Street, his talents were already known to have no bounds. "Edgar Miller is an artist who works in as many media as the world has made known."[235]

Miller, whose work at the School of the Art Institute and Iannelli's studio showed a clear inclination toward modernism, won the Art Institute's

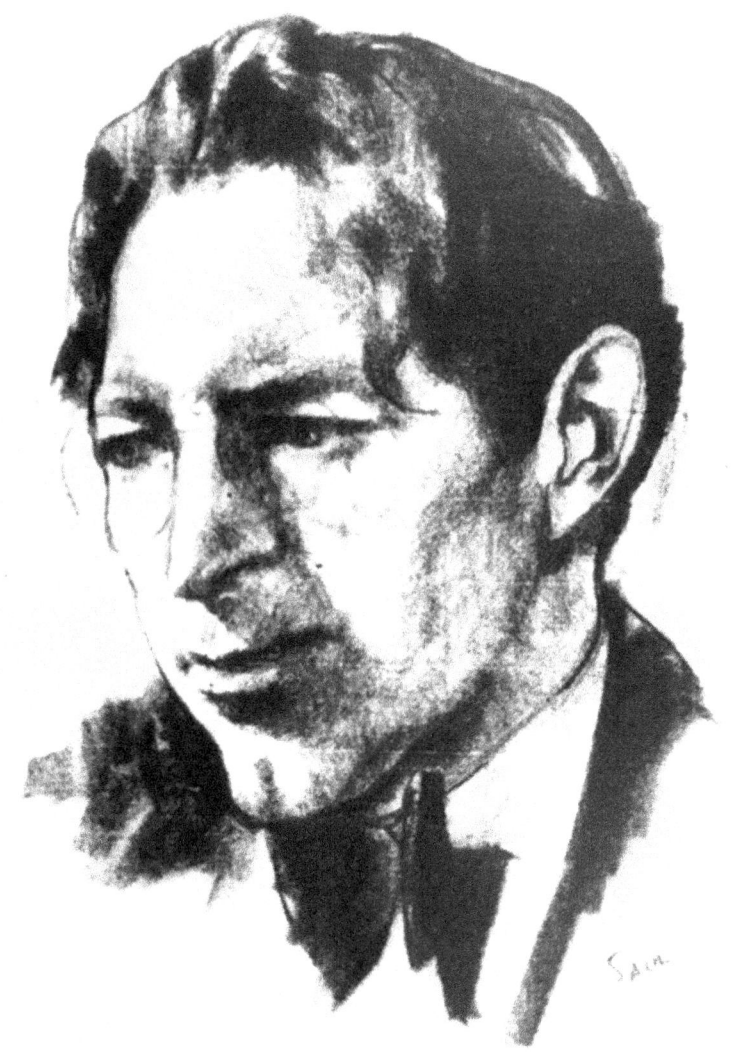

Portrait of Edgar Miller by Sol Kogen, circa 1928. "*Edgar Miller, Designer-Craftsman,*" Architecture *LXVI, no. 2, (August 1932).*

prestigious Logan Medal for his innovative work on a stained-glass panel that is still displayed in the Art Institute's permanent collection. He became one of the most well-known Chicago artists of his time and contributed significantly to the city's modern art movement of the 1920s, '30s and '40s.

In the mid-1920s, Miller operated a small art gallery at 19 West Pearson Street in Towertown, quaintly referred to as the House at the End of the Street. There he exhibited his own work as well as the work of other

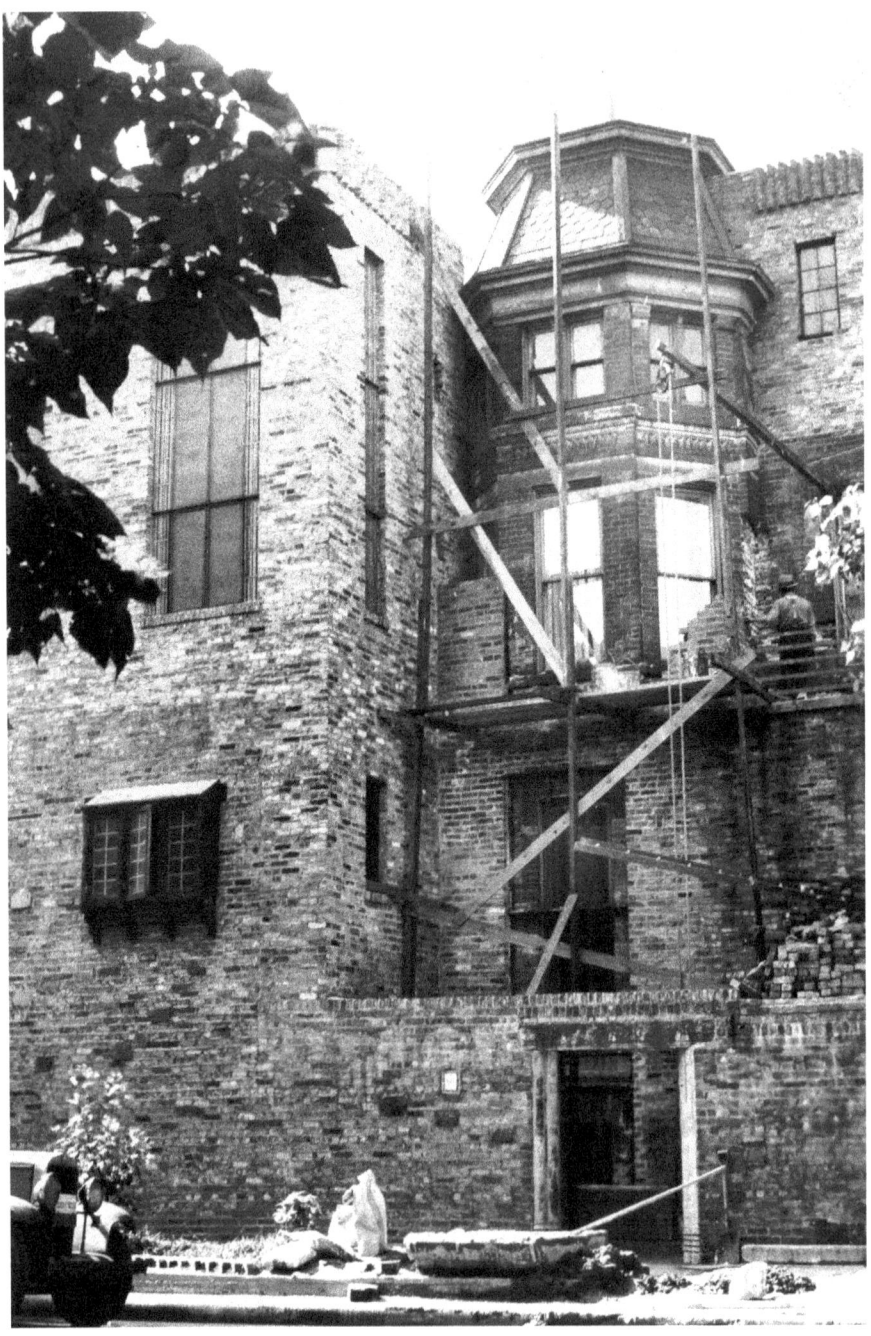

Workmen remodeling Carl Street Studios, 155 West Carl Street (now West Burton Place), circa 1930. *Paul Hanson, Chicago History Museum, Ichi-22776.*

modernist artists, including Lionel Feininger, Rudolph Weisenborn, John Storrs and John W. Norton. The diversity and breadth of Miller's artistic venue were unmatched. He excelled at oil painting, watercolor, pastels, mural painting, plaster reliefs, sculpture, steel and copper work, ceramics, textiles and batik (for which he would win another Logan Medal), mosaics, printmaking of every type, wood carving and stained glass. Miller would use many of his talents in these diverse media at the artist colonies on Carl Street and elsewhere.

Work began on the Carl Street Studios complex in 1927, shortly after Sol purchased the property. Unlike the Tree Studios, Kogen and Miller conceived of an artist studio complex whose interior and exterior spaces would themselves be innovative works of art and not merely functional spaces for the production of art. To help build the complex, they recruited a highly talented and versatile Mexican immigrant, Jesus Torres. They began by gutting the three-story mansion, including the basement. Miller is generally credited with designing the interior space plan for all of the studio units in the former mansion, which included using basement spaces as primary living areas, a novel concept at the time. The studios featured duplex spatial configurations that provided for large, two-story living room / studio spaces with adjacent accessory rooms, such as small kitchens and dining rooms, and lofted bedrooms and bathrooms above.

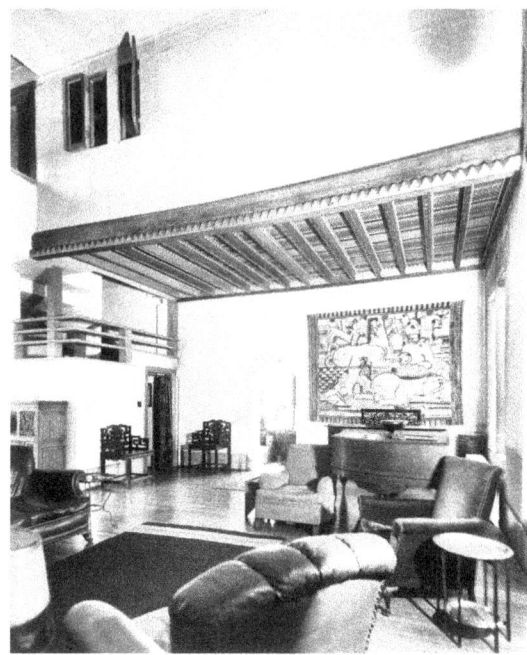

Carl Street Studios, Unit 2 living room, circa 1931. *Chicago Architectural Photographing Co., Maurice L. Bein Papers, Burnham & Ryerson Archives, The Art Institute of Chicago, Digital File #198505_150204-138.*

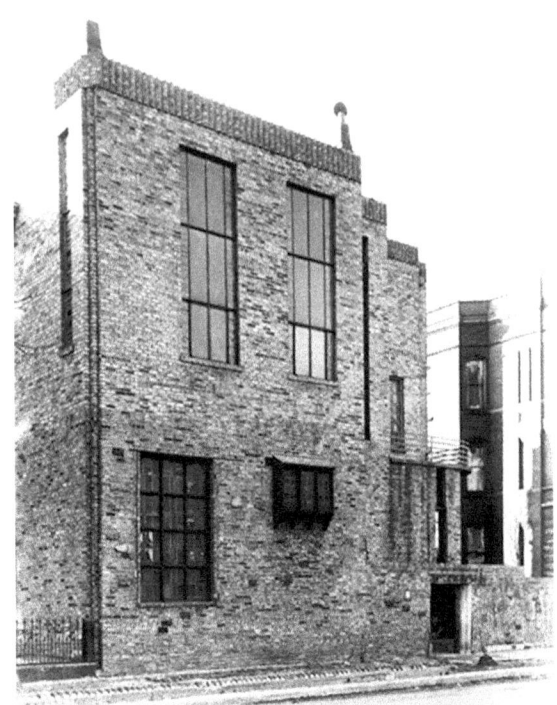

Carl Street Studios, front façade, circa 1931. *Chicago Architectural Photographing Co., Maurice L. Bein Papers, Burnham & Ryerson Archives, The Art Institute of Chicago, Digital File #198505_150204-118.*

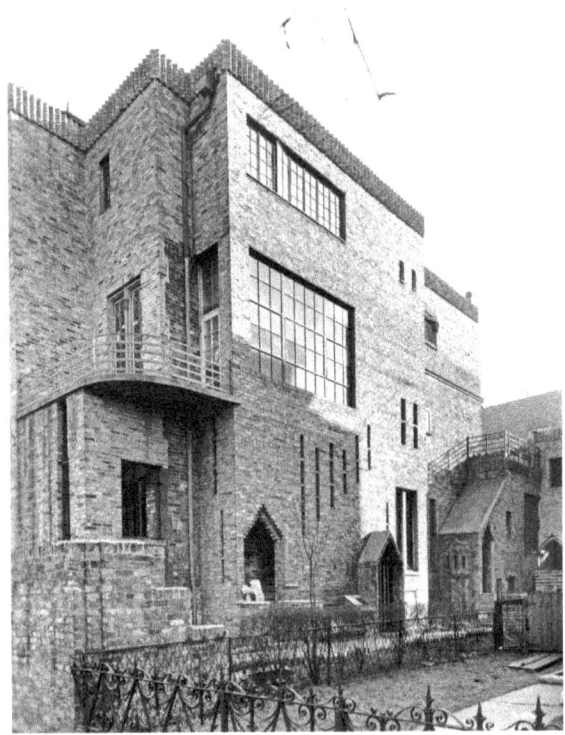

Carl Street Studios, West façade, circa 1931. *Chicago Architectural Photographing Co., Maurice L. Bein Papers, Burnham & Ryerson Archives, The Art Institute of Chicago, Digital File #198505_150204-119.*

The exterior walls of the mansion were masked with a new face of common brick and featured artistic textural elements and designs.

Kogen and Miller met the challenge of maximizing light in each studio while maintaining privacy. In some units, soaring two-story windows of stained, painted and/or obscure glass, each rendered by Miller, were installed. They pioneered using glass block and molded textured glass for primary living-space windows. Interior walls composed mainly of plaster and fireplaces were aesthetically enhanced with painted murals, plaster reliefs and hand-carved wood elements. Kogen and Miller employed myriad colorful marbles, terrazzo and Rookwood, Grueby and Batchelder tiles on all manner of surfaces—floors, walls, baseboards, fireplaces and counters. They used decorative copper and steel work in doors, windows and light fixtures. The exterior door of each unit enjoys its own distinctive personality, and many incorporate intricate, hand-carved elements by Miller and Torres. Collectively, the doors contribute to the asymmetrical flavor of the building.

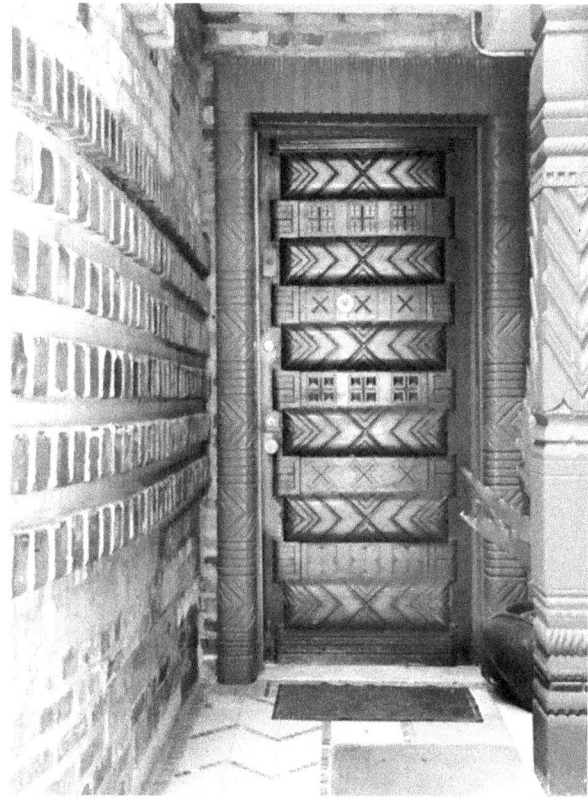

Carl Street Studios, door to unit 14. *K.M. Stolte (2018).*

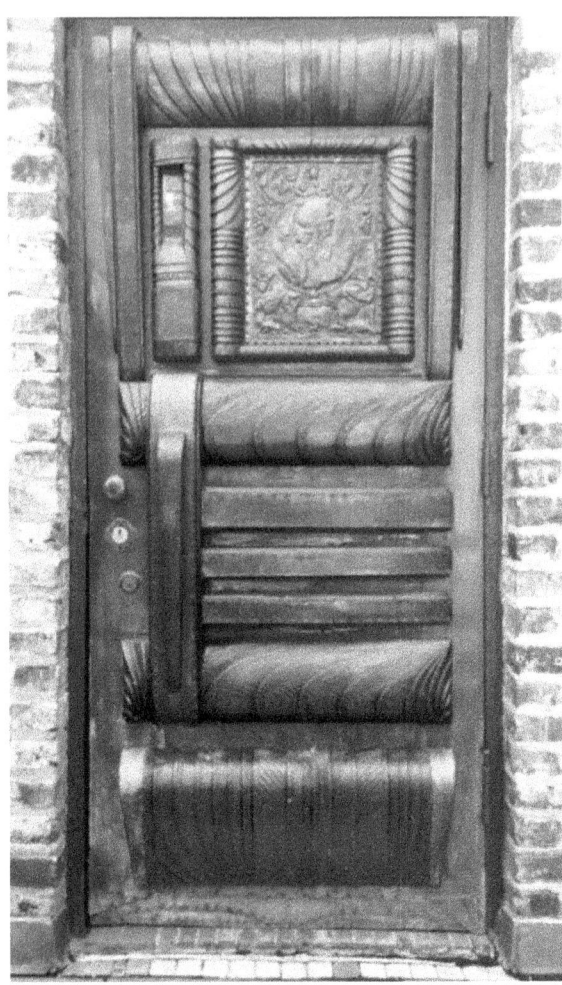

Carl Street Studios, door to
unit 16. *K.M. Stolte (2018).*

After work on the six studios in the former mansion was completed,
Kogen and Miller constructed an additional four-story building adjacent
to the northeast corner wall of the original mansion, adding three
additional studios. They then renovated the existing two-story stables and
coach house (probably former "fire shanties") at the back of the property
to include two additional stories and eight studios. These additional
structures at the periphery of the property had the intended effect of
enveloping an east courtyard. Architectural flourishes, such as interesting
brick and tile work, mosaics, ceramic reliefs and wood carvings by Miller
and Torres, ornamented these new structures. The sidewalk in front of
the building was replaced with a dramatic walkway of colorful tiles and
marble slabs.

Much of the high-grade materials used in the building were reclaimed by the artists from demolished mansions in the area, demolished buildings from the 1933 Century of Progress World's Fair and the Maxwell Street market vendors. In a 1993 interview, Miller recalled, "Here was secondhand material like good wood, tile, and marble that was distinguished as hell, ready to be destroyed. We salvaged it."[236] Kogen and Miller brought the salvaged material back to the Carl Street complex and stored it in various

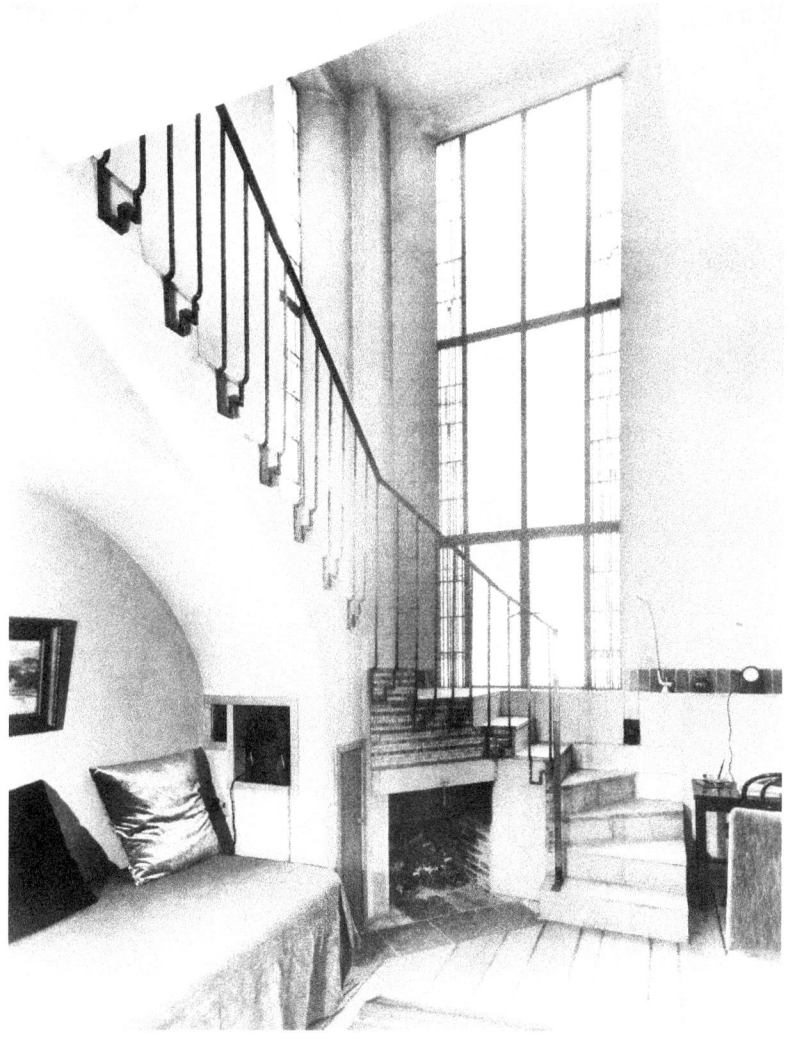

Carl Street Studios, unit 7 interior, circa 1931. *Chicago Architectural Photographing Co., Maurice L. Bein Papers, Burnham & Ryerson Archives, The Art Institute of Chicago, Digital File #198505_150204-137.*

locations on the property, the best of it in Miller's studio in the rear coach house, where he and Torres carved, molded and painted it into useful and beautiful objects that would be used to adorn the studios and the exterior façades of the building.

> *The atelier at the courtyard's end is like an antique shop in a refreshing present tense. Hundreds of objects, newly made and in the process, are in sight. Gorgeous painted ceramics, etched glass, clay animal grotesques, a great church window with sober saints, panels of engraved polychrome wood, drawings of things imagined and things to be made, book illustrations, carvings of wood and stone, plaster reliefs, elegant or humorous—a delectable confusion to which strength or delicacy of color and form have been beautifully brought. A Mexican assistant [Jesus Torres] labors, brush in hand, on the rounded surfaces of a great clay bowl, converting it into an object of distinction. Miller himself cuts with undisguised joy into the hard fabric of a chance fragment of stone, from which will presently emerge an unbelievable rabbit. Thus it goes on in that fascinating place— materials of every sort taking beautiful and appropriate form under the urge of a powerful imagination.[237]*

Kogen had a particular affinity for ceramic tiles, especially those imported from England, Germany and the Netherlands. They were widely in use during the 1910s and 1920s, but by the time of the Great Depression, they became a drag on the market. Practically all building projects in America came to a sudden halt, and many of the companies that sold ceramic tiles went bankrupt, providing Kogen the unique opportunity to purchase entire stocks for a fraction of their former value.[238] Under Studio 8, Kogen built a subterranean storage vault where "hundreds of thousands of pieces of tile [are] stacked on shelves—more than Kogen or anyone else is likely ever to use."[239] That prediction, made in 1956, was quite true. Even now, tens of thousands of ceramic tiles and pieces of marble, slate and terrazzo remain untouched in the storage vault.

The configurations of the buildings created an east courtyard completely enveloped by the original house, the front addition and the modified stables/ coach house structure at the rear. This courtyard is paved with tiles and pieces of marble, flagstone and terrazzo and incorporates several raised planting beds with trees, shrubs and flowers. It is decorated throughout with carved doors, soaring stained-glass windows, a large art deco fresco resembling cave paintings, mosaics, friezes and other sculptural elements. There is a

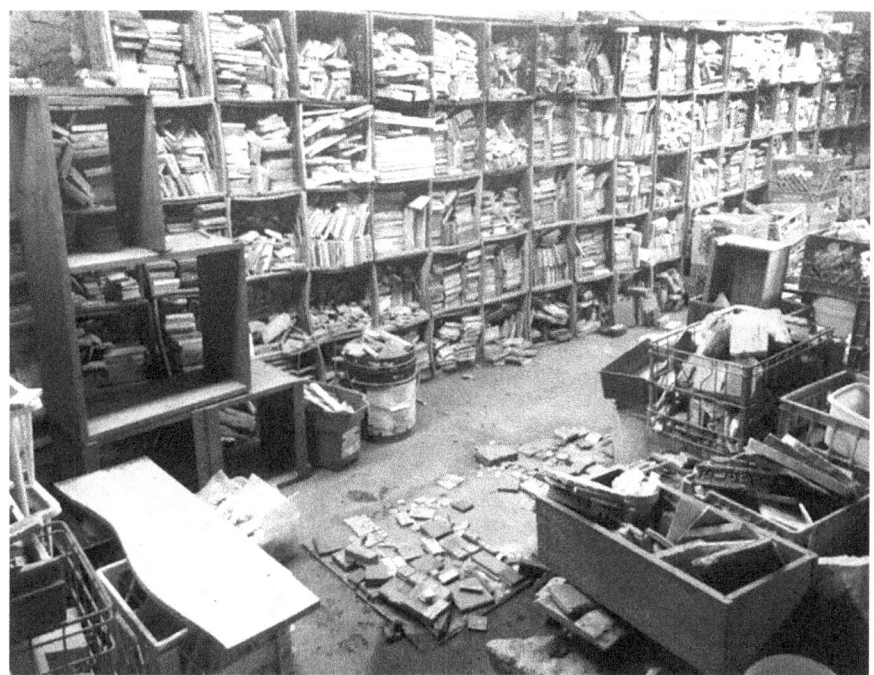

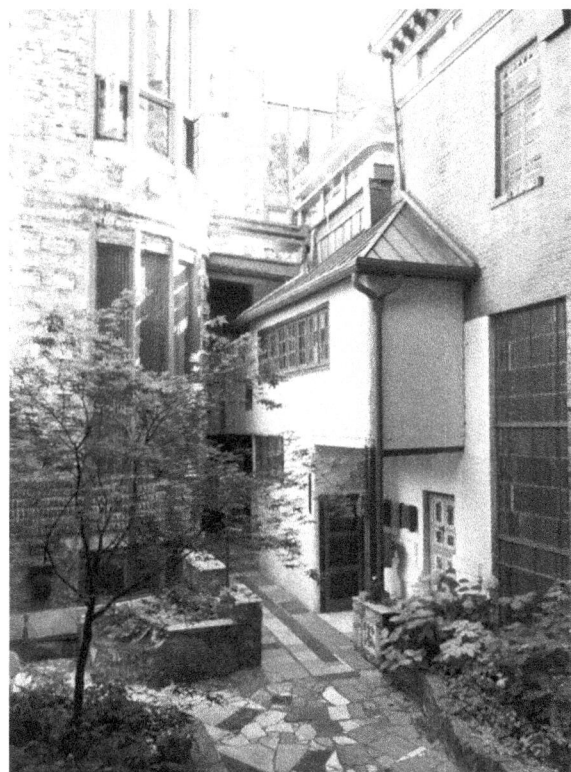

Above: Carl Street Studios, underground tile vault. *K.M. Stolte (2018).*

Left: Carl Street Studios, east courtyard. Scores of artists on West Burton Place congregated periodically in the east courtyard for pig or goat roasts. *K.M. Stolte (2018).*

large marble-topped table supported by brick columns in the center of the courtyard and a marble-topped sideboard built into a wall nearby (these were later additions). The walkway leading from the east courtyard to the front wall entry gate consists of the same array of tile, marble and stone and spills beyond the entry gate onto the outer sidewalk that runs the entire length of the front façade and privacy wall.

The west courtyard is bounded on the east by the original house and on the west by an iron fence supported by a series of brick columns. (After ninety years of growth, a large elm tree planted near the iron fence has essentially swallowed part of the fence and one of the brick columns within its girthy trunk.) The west courtyard is paved with tile and marble and incorporates three planting beds and a twenty-seven-foot-long koi pond with a fountain.

Each of the studios in the complex has at least one door that opens to these courtyards or to an outside walkway at the third-floor level in the rear of the east courtyard. Kogen and Miller intended the courtyards to offer

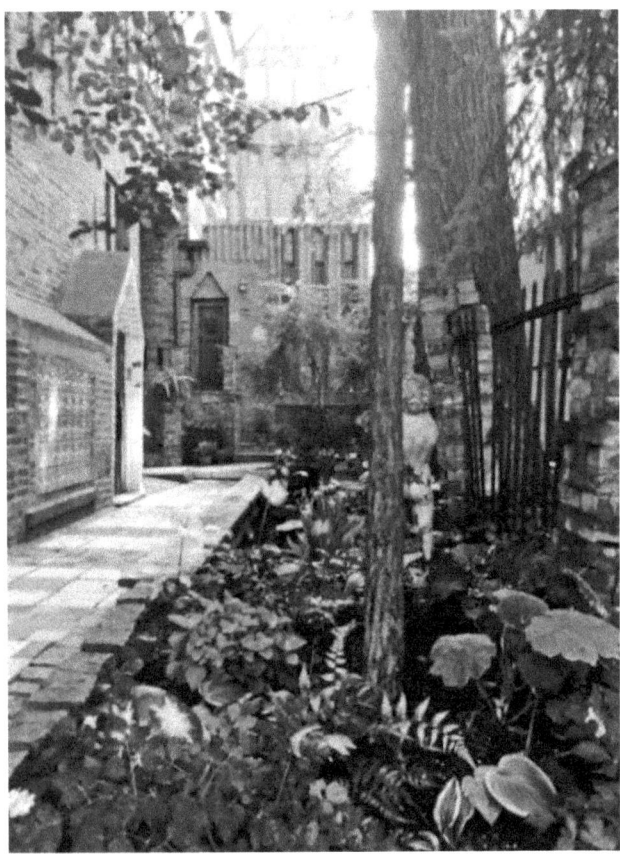

Carl Street Studios, west courtyard. *K.M. Stolte (2018).*

idyllic spaces for communal socialization of the resident artists, and by all accounts their objectives have been met for the past ninety years.

As a result of the stock market crash of 1929, Sol Kogen's financial position was severely impacted. Consequently, during the Depression, Kogen relied more and more on Carl Street Studios as a means of generating revenue.[240] In the mid-1930s, Miller and Kogen had a dispute regarding their "partnership," and Miller markedly diminished his work at Carl Street Studios. Some writers have argued, erroneously, that Miller discontinued work altogether in 1935 and that he had no hand in designing the final eight units in the coach house and stables at the back of the property (Studios 10–18; there is no Studio 13 due to an anachronistic superstition prevalent in the 1930s and '40s).[241] Compelling evidence exists, however, that shows Miller continued working on some aspects of the complex after 1935 and that he was still at Carl Street Studios, at least for a time, when the coach house / stables were being converted into artist studios.

For example, a windowpane in the second-floor front bay window of Studio 8 was signed by Miller and dated 1936. The primary door of Studio 8 is also dated 1936, and the door to Studio 11 in the rear coach house, which bears carvings unmistakably by Miller's hand, is dated 1940. Studio 11 also has a very large stained-glass window by Miller. A five-foot decorative wooden panel carved and painted by Miller overlooks the staircase of Studio 12 in the coach house. It would appear, therefore, that Miller's artistic association with Carl Street Studios continued to some extent after 1935 and that he contributed to some of the rear studios. Indeed, according to the 1932 account quoted above, Miller's own atelier was located in the coach house from the outset,[242] and one would expect that he had primary design responsibility for the studio space that he occupied for eight years. Moreover, a newspaper article published in early 1934, when Miller was indisputably present, states, "The great old barns in the rear of the building are being modernized in the same captivating manner."[243]

With Edgar Miller receding, if not entirely gone, from the scene after 1935, ongoing work in the studio complex was continued by Kogen and the versatile Jesus Torres, who had been Miller's primary apprentice. Most of the coach house units are dominated by the work of Torres, though they also feature some artworks by Miller. Work on the building would progress in one form or another for several decades, the last major structural project being completed in 1964, long after the deaths of Kogen and Torres, when a bedroom / dressing room addition was made to Studio 4 in a space that had once been part of the west courtyard terrace.[244]

The Carl Street Studios proved to have great appeal for Chicago's artistic community. According to Sol Kogen, "First I fixed up the coach house for Edgar Miller and John Norton. Then others started coming, and I built studios for them on other parts of the property."[245] In addition to Miller and Norton, notable local artists Edgar Britton, Edward Millman, Stewart Rae, Taylor Poore and Eleanor de Laittre Shephard abandoned Towertown and settled at Carl Street Studios in the 1930s.[246] Internationally famous painter and Art Institute instructor Boris Anisfeld, who had previously lived at the Tree Studios, occupied Studio No. 1 from 1934 until his death in 1973. Anisfeld is said to have sometimes paid his rent to the Kogens with his own paintings.[247] Mark Tobey, another modernist painter of international repute, resided at Carl Street Studios for a time.

Well-known ballet dancer and choreographer Adolph Bolm, jazz singer Wee Bonnie Baker, pioneering television personality Dave Garroway and film critic Roger Ebert lived at Carl Street Studios. So too did one of the country's first celebrity chefs, Henri Charpentier. A world-renowned French chef even before he came to America in 1907 to manage the kitchen at Delmonico's, Charpentier had been a chef at the Savoy in London, the Metropole in Moscow, Vier Jahreszeiten in Munich, Maxim's in Paris, the Quirinale in Rome and, earlier in his career, a restaurant at Monte Carlo where he serendipitously invented crêpes Suzette for the future Edward VII of England. (His warm relations with the English royal family led to annual Christmas cards from Buckingham Palace until his death in 1961.) Following his years as chef at Delmonico's—then America's most famous restaurant— he operated his own popular New York restaurant, Henri's, for almost two decades. At age fifty-eight, Charpentier moved to Chicago in 1938 to open and operate the Café de Paris, located downtown. Before, during and after his eight-year stint in Chicago, Charpentier wrote several well-regarded cookbooks. In 1946, he moved to California, where he ended his illustrious culinary career by operating a tiny restaurant out of his own home. It seated no more than twelve persons and required reservations months and, for certain dates, even years in advance.

The popularity of the Carl Street Studios with Chicago artists during the Depression led others to purchase old run-down buildings on West Burton Place to create their own studios. One of the first was William Giuliani, a retired baritone from the Metropolitan Opera. He and his wife purchased a three-story rooming house together with a barn at 151 West Carl Street, adjacent to Sol Kogen's complex.[248] Between 1932 and 1935, the Giulianis remodeled their studio building in a manner similar to that employed next door at Carl Street Studios, using many of the same materials and design concepts. The floors and other surfaces of the studio units feature random arrangements of title, terrazzo and marble. There are a few two-story stained-glass and painted windows in units at the rear of the building.

The front façade incorporates a curved window bay with stacked windows that were originally part of the Swift & Company Bridge and Service Building at the 1933–34 Century of Progress World's Fair. The curved window bay leads to an inset front entrance with a small cantilevered concrete, scalloped-edged roof. The common brick of the front façade is interrupted intermittently by random imbedded stones and bricks with contrasting color and texture. The building comprised at least four studio units in the main building and two units in the converted two-story barn at the rear of the property.

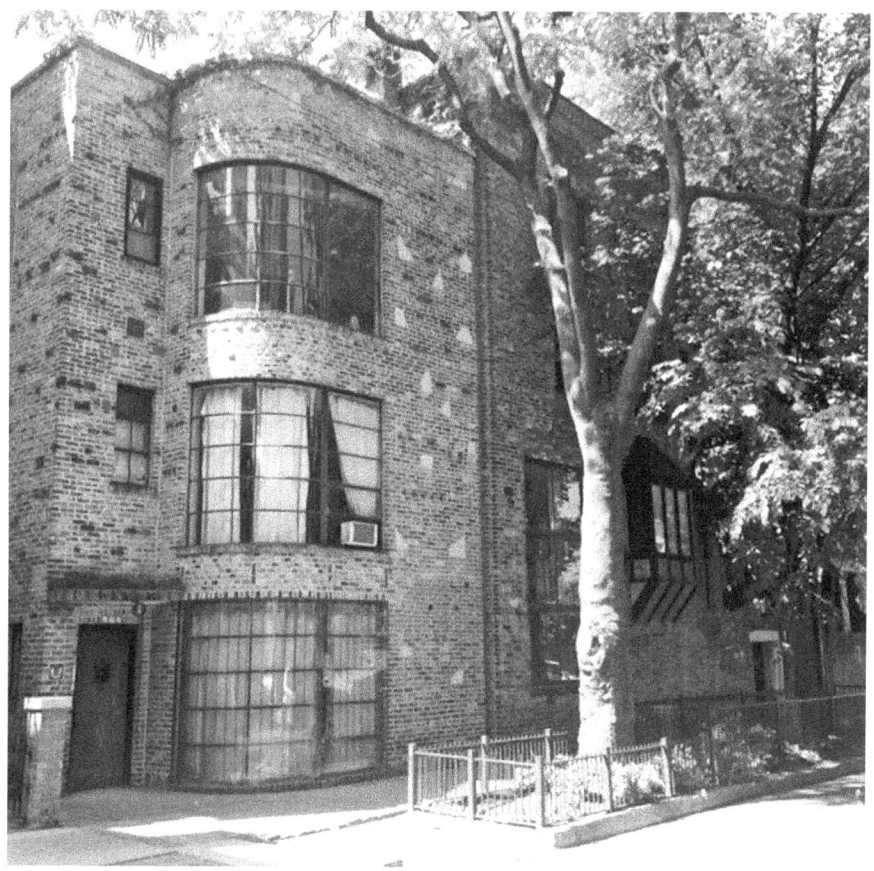

151 West Burton Place. *K.M. Stolte (2018).*

A group of seven commercial artists led by Clive Rickabaugh and Carl Peter Koch purchased the properties at 152–156 West Burton directly across from Carl Street Studios and created an artists' cooperative.[249] The combined property consisted of two three-story rooming houses and three coach houses at the rear.[250] These artists erected a six-foot-high brick wall across the entire front perimeter of the parcel, creating a series of private courtyards adorned with friezes, sculptures and planting beds. The multi-structure complex, as remodeled, constituted an eclectic collection of architectural styles, including elements of art deco, art moderne, arts and crafts and the international style.

In 1939-40, Norman Johnson purchased the three-story Italianate house at 161 West Burton Place, originally built in 1879, and remodeled it into one of the finest examples of art moderne architecture in the Midwest.[251] The educated consensus is that Johnson employed progressive architect Andrew Rebori to redesign the house and supervise the remodeling effort.[252] Rebori had been consulting architect for Kogen and Miller's Carl Street Studios two doors down, and the remodeled Johnson building bears an uncanny resemblance to other residences designed by Rebori in the Gold Coast neighborhood. Like Rebori's own home and studio he designed and built at 1328 North State Street, later owned by painter Richard Florsheim, the front façade of 161 West Burton is dominated by a corner window bay with an expansive curved glass block mass extending vertically for two stories, another shorter curved glass block mass at the third-floor level and an inset front entry, albeit rotated to the west. The dominant curved window bay creates a bookending effect with the corresponding curved window bay of the Giuliani studios at 151 West Burton.

The east, north and west façade walls are of common brick punctuated randomly with bricks and stones of contrasting colors and textures. The west façade, facing an alley, features an enormous two-story window with opaque glass panes and several uniform smaller casement windows, all with opaque glass. The southwest corner is curved and incorporates several slits in the brick to permit light into an enclosed, curving, outside staircase leading to a long terrace at the second floor in the rear of the building. (As discussed below, Rebori employed a similar series of slit windows in a curving stairwell at the Frank Fisher Studios). The Johnson studios contained five handsome units. Some of the units incorporated wood trim elements carved by Edgar Miller, and all units reflect an art moderne design scheme.

At the opposite end of the street, at the intersection of West Burton Place and LaSalle Street, Theophil Reuther, an artist, purchased and

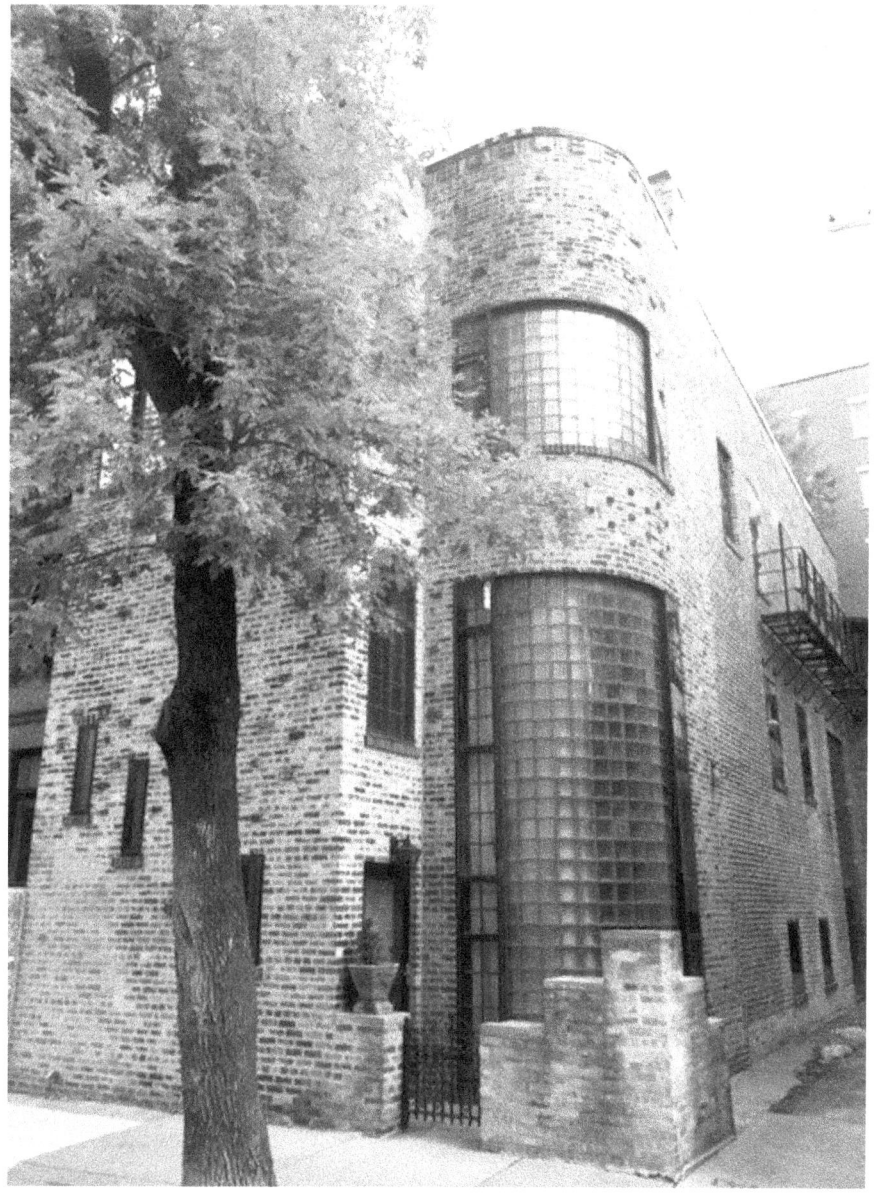

161 West Burton Place. *K.M. Stolte (2018).*

remodeled an old 1892 three-flat in 1940 that he called the Theophil Studios. Reuther engaged architect Frank Lapasso to redesign the three-flat. Lapasso adopted an art moderne vernacular for both the exterior façades and the six studio interiors.

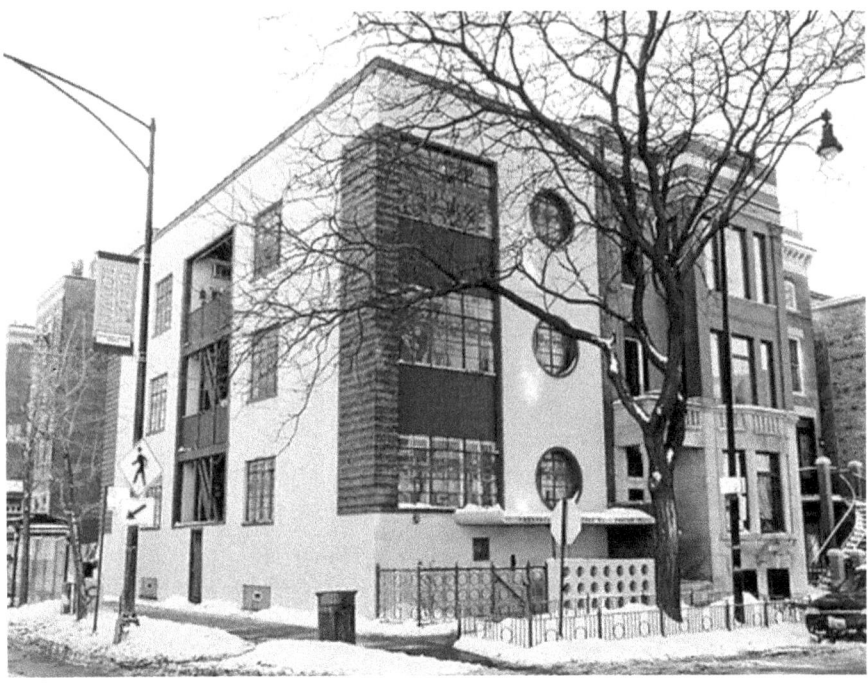

Theophil Studios, 143 West Burton Place. *K.M. Stolte (2016).*

The principal (north) façade features a vertical stucco panel on the western half with three large circular stacked windows. On the eastern half of the front façade is a red brick and wood panel with three rectangular sets of casement windows. The southern façade of the building facing the alley essentially repeats the same arrangement. Portions of all of the windows have some stained-glass ornamental elements. The front entrance is reached by stepping down a few flights to a below-grade doorway over which Lapasso placed a linear cantilevered overhang etched with the name *Theophil Studios.* Near the entryway door are several sculptural elements made by Edgar Miller, one of which is a highly stylized terra-cotta frieze of a horse that ranks among the best of Miller's works.

The last major remodeling on the block was on the coach house behind 158 West Burton Place. The house in front was never remodeled and retains its original 1880s façade. The coach house, reputed to sit on the smallest lot on record in Chicago (eighteen feet by twenty-four feet), was initially built by architects Glicken & Glicken in 1938. In 1965, architect Ron Dirsmith purchased the coach house and renovated it in a highly stylized, hip scheme featuring a curved, cantilevered floating stairway, a wood-burning fireplace resembling an igloo, rough terrazzo floors throughout and a twelve-piece series of art glass windows tracing man's evolution by artist Robert White.[253] The back (alley) wall of the structure contains highly idiosyncratic windows comprising multicolored, jewel-like cut glass embedded in stucco panels. Dirsmith named this structure the Sun House and said of it, "The whole place is a four-story piece of sculpture."[254]

Alan Artner, the art critic for the *Chicago Tribune* for almost forty-five years and a resident of West Burton Place for even longer, aptly characterized the West Burton Place artist colony in an August 1975 article calling for the landmarking of the block: "I am aware of no other local structure of this century, excepting those created for the 1933 World's Fair, that had as much collaboration by Chicago artists as did the Kogen Studios. Certainly, they are patchworks on a large scale, eccentric flights of fancy given form, and few of the artists who worked on them are among our biggest names. But everywhere there are naïve, aspirant, human touches left by men and women who lived where they worked and loved where they lived."[255]

The artist colony that nestled on West Burton Place was a socially cohesive group. Because of its small geographic size—a single block—the consolidation of artists who lived and worked on West Burton Place was far denser than it was in Towertown, where the artists were spread out over a thirty-six to forty-block area. In its heyday, it was estimated that more than one hundred artists lived on West Burton Place.[256] And like the artists a generation before at the Fine Arts Building and Eagle's Nest Camp, the Burton Place artists liked to play.

> *The hundred residents of the block celebrate Halloween, New Year's Eve and Christmas together. Usually the Halloween and New Year's parties are given in one of the larger studios. If one of the residents play the piano well, he plays for the group. Perhaps someone else dances well—then the entertainment includes dancing. Everyone contributes—it's everybody's party. Ever since the first studios were built, it's been the custom to have an outdoors barbeque on Christmas Eve. Everyone from the block joins the fun. A huge pit is dug in one of the many courtyards.....Sometimes a pig is roasted, other years it's a lamb. Sometimes both revolve on the glowing spit. Sweet potato pies, salad and coffee are set on a long wooden table deep in the shadows under the protecting roof of an archway.[257]*

There were also two-day art fairs held on West Burton Place, in which more than one hundred artists exhibited their works and competed for prizes.[258] Proceeds from the gate paid for a street cleaner, and the rest was given to a charity.

Just as the Fine Arts Building and Towertown artists socialized, dined and played at the Cliff Dwellers and Dil Pickle Clubs, respectively, the more successful of the Burton Place artists became members of the Tavern Club,

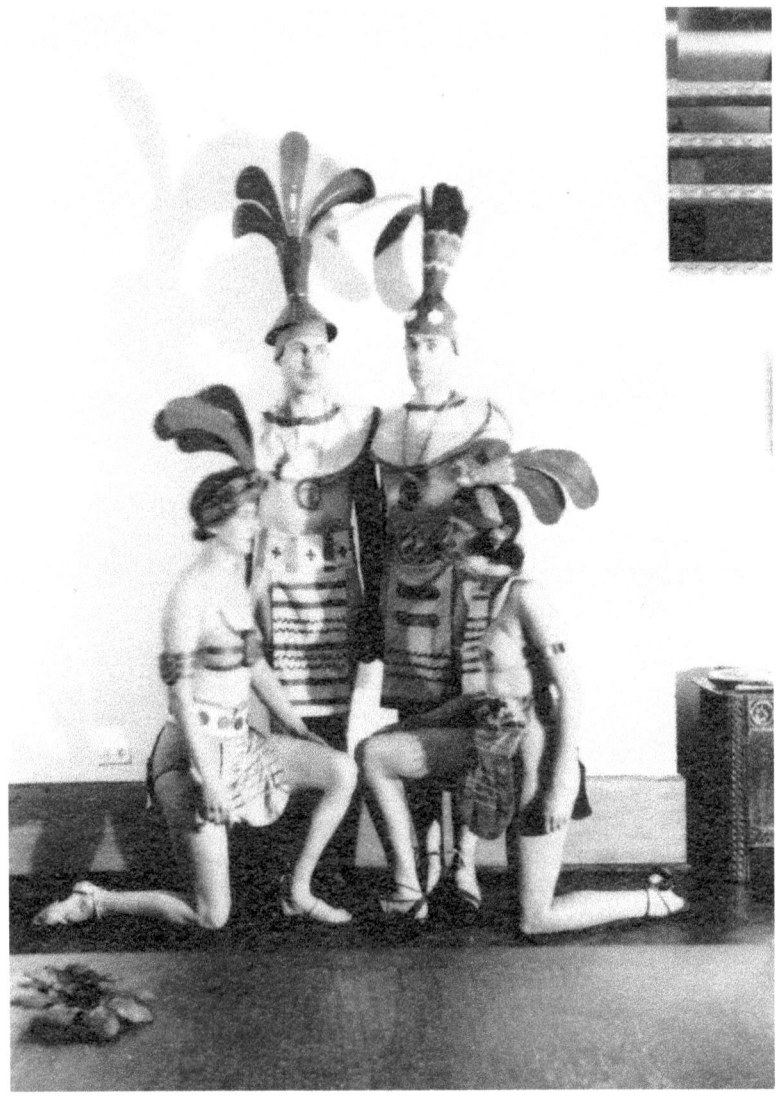

Clockwise, Edgar Miller, Taylor Poore, Dorothy Miller and Madge Poore in costume at Carl Street Studios, Unit 2, circa 1929. *Photographer unknown, Taylor Poore Papers, Newberry Library.*

located on the top floors of 333 North Michigan Avenue. Formed in 1928 by a prominent group of Chicago businessmen, artists and architects, the Tavern Club offered dining facilities, game rooms, several bars and a large outdoor terrace overlooking the Chicago River and the Miracle Mile where members and their guests danced on summer nights into the early mornings. Among the club's members were Burton Place artists and architects Edgar Miller, John Warner Norton, Taylor Poore, Andrew Rebori and others.

In 1933, the Tavern Club commissioned Edgar Miller to paint a large, playful mural titled *Love through the Ages* on the walls of one of the club's dining rooms. This mural depicted several scenes featuring historic personages engaged in both prurient and violent activities. There were vignettes depicting ancient Egyptian, Greek and Roman lovers, medieval coquets and Henry VIII with his six wives. More violent, less loving scenes included Spanish conquistadors battling Aztecs, cowboys shooting at Native Americans and one particularly prescient scene titled "The Rape of Peace," in which Hitler, Mussolini, Hirohito, Stalin and other dictators are tearing apart a woman representing world peace.[259] A more appropriate title of the Miller mural would have been *The History of Love and War*. In May 1959, Edgar Miller disassembled the mural and framed the various mural panels, which the Tavern Club sold at an auction held at the club. Miller then painted another version of *Love through the Ages* to replace the old version. John Norton was commissioned by the club to paint a large mural in another room.

The Tavern Club presented frequent periodic art exhibitions. These exhibitions featured the works of hundreds of artists and architects during the club's eighty-year existence, including John Storrs, Edgar Miller, John Norton, Thomas Tallmadge, John Holabird, Louis Skidmore, James Sessions, Rockwell Kent and Francis Chapin. In 1953, the club held a festive "Painting Marathon of the Ages," in which 8 artist members, including Miller and Ivan Albright, painted large scenes while 150 other club members, press photographers and television crews watched. Prizes were awarded to the first artist to finish the painting and to the artist with the best design.[260] The party at 333 North Michigan Avenue ultimately ended, and the Tavern Club closed its doors during the economic recession of 2008.

Sol Kogen died in 1957, and the Carl Street Studios complex was operated first by Kogen's wife, Florence. With her death, his daughter operated the site. In 1985, Kogen's daughter sold the building to a Chicago entrepreneur, Mark Mamolen, who together with others located Edgar Miller in San Francisco and invited the artist back to Chicago to continue work on both the Carl

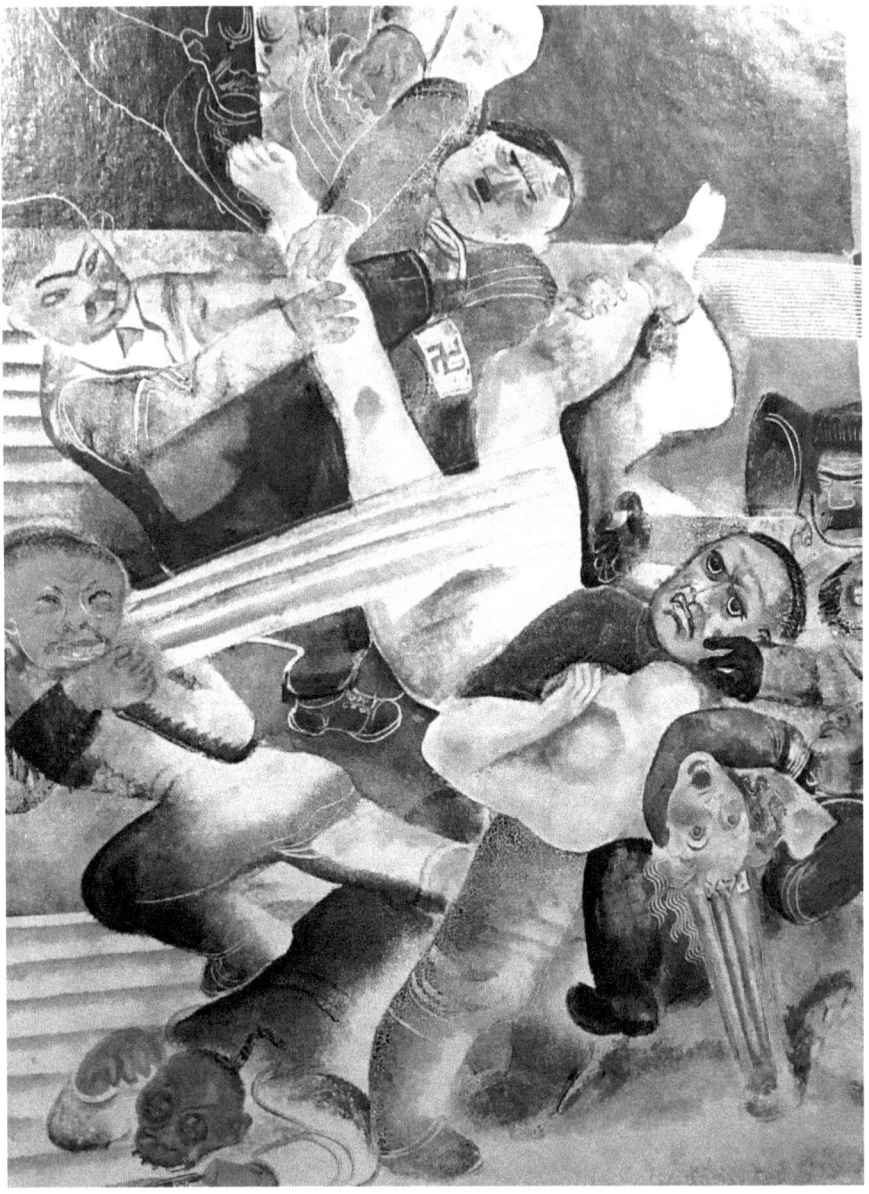

"Rape of Peace" by Edgar Miller, a panel from Miller's *Love through the Ages* mural at the Tavern Club, 1933. *K.M. Stolte (2019).*

Street Studios and the Kogen-Miller Studios. Miller, by then long forgotten by the Chicago art scene and in his mid-eighties, relished the opportunity to leave retirement and continue the projects he had started almost sixty years

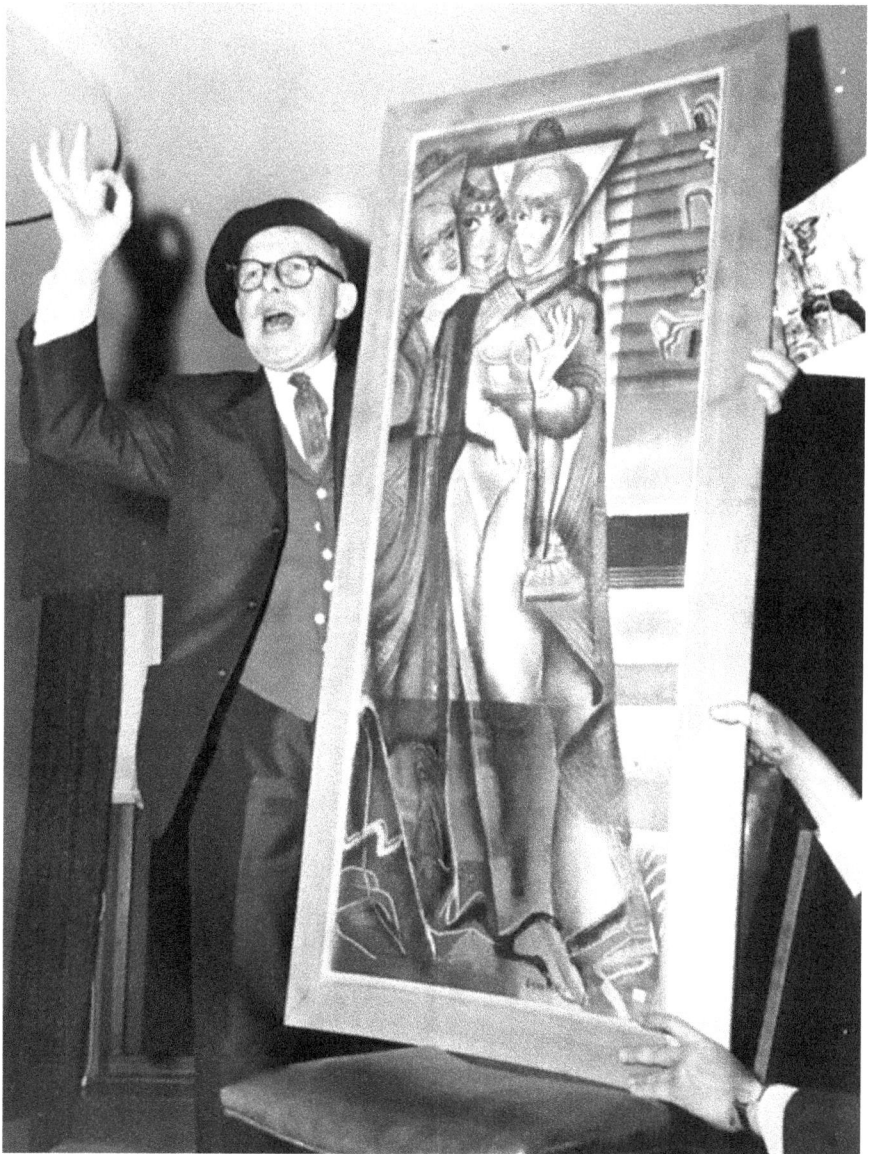

Artist Earl Clifford Gross auctioning a panel of Edgar Miller's *Love through the Ages* mural at the Tavern Club, May 17, 1959. *Photographer unknown, author's personal files.*

before. From this time until the early 1990s, Miller lived at both complexes and executed stained-glass work, murals, carved doors and other art pieces for the buildings. Many of the studios were further enhanced by these later works by Miller, who eventually died in Chicago in 1993 at the age of ninety-three.

West Burton Place was placed in the National Register of Historic Places in 2007 and was designated as a Chicago Historical Landmark District in April 2016.

JESUS TORRES

Among the most versatile artists who worked at the Burton Place artist colony was Jesus Torres. Born near Mexico City in June 1898, Torres immigrated to the United States as a nineteen-year-old and toiled as an itinerant worker in farm fields in Texas, Oklahoma and Minnesota for several years.[261] He made his way to Chicago, settling in a neighborhood of other Mexican immigrants on North Clark Street and worked as a laborer at the Chicago Stockyards.[262] Shortly thereafter, he registered for classes in English at Hull House and also studied art there under Morris Topchevsky, a close friend and colleague of well-known Mexican artist Diego Rivera.[263]

> *One day Topchevsky gave a mound of clay to the little Mexican, Torres, supposing it would be molded into some awkward piece, perhaps a bowl. But the monosyllable Jesus sculpted a head. In this mode of expression, the Mexican was not inarticulate. His hands had given voice to an artist's mind. Even before the head of clay was baked in the kiln it was sold to a member of the Hull House family. Torres had found his highway to the future.*[264]

Following his art instruction at Hull House, Torres excelled at sculpture and ceramics. In the spring of 1931, he was invited to participate in a major downtown exhibition of religious art by the Renaissance Society of the University of Chicago, an exhibition in which the cream of Chicago's art community displayed their works. Torres exhibited seven sculptural and ceramic works: two heads of Christ, the head of the Madonna, the Crucifixion, and three tiles depicting a scene at Gethsemane, the Cross and Dove and a Station of the Cross.[265] He also exhibited his work at the Art Institute.[266] From ceramics, Torres moved on to master the arts of wood carving, metalwork and, ultimately, interior decorating.

By 1932, Sol Kogen and Edgar Miller had hired Torres as Miller's principal apprentice at the Carl Street Studios. There he worked with Miller making decorative tiles in the building's kiln and setting tile in

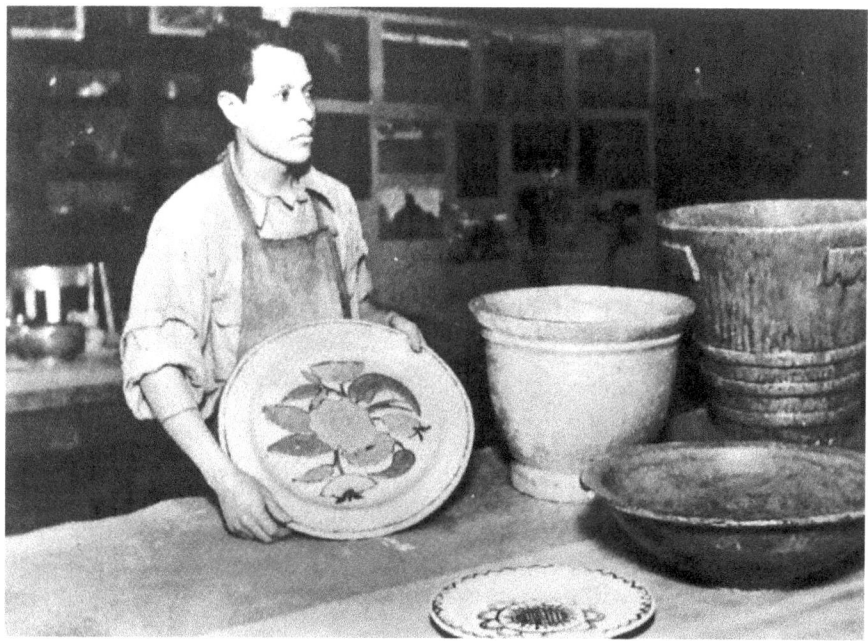

Jesus Torres, Hull House pottery studio, circa 1925. *Photographer unknown, University of Illinois, Special Collections.*

floors, fireplaces and bathroom and kitchen counters and walls. He carved geometric and figural designs in decorative trim, structural supports, balustrades and stairway railings. His unique, vibrant and colorful tile work and deeply carved doors and copper reliefs are among the most dramatic and stylistic artwork in the complex. Torres's muscular carving style set a contrast to Miller's lighter and more nuanced hand and enhanced the dynamic mixture of ethnic and cultural influences at the studio complex. He brought to Carl Street "designs [that] reflected his early ancestry—that of the Aztecs. It was imaginative but withal geometrical."[267]

After Miller reduced his work at Carl Street Studios in the mid-1930s, Torres became the principal artist and continued work on the studios into the 1940s. Torres worked with Kogen and Miller on other studio buildings on West Burton Place and elsewhere. As his fame grew, Torres received commissions to decorate the interiors of hotels, restaurants and dining rooms in Minneapolis, Milwaukee and other cities. In 1943, he was invited by the Pullman Palace Car Company to decorate the interiors of at least five luxury train cars, and his efforts were widely publicized.[268] By the time

Torres died prematurely at age fifty in 1948, the former immigrant field hand had achieved "international fame as a wood carver and artist in copper and brass."[269]

THE KOGEN-MILLER STUDIOS

In June 1928, Chicago industrialist Max Woldenberg hired Kogen, Miller, Torres and Edgar Britton to remodel an old Victorian mansion and rear barn and stables into artist studios in the same vein as their work at Carl Street Studios.[270] This nine-studio complex, located at 1734 North Wells Street, is usually referred to as the Kogen-Miller Studios; the large residence occupying the converted barn and stables is known as the Glasner Studio, named for its first resident. The artists employed similar design concepts at the Kogen-Miller Studios as they had adopted at Carl Street. They used common brick, punctuated in random places by ceramic tiles, stones and bricks of contrasting color and texture, to resurface the original Victorian house, a smaller separate structure they built on the property, the rear barn and stables and the high privacy wall at the front. The front wall is interrupted by a heavy wooden entry door, painted a voluptuous red, carved by Miller with highly stylized animals, plants and abstract elements.

The buildings on the property are arranged to create distinct courtyard spaces, paved with brick, ceramic tiles and pieces of marble and terrazzo in the same charmingly haphazard manner as the courtyards at Carl Street Studios. The courtyards are adorned with a small koi pond, planting beds and sculptural works.

Similar to Carl Street, the principal spatial layout scheme for each studio unit generally consists of a large studio / living room that extends upward two stories, with accessory rooms such as lofted bedrooms, kitchens and bathrooms sometimes surrounding the larger room, or other times up (or down) a flight of stairs.[271] The studio / living rooms are dominated by large two-story windows of stained, painted and opaque glass rendered by Miller. Curved staircases of vibrantly colorful tile, probably the work of Torres, usually incorporate either elaborately carved wood railings by Miller and/or Torres or very sleek, modern railings composed of steel. Unit doors feature geometric or figural carvings by Miller or Torres. Some studios have hanging chandeliers made of stained and painted glass crafted by Miller. All have wood-burning fireplaces constructed of brick or faced

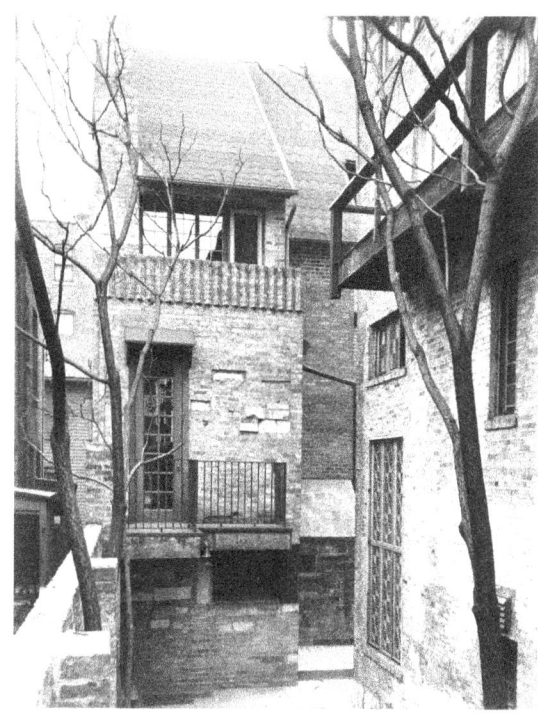

Kogen-Miller Studios, south courtyard, circa 1931. *Chicago Architectural Photographing Co., Maurice L. Bein Papers, Burnham & Ryerson Archives, The Art Institute of Chicago, Digital File # 198505_150204-127.*

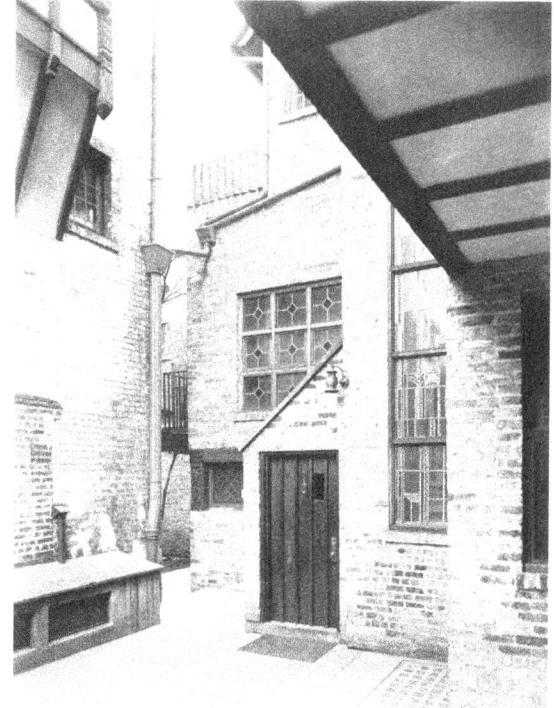

Kogen-Miller Studios, West courtyard, circa 1931. *Chicago Architectural Photographing Co., Maurice L. Bein Papers, Burnham & Ryerson Archives, The Art Institute of Chicago, Digital File # 198505_150204-125.*

with hand-painted tiles. Some studio rooms include beamed ceilings, the beams carved and painted by Edgar Miller.

The Glasner Studio, converted from the rear barn and stables, includes all the architectural and design features identified above, but in spades. The four-story structure, which sits on a deceptively small footprint, is indisputably Edgar Miller's masterpiece. Almost every surface is decorated by Miller in some fanciful manner, and visitors to the Glasner Studio are often overwhelmed by the breadth, scope and quality of the art surrounding them.[272] This studio contains several public living spaces on each of its four floors and bedrooms on two. The main living room is graced by a carved beamed ceiling painted by Miller with a series of images tracing the history of science, finishing with an image of the splitting of the atom.

The top floor of the Glasner Studio comprises an enormous room with a high, beamed cathedral ceiling, a large fireplace faced with ceramic tiles containing figures of horses and antelopes painted by

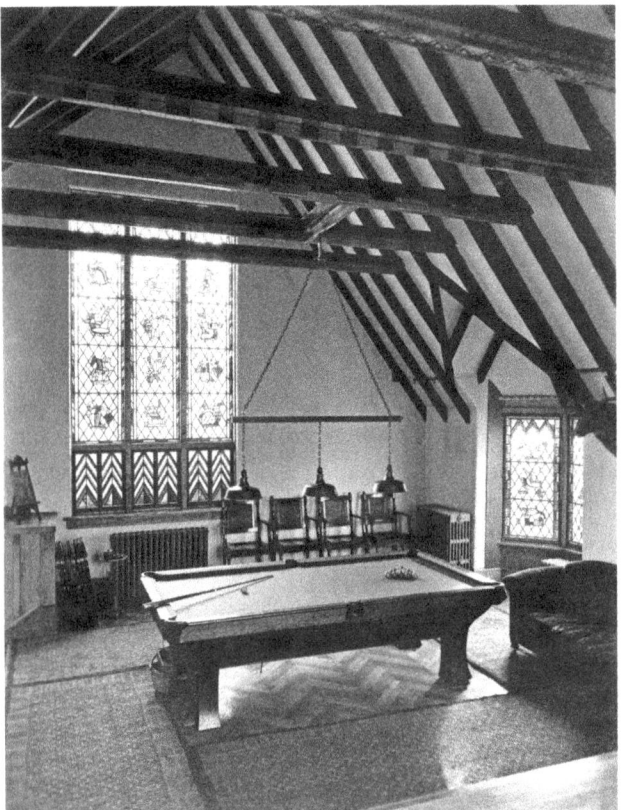

Kogen-Miller Studios, Glasner Studio fourth-floor interior, circa 1931. *Chicago Architectural Photographing Co., Maurice L. Bein Papers, Burnham & Ryerson Archives, The Art Institute of Chicago, Digital File # 198505_150204-131.*

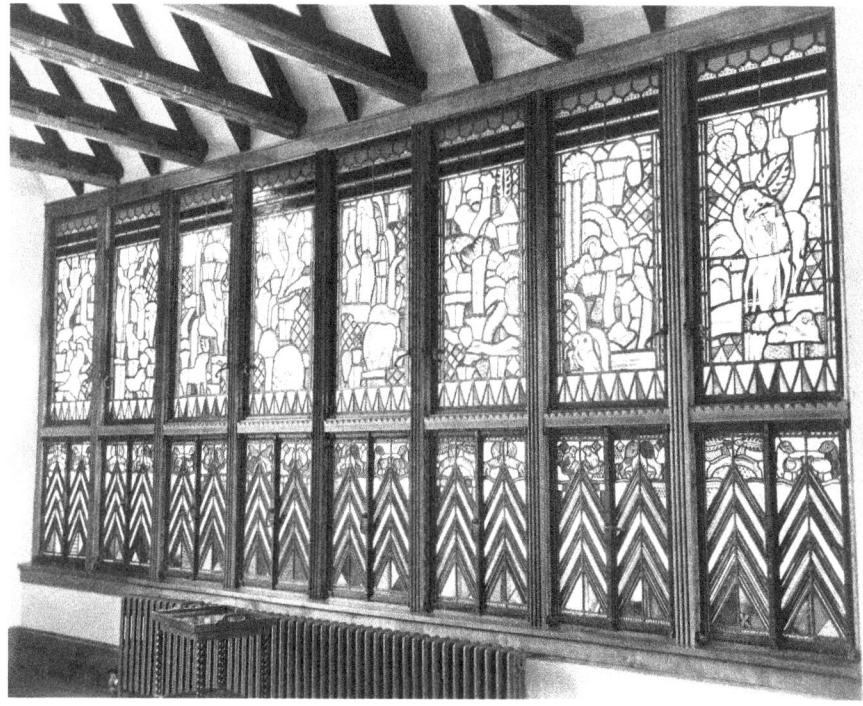

Kogen-Miller Studios, Glasner Studio fourth-floor interior, "Garden of Paradise" window. *Chicago Architectural Photographing Co., Maurice L. Bein Papers, Burnham & Ryerson Archives, The Art Institute of Chicago, Digital File #198505_150204-144.*

Miller and several stained-glass windows, also by Miller. As impressive as the spatial dimensions and ornamental features of this room are, it is dominated by the most stunning achievement of Edgar Miller's artistic career—a massive, eight-bay, stained- and painted-glass window depicting a Garden of Paradise theme. It does not take an expert to conclude that this awe-inspiring window is one of the finest secular art windows in America.

Work at the Kogen-Miller Studios was completed in 1932. The Glasner Studio is now the headquarters of the Edgar Miller Legacy, a not-for-profit organization established to promote and educate the public about the art of Edgar Miller.

THE FISHER STUDIOS

Fortuitously, just as Edgar Miller was diminishing his work at Carl Street Studios, he was approached by his friend and past collaborator, architect Andrew Rebori, about a new artist studio building to be constructed at 1209 North State Street. Frank F. Fisher Jr., an executive with Marshall Field & Company, engaged Rebori to design and supervise the construction of a studio building for artists on the site. By the time they were finished in 1937, architect Rebori and artist Miller would unveil one of the finest art moderne buildings in the United States. It attracted immediate attention in the country's architectural community and enjoyed a four-page photospread in *Architectural Forum* a few months after construction was complete.[273]

Andrew Rebori was born in New York City in 1886, the son of Italian immigrants. His father, an army engineer, died when Rebori was three years old, dooming his mother, two sisters and himself to impoverished circumstances for many years.[274] During his high school years, Rebori worked as a draftsman with two different architects in New York City. Through the help of one of these architects, in 1905 Rebori received a scholarship to attend the School of Architecture at the Massachusetts Institute of Technology, the most respected architecture program in the country. In 1907, he won a prize from the Boston Society of Architects and was a finalist for a prize at Columbia University. The following year, he won a Lowell Traveling Scholarship, which allowed him to study a year abroad, first at the École de Beaux-Arts in Paris and then at the American Academy in Rome.[275]

On his return to the United States, Rebori worked for a short time with Cass Gilbert in New York. He later moved to Chicago and worked in the office of Jarvis Hunt until about 1920. Thereafter, he formed his own architectural firm, Rebori, Wentworth, Dewey & McCormick. Each of his three partners was from a socially prominent family in Chicago, one of which Rebori himself entered when he married the niece of Colonel Robert McCormick, the publisher of the *Chicago Tribune*.[276] During some of this period, Rebori and his wife lived in one of the larger units at the Tree Studios.

Given its makeup, Rebori's firm was geared toward the needs of Chicago's elite and received several lucrative commissions in the 1920s. After 1926, Rebori's interest in art deco and modernist architectural design became more and more apparent.[277] Rebori's firm suffered financially after the stock market crash of 1929 and later dissolved altogether in the early years of the Depression.[278] Despite these setbacks, Rebori managed to receive some commissions for work associated with the 1933 Century of Progress World's Fair and, for what it was worth financially, collaborative work at the artist colony at Carl Street Studios and West Burton Place. His work on Burton Place made him the ideal candidate when Frank Fisher went looking for an architect for his new studio building on State Street.

The Fisher Studios is a four-story brick structure containing thirteen duplex studios on two tiers. These consist of ten more or less identical one-bedroom units in the center of the building, one two-bedroom unit at the front and two three-bedroom units, one at the front and one at the back.

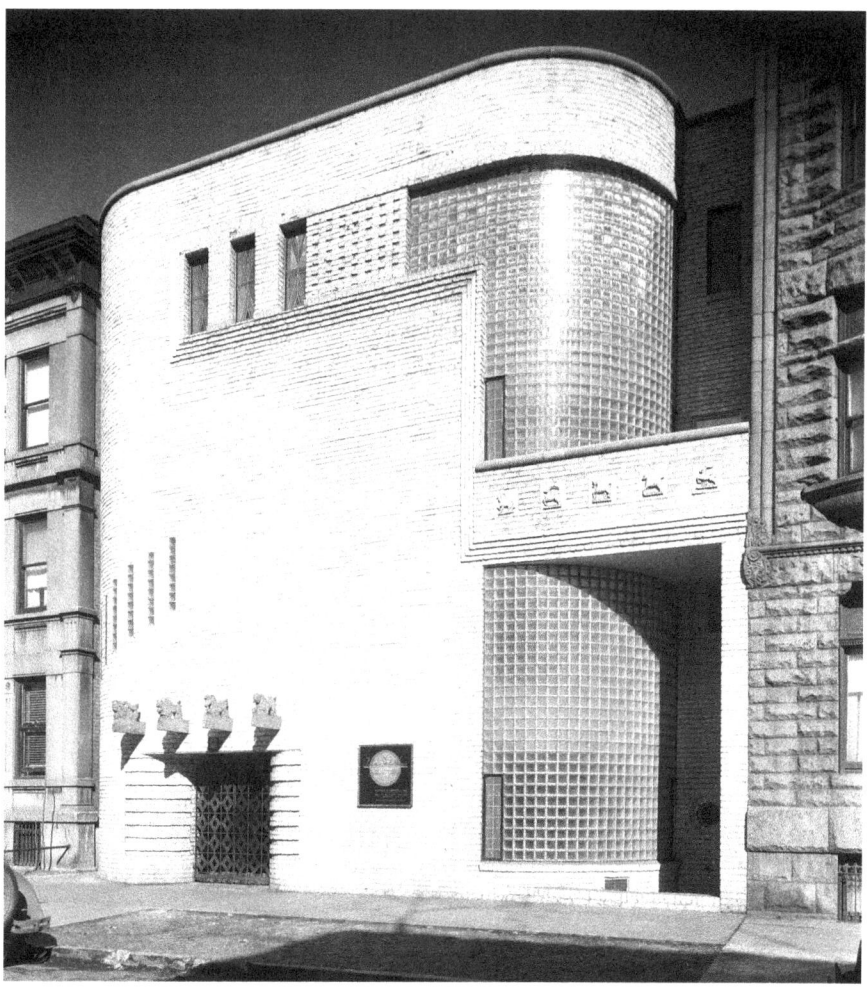

Frank Fisher Studios, front façade, 1936. *Heidrich-Blessing Co.,* Architectural Forum *(May 1937), Chicago History Museum, HB-03929-A.*

169

The bottom-tier studios are accessible from a courtyard on the ground floor beyond the front gate. The second-tier studios are accessible from a third-floor outdoor walkway accessible by an elegant brick curving staircase. The entire exterior of the building was painted white.

Rebori and Miller designed the front (west) façade and northern façade to have an elegant, streamlined appearance typical of art moderne architecture of the period.[279] Of the window surface in the Fisher Studios, 90 percent is composed of glass block, with a few other casement-type windows featuring panes of stained glass and painted figurative and other decorative elements by Edgar Miller. The two front studios have enormous two-story, curving glass block windows on the southern end that dominate the front façade of the building. The northern portion of the front façade (concealing the curved staircase leading to the third-floor outdoor walkway) features a series of narrow slit windows of glass block. Over the front gate were placed decorative wooden mullions with stylized animals carved by Edgar Miller extending horizontally from the brick wall. To the south at the third-floor level of the façade appear a corresponding series of reliefs of animals sculpted by Miller.

The ten one-bedroom units in the center of the building each incorporate an expansive, two-story wall of glass block, providing ample northern light that artists tend to favor. Rebori and Miller enhanced the aesthetics of the courtyard façades with linear courses of brick extending from the wall surface, creating vertical and horizontal shadows on the white surfaces. The interiors of the studios were designed by Rebori and Miller to mimic some of the same art moderne design schemes Kogen and Miller used at Carl Street Studios and the Kogen-Miller Studios, including elegant winding staircases, curved plaster walls and the lack of any moldings.

The Fisher Studios building was designated a Chicago Historical Landmark in 1996. Despite this, in 1999 a developer purchased the building and began "renovations." Those renovations included tearing out the old metal casement windows (featuring Miller's stained-glass work and paintings of stylized animals) and tossing them into trash heaps in the courtyard.[280] Incensed local residents contacted the city, which filed a legal action seeking an immediate temporary restraining order. The court summarily granted the injunction and later ordered the developer to pay tens of thousands of dollars for repair of the windows. Regrettably, some of the windows were beyond repair. The Fisher Studios are now condominiums.

Artists and others associated with the arts occupied the Old Town artist colonies discussed herein and other pockets of the larger Old

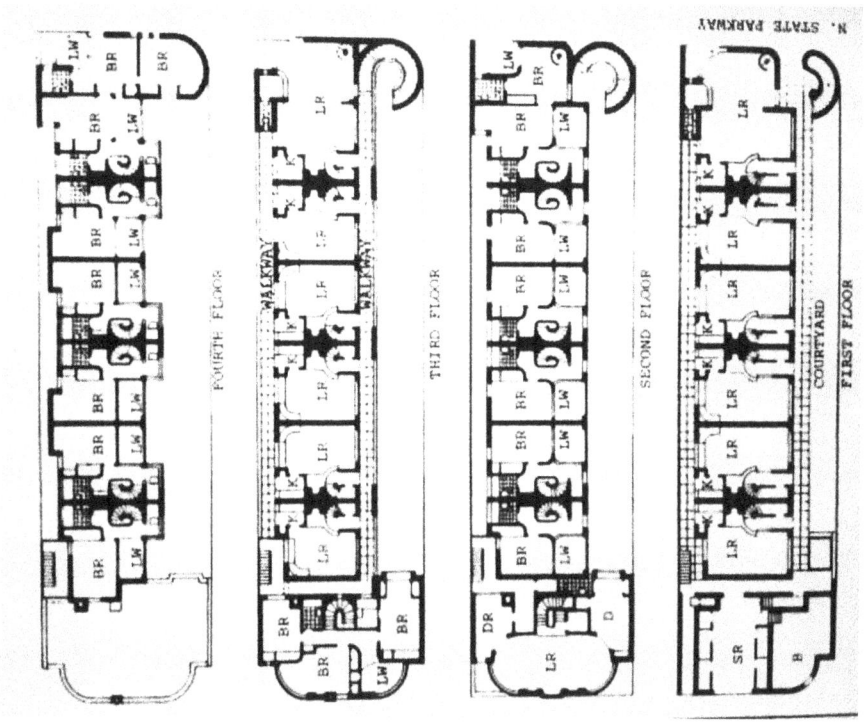

Frank Fisher Studios, first-floor diagram. Architectural Forum *(May 1937)*.

Town neighborhood from the late 1920s through the present day, but the concentration of artists in Old Town has diminished considerably over the decades. Old Town is still host to two major annual art exhibitions on its streets and is home to a few organizations that encourage and promote the interests of artists and art patrons. But the days of Old Town as a bohemian mecca are long over. During the 1950s, '60s and '70s, North Wells Street boasted a large collection of unique and hip shops (Crate and Barrel was born there with real crates and real barrels), night clubs and restaurants. Visitors to the neighborhood in the 1950s and '60s brushed shoulders with Mike Nichols and Elaine May and in the 1970s and '80s with Dan Aykroyd, Gilda Radner, Harold Ramis, John Candy, Eugene Levy, Catherine O'Hara and other comedians from the Second City Comedy Club a few steps from North Avenue.

Wells Street remained a magnet for creative types, first beatniks, then hippies and finally curious preppies, until about 1980. Now, the art galleries, headshops and kitschy salons are gone. Populated by huge, nondescript, loud bars, North Wells Street has devolved from being a

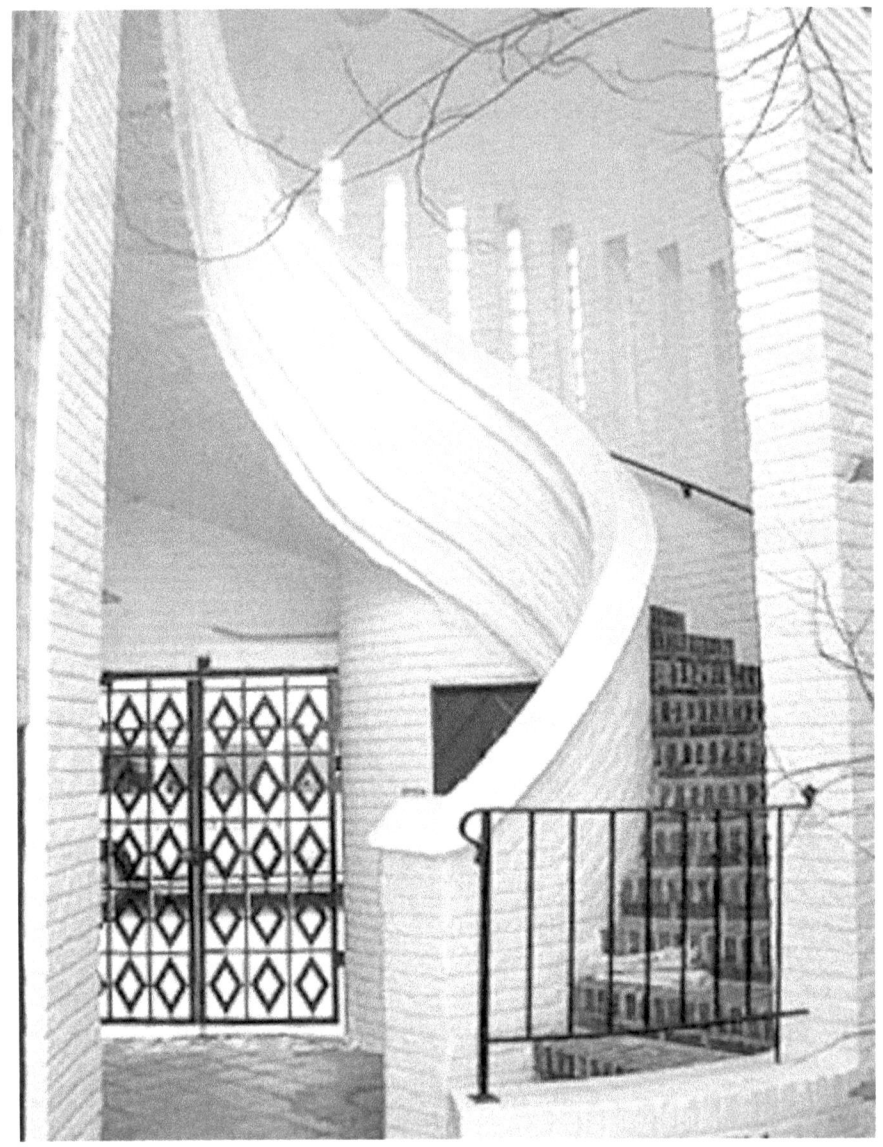

Frank Fisher Studios, courtyard staircase. *K.M. Stolte (2017).*

center of culture and the avant-garde in Chicago to a ruckus party place for millennial suburbanites who stand in long lines just to gain entrance and have a few beers—a small but poignant exemplar of what Lorado Taft had in mind when he created his *Fountain of Time* one hundred years ago: "Alas, Time stays, we go."

Conclusion

The Fine Arts Building is still home to dozens of artists and art-related organizations. The building's Studebaker Theatre, long shuttered, is again open for live performances. A few artists still live at the Carl Street Studios and the other buildings on West Burton Place. The recently established Edgar Miller Legacy, a not-for-profit organization established to reacquaint the public with Edgar Miller and his art, now occupies his masterpiece: the Glasner Studio at the Kogen-Miller Studios complex. The Eagle's Nest Camp, the Ox-Bow summer school and Lorado Taft's Midway studios still cater to the needs of students of the arts. But the tight, cohesive and interactive collectives of artists that once roasted goats on Christmas Eve at Burton Place, frolicked like modern-day bacchanals through the woods at the Eagle's Nest Camp or danced on languid Friday afternoons at the Little Room with the likes of Isadora Duncan are no more.

Chicago's present-day artists live and work in looser communities, such as Pilsen, Wicker Park and Bridgeport. There are a few small communal-type live/work artist enclaves that have popped up in these neighborhoods in the last twenty years—one artist collective on Halsted Street in Pilsen was quite in vogue about twenty years ago—but they lack the fraternal intimacy and collaborative interaction that differentiated the Tree Studios, 57th Street Artist Colony, Eagle's Nest Camp and Carl Street Studios from run-of-the-mill apartment complexes inhabited by creative types.

Ragdale, the former Lake Forest country estate of architect Howard Van Doren Shaw, perhaps comes closest to the communal, interactive spirit of the older artist colonies. Founded in 1976, this not-for-profit organization offers thirteen artists-in-residence at any given time the opportunity to enjoy uninterrupted time for creative work, a supportive environment, dynamic artist exchanges, fifty acres of idyllic prairie and a family-style dinner each evening.[281]

The art and architecture of several of the artist colonies still intrigue and dazzle the public. The graceful Queen Anne façade of the original Tree Studios building informs tourists of a more genteel era in Chicago. In the turn-of-the-twentieth-century murals that grace the walls of the Fine Arts Building, the viewer will glimpse the sense of classical beauty the Edwardian triumvirate—Taft, Grover and Clarkson—believed would uplift and enrich the citizenry. Taft's *Fountain of Time* still astonishes anyone who ventures to the far west end of the Midway, and his colossal statue of Chief Black Hawk stands on the banks of the Rock River as a noble sentinel of a bygone era. The Carl Street Studios and the Kogen-Miller Studios periodically open their gates for tours to allow the public to enjoy the more eclectic art and design works of Edgar Miller, Sol Kogen, Jesus Torres and other artists who once lived and worked there. And at the root of all these residual reminders of a long tradition of artist enclaves in Chicago is arguably the city's most spectacular cultural achievement: the World's Columbian Exposition of 1893.

Notes

Introduction

1. *Little Review* 3, no. 6 (September 1916).
2. Smith, *Chicago's Left Bank*, 3, quoting H.L. Mencken in *The Smart Set*.

Chapter 1

3. *G.P.A. Healy Centenary Exhibition*, 2.
4. Ibid., 2–3.
5. Andreas, *History of Chicago*, 559–60.
6. Healy, *Reminiscences*, 53.
7. Ibid., 57–58, 63–67.
8. Ibid., 67, 71.
9. Andreas, *History of Chicago*, 559.
10. Ibid.
11. Taft, *History of American Sculpture*, 201–02.
12. Andreas, *History of Chicago*, 556.
13. Dryer, Illinois Art Project.
14. Andreas, *History of Chicago*, 557.
15. Dryer, Illinois Art Project.
16. Ibid.

17. Encouraged by the success of the Art Exhibition, a few local artists and patrons formed the Chicago Art Union, with its objective the encouragement of fine art in the West. This group held an exhibition at 113 Lake Street, the same building where George Healy had established his studio, on December 5, 1859. The Art Union exhibition closed about a month later. It included forty-seven works of art by Healy, Volk, Howard Strong and S.P. Tracy (Dryer, Illinois Art Project). A similar exhibition of the works of local and nonlocal artists was held in December 1862 in a gallery opened by Leonard Volk (Dryer, Illinois Art Project).

18. *Chicago Tribune*, May 2, 1867.

19. Andreas, *History of Chicago*, 558.

20. Ibid.

21. Buechele and Lowe, *School of the Art Institute of Chicago*, 17–18.

22. Many of the museum's first important paintings—by Meindert, Hobbema, Jan Steen and Jean Francois Millet—entered its collection in 1894 as gifts. The institute's trustees began purchasing major old master paintings within the next decade. Its famous, first-rate collection of impressionist masters came by way of bequests from Bertha Honore Palmer in 1922 and the Ryerson family in 1933. The institute's modernist collection started in earnest with the bequest of twenty important paintings and three sculptures in 1931 by Arthur Jerome Eddy.

23. Smith, *Chicago's Left Bank*, 108.

24. Ibid.

25. Ibid., 109.

26. J.W. Ziegler, *World's Columbian Exposition* (Chicago: Monarch Book Company, 1893), 408–10.

Chapter 2

27. Baum and his family moved to Chicago's Humboldt Park neighborhood in 1891. After several years of writing for Chicago newspapers and magazines and authoring a handful of children's books, Baum published the first of thirteen Oz novels in 1900. Some believe that Baum had the buildings of the Columbian Exposition in mind when he described the Emerald City, but it is just as likely, if not more so, that the group of soaring towers of the Chicago Loop was his model.

28. Ziegler, *World's Columbian Exposition*, 333–34.

29. Ibid., 11–13.

30. Ibid., 604.
31. *Harper's Weekly*, no. 1917, September 16, 1893.
32. "Art Galleries and Annexes," in *World's Columbian Exposition Official Catalogue*, part X.
33. Ibid.
34. Ibid.
35. Ibid.
36. *Revisiting the White City*, 11 ("At the World's Columbian Exposition, visitors were invited to see the largest and most elaborately selected exhibition of American Art ever assembled in this country.").
37. Ibid.; Walton, *World's Columbian Exposition Official Illustrated Publication*, 25. The artworks on display included sculpture, oil paintings, watercolor paintings, etchings and engravings.
38. The estimates that appear in this section are based on an analysis of "Art Galleries and Annexes" in *World's Columbian Exposition Official Catalogue*, part X.
39. This is not meant to be a judgment on the *merits* of the works by Chicago painters, only the number of paintings by Chicagoans displayed at the fair.
40. The fifty-seven-page section of the book devoted to the fine arts mentioned three artists from Chicago, Charles Abel Corwin, Frederick Freer and Grover, and included engraved copies of paintings by the latter two.
41. Bulliet, "Artists of Chicago Past and Present, No. 96."
42. *Chicago Tribune*, November 1, 1893, 4.
43. *Revisiting the White City*, 63.

Chapter 3

44. "Giverny: The Colony of American Artists." The Terra Foundation is a philanthropic organization established by Daniel Terra to promote American visual art and provide educational programs toward that aim. The foundation is based in Chicago but has an important presence in Paris and Giverny.
45. Corn, *Great American Thing*, 17–18. Chicago writer Sherwood Anderson expressed similar sentiments, characterizing artists as "an outlaw people. Those of us who write words, tramp the boards on the stage, spread paint on canvas, chip, carve and hammer, trying to reach into unreality through the real, do not belong. There is the world

around us and it is not our world. We never made it. It keeps saying to us 'you must have bread and clothes. Come to terms then.'" Sherwood Anderson, "Review of Margaret Anderson's *My Thirty Years War*," *New Republic* (June 11, 1930).

46. Evelyn Waugh, *Brideshead Revisited* (New York: Penguin 1962), 62–63.
47. Floyd Dell, "At the Institute," *Friday Literary Review* (April 4, 1913).

Chapter 4

48. "The North Side Is to Have an Art Palace," *Chicago Tribune*, August 5, 1894.
49. Peterson and McDonogh, *Global Downtowns*, 39.
50. Commission on Chicago Landmarks, *Tree Studios: Preliminary Staff Summary of Information* (1980), 1.
51. Chicago Department of Cultural Affairs, *Capturing Sunlight: The Art of Tree Studios* (1999), 10.
52. Ibid.
53. "The North Side Is to Have an Art Palace."
54. Alan Artner, "In Celebrating Tree Studios' Past, Exhibit Can Also Impact the Present," *Chicago Tribune,* July 20, 1999.
55. Commission on Chicago Landmarks, *Tree Studios*, 5.
56. Keegan, "Artists in Residence."
57. "Tree Studios," *Architectural Record* 51 (1922): 259.
58. "A Marked Advance in Studio Designing," *Construction News* (November 22, 1913): 7.
59. Ibid., 8–9
60. Several artists lived and worked at the complex for decades at a time. For example, sculptor/painter Louis Grell occupied at least three units at the Tree Studios from 1916 until his death in 1960.
61. Commission on Chicago Landmarks, *Tree Studios*, 7.
62. Bohan, "Pauline Palmer."
63. Ibid.
64. Ibid.
65. Ibid.
66. Chicago Department of Cultural Affairs, *Capturing Sunlight*, 14.
67. Bohan, "Pauline Palmer."
68. Ibid.

69. When Studebaker outgrew the building on Wabash Avenue, it moved its entire operations to the company's home base in South Bend, Indiana, where it ultimately manufactured Studebaker automobiles.

70. Fletcher, *Some Went This Way*.

71. Ibid.

72. Smith, *Chicago's Left Bank*, 38.

73. Ibid., 156.

74 Irving Kane Pond, *The Autobiography of Irving K. Pond – The Sons of Mary and Elihu* (Chicago: Hyoogen Press, David Swan & Terry Tatum, eds. 2009). Pond's descriptions of his interactions with Frank Lloyd Wright, Louis Sullivan and Danial Burnham are refreshingly presented without any varnish.

75. "The Little Roomers."

76. Anna Morgan, *My Chicago* (Ralph Fletcher Seymour, 1918), 189.

77. See generally *The Book of the Fine Arts Building* (Chicago: Fine Arts Building, 1911).

78. The Cordon Club, a female counterpart to the Cliff Dwellers, was founded at the Fine Arts Building in October 1915 and soon had four hundred members, including most of the grand dames of Chicago society and many female artists, musicians, composers, writers and editors (*Chicago Tribune*, October 24, 1915). The club maintained its quarters in the building for many decades.

79. Fuller, "At St. Juda's."

80. Fuller, *Bertram Cope's Year*.

81. Fuller, unpublished diary.

82. Stilson, *Art and Beauty in the Heartland*, 77.

83. Newlin, *Hamlin Garland*, 247–48.

84. Ibid., 248.

85. "Chicago's New Club of the Arts.

86. Smith, *Chicago's Left Bank*, 23.

87. Hecht, *Child of the Century*, 233.

88. Highleyman, "Margaret Anderson and Jane Heap"; Anderson, *Fiery Fountains* (providing a lively and touching remembrance of Anderson's relationship with LaBlanc); Anderson, *Strange Necessity*.

89. Prince, *Old Guard and the Avant-Garde*, 146.

90. Anderson, *My Thirty Years' War*, 35.

91. Anderson, "Announcement," 2.

92. "'Meant It,' Says Miss Anderson: Editor of *Little Review* Stands Pat in Face of Federal Scrutiny," *Chicago Tribune*, January 27, 1916, 9.

93. "Editress Can't Pay Rent; Makes Her Home in Tent," *Chicago Tribune*, August 6, 1915, 14; Olson, *Chicago Renaissance*, 27.

94. "Miss Anderson Faces a Dilemma." *Republic*, August 31, 1915, 5; "Ours Is the Life; Others Are Odd; Miss Anderson," *Chicago Daily Tribune*, August 9, 1915, 13. The latter article featured a half page of photographs of Anderson and her coterie at camp on a Lake Michigan beach.

95. Hansen, *Midwest Portraits*, 105.

96. Prince, *Old Guard and the Avant-Garde*, 40.

97. Gapp, "Death of Bohemia."

98. Historic American Buildings Survey, Columbian Exposition Store Buildings, 3.

99. Ibid.

100. Duffey, *Chicago Literary Movements*, 14–15.

101. Gapp, "Death of Bohemia."

102. Ibid.

103. Ibid.

104. Lord, *Summer to Be*, 57–58.

105. Davis, "Genuinely Civilized Oddballs."

106. Ibid.; Levitt, "Migration of the Hipster."

107. Prince, *Old Guard and the Avant-Garde*, 142.

108. Meier, "Theatrical Laboratory for Testing Plays," 8–9.

109. Davis, "Genuinely Civilized Oddballs."

110. Smith, *Chicago's Left Bank*, 158–59.

111. Prince, *Old Guard and the Avant-Garde*, 39; Williams, "Lorado Taft," 216.

112. Ibid.

113. Smith, *Chicago's Left Bank*, 159.

114. Ibid.; Taft, *Lorado Taft*, 44–46.

115. Smith, *Chicago's Left Bank*, 159; Prince, *Old Guard and the Avant-Garde*, 40.

116. Taft, *Lorado Taft*, 36.

117. Prince, *Old Guard and the Avant-Garde*, 40.

Chapter 5

118. Chandler, "Eagle's Nest Camp," 195–97.

119. Ibid., 197.

120. "Eagle's Nest Artist Colony."

121. Ibid.; Smith, *Chicago's Left Bank*, 157.

122. Stilson, *Art and Beauty in the Heartland*, 2.

123. Lowden and Heckman, *Lorado Taft's Indian Statue*, 16.
124. McGuire, "Eagle's Nest Association," 56.
125. Palmer, "Account of the Eagle's Nest Colony."
126. Ibid.
127. Ibid.
128. Ibid.
129. "Eagle's Nest Artist Colony."
130. Monroe, "Eagle's Nest Camp," 5–10.
131. "Eagle's Nest Artist Colony."
132. Monroe, "Eagle's Nest Camp," 10.
133. Lord, *Summer to Be*, 57.
134. Palmer, "Account of the Eagle's Nest Colony."
135. Smith, *Chicago's Left Bank*, 157–58.
136. Ibid., 158; Palmer, "Account of the Eagle's Nest Colony."
137. Smith, *Chicago's Left Bank*, 158; Palmer, "Account of the Eagle's Nest Colony."
138. Weller, *Lorado Taft*, 114.
139. Ox-Bow School of Art & Artist Residency, "History."
140. Ibid.
141. "Ox-Bow at 100," *American Craft Magazine*.
142. Ibid.
143. Ibid.; Ox-Bow School of Art & Artist Residency, "History."

Chapter 6

144. Zorbaugh, *Gold Coast and the Slum*, 4.
145. Ibid., 10–11.
146. Ibid., 12.
147. Drury, unpublished, undated manuscript about Towertown.
148. Sharp, *Old House Handbook*, 19.
149. Ibid.
150. Smith, *Chicago's Left Bank*, 13.
151. Ibid., 167.
152. Prince, *Old Guard and the Avant-Garde*, 64.
153. Hecht, *Child of the Century*.
154. Steffes, "Bertrand Goldberg in Towertown."
155. Strykowski, "Woman's World."
156. Administrative History of the Three Arts Club Records.

157. Bruegmann, *Architects and the City*, 431–30; Gapp, "Death of Bohemia."

158. "Chicago's Arts Club Is Saved," *Prescott Courier*.

159. Jones, Willis-Morton and O'Brien, *Chicago's Gold Coast*, 107.

160. Stamper, *Chicago's North Michigan Avenue*, 47.

161. Ibid.

162. Ibid.

163. Description of Harriet Moody's Papers, 1906–1932, University of Wyoming Library; description of Harriet Moody's Papers, 1899–1930, University of Chicago Library.

164. Whitaker, "Anatomy of a Restaurateur."

165. Smith, *Chicago's Left Bank*, 40; Jan Whitaker, "Anatomy of a Restaurateur."

166. Sharp, *Old House Handbook*, 17; Gapp, "No Longer on Top."

167. De la Croix, *Chicago Whispers*, 56; Zorbaugh, *Gold Coast and the Slum*, 87–89.

168. Prohibition began in 1920, not 1917.

169. De la Croix, *Chicago Whispers*, 37, quoting Ben Reitman from a *Chicago Times* article dated August 23, 1937.

170. Ibid.

171. Franklin Rosemont, "Introduction," in Beck, *Hobohemia*, 6–7.

172. Lieberman, *Chicago Evening American*, March 14, 1922.

173. Drury, unpublished, undated manuscript about Towertown.

174. Ibid.

175. Some bloggers have attempted to track the career of this interesting woman and have surmised that her last name was actually Collie (taken after a short marriage) and that her maiden name was Lieberman.

176. Selzer, *Chronicles of Old Chicago*, 130.

177. Drury, unpublished, undated manuscript about Towertown.

178. Ibid.

179. "Green Goose Disappears," *Lincoln Journal Star*, November 5, 1921; "Green Goose Is Lost; Owner Heartbroken," *Buffalo Times*, November 9, 1921.

180. Lieberman, *Chicago Evening American*, March 14, 1922.

181. Ibid.

182. Ibid., 131–32.

183. Collier's mother's name was Nellie, giving the assumed name added significance, that is, "Nellie's Child."

184. "Five Named in P.G.&E. Robbery," *San Francisco Examiner*, December 8, 1924, 5; "Ryan Bares $18,000 Theft Details," *San Francisco Examiner*,

December 29, 1924, 1; "Woman Tells of New Holdups," *San Francisco Examiner*, January 11, 1925, 1.

185. "PGE Bandit Slain in N.Y.," *San Francisco Examiner*, December 1925, 9; "Poem in Wood—T'is World's Most Beauteous Limb," *New York Daily News*, December 8, 1925, 123.

186. Kogan, "Last Call at Ric's."

187. Smith, *Chicago's Left Bank*, 154.

188. Rick Kogan, "Ask Rick: Your Questions Take Us Back in Time," *Chicago Tribune*, October 28, 2018, section 4, 3.

189. Ibid., 155.

190. Ibid.

191. Kogan, "Ask Rick."

192. Kogan, "Last Call at Ric's."

193. Ibid.

194. Bulliet, "Artists of Chicago Past and Present, Frederic Milton Grant," 4R.

195. Letter from Frederic Milton Grant to Nita Herczel of the Union League Club of Chicago, November 4, 1958, Union League Club Archives.

196. *American Art News* 13, no. 29 (April 23, 1915): 5.

197. Bulliet, "Artists of Chicago Past and Present, Frederic Milton Grant," 4R.

198. Jewett, "Color Work of F.M. Grant."

199. Jewett, *Chicago Tribune*, May 11, 1952.

200. Ness and Orwig, *Iowa Artists of the First Hundred Years*, 88.

201. Bulliet, "Artists of Chicago Past and Present, Frederic Milton Grant," 4R.

202. Letter from Frederic Milton Grant to C.J. Bulliet, April 17, 1936, Smithsonian Institution, Archives of American Art.

203. Grant provided snapshots, together with identifying information, of these musical transcriptions to the archives of the Union League Club of Chicago, where they remain.

204. Bulliet, "Artists of Chicago Past and Present, Frederic Milton Grant," 4R; letter from Barbara R. Anderson to Keith M. Stolte, January 25, 2006, personal files of the author.

205. Grant, unpublished essay, December 8, 1958.

206. Kushner and Orcutt, *Armory Show at 100*, 365–67.

207. Prince, *Old Guard and the Avant-Garde*, 95–96.

208. Smith, *Chicago's Left Bank*, 165.

209. "The Cubist Art," *Chicago Tribune*, April 2, 1913.

210. "May Bar Youngsters from Cubists Show," *Chicago Record-Herald*, March 27, 1913.

211. Levitt, "Return of the Armory Show."

212. Letter from William French to Charles Hutchinson, February 22, 1913, in Kushner and Orcutt, *Armory Show at 100*, 368.

213. Ibid.

214. Prince, *Old Guard and the Avant-Garde*, 98–101.

215. Eddy, *Two Thousand Miles on an Automobile*.

216. Ibid.

217. Smith, *Chicago's Left Bank*, 165.

218. "Students Burning Futurist Art and Celebrating Cubists' Departure," *Chicago Daily Tribune*, April 17, 1913.

219. Kushner and Orcutt, *Armory Show at 100*, 372–73.

220. This tension is the subject of Prince's *The Old Guard and the Avant-Garde*, which superbly addresses the topic from several angles.

Chapter 7

221. National Register of Historical Places, "West Burton Place Historical District," Section 7 (U.S. Department of the Interior, National Park Service, 2007), 7.

222. Ibid., 8.

223. Ibid.

224. Ibid., 8–9.

225. Ibid., 3–6.

226. "Studio Building Is Planned for 155 Carl Street," *Chicago Daily Tribune*, August 21, 1927.

227. Roberts, "There's No Place Like Burton Place," 42–3.

228. Ibid., 43.

229. Ibid.

230. Ibid., 44.

231. Ibid.

232. Ibid.

233. Matsoukas, "Kogen-Miller Studios," 197. An unfortunate and somewhat silly controversy has existed for over seventy years involving precisely what credit each man should receive for the work done on the artist studios they created. It is fair to say that both men's comments to the press stinted the other's contribution, and their respective positions were repeated by family members and other adherents over the years. Suffice it to say both men, together with Jesus Torres, made invaluable

contributions and that the studios as designed and built would not exist without all three men working in tandem.

234. Mix, "Burton Place," 33.
235. Ibid.
236. Malkind, "Always an Artist."
237. Reed, "Edgar Miller," 63.
238. Roberts, "There's No Place Like Burton Place," 45.
239. Ibid., 45.
240. Ibid., 44.
241. Cahan, Williams and Vertikoff, *Edgar Miller and the Handmade Home*, 200. Despite the minor error, this beautifully illustrated book provides the most comprehensive discussion and illustration of Edgar Miller's (and Sol Kogen's and Jesus Torres's) work at the Carl Street Studios and other buildings.
242. Reed, "Edgar Miller," 63.
243. Bargelt, "Old Apartment House," C4.
244. Poore, "Imagination Keys Revamping," E16.
245. Ibid.
246. Mix, "Burton Place," 33.
247. Bowley, "Montmartre Look," 20. Today, some of Boris Anisfeld's canvasses could pay for one or two decades' worth of rent. By 1966, Kogen's family owned five Anisfield paintings; Mix, "Burton Place," 36.
248. Mix, "Burton Place," 34
249. Ford, "Artist Colony."
250. Mix, "Burton Place," 34.
251. Shepard, "Drabness Gone in this Neighborhood." This publication includes a photographic comparison of the building before and after the 1940 remodeling.
252. Commission on Chicago Landmarks, *Landmark Designation Report for the West Burton Place Historical District*, 26.
253. Mix, "Burton Place," 37.
254. Ibid.
255. Artner, "Kogen History."
256. Smith, *Chicago's Left Bank*, 161.
257. Ford, "Artist Colony One Big Happy Family."
258. Mix, "Burton Place," 36.
259. Dedmon and Boyden, *Our 50th Year View*, 27.
260. Ibid.
261. "Jesus Torres Obituary," *Chicago Tribune*, June 14, 1948, C5.

262. Flavin, "Aztecs' Glory Finds Rebirth."

263. Ibid.

264. Ibid.

265. *Festival of Religious Art: Religious Art by Artists of Chicago and Environs*, Exhibition Program (Renaissance Society 1931).

266. "Jesus Torres Obituary."

267. Genevieve Flavin, "Aztecs' Glory Finds Rebirth in Torres' Art," S11.

268. Ibid.; "Thousands Acclaim Spectacular Exhibition of New Equipment," *Rock Island Lines New Digest* VI, no. 12 (December 1947): 4, 8–9.

269. "Jesus Torres Obituary."

270. Cahan, Williams and Vertikoff, *Edgar Miller and the Handmade Home*, 52. The purchasing arrangement for this property was somewhat curious. While records show that Kogen and Miller and Miller's wife, Dorothy, purchased the property and secured a mortgage, it was announced a few weeks later that Woldenberg actually owned it. See also "Woldenberg to Install Studios at 1734 Wells," *Chicago Tribune*, June 17, 1928. At some point, the ownership later reverted to Kogen, who leased the studio being constructed in the rear stable building to another Chicago industrialist, Rudolph Glasner (Cahan, Williams and Vertikoff, *Edgar Miller and the Handmade Home*, 53).

271. Matsoukas, "Kogen-Miller Studios," 197.

272. Cahan, Williams and Vertikoff, *Edgar Miller and the Handmade Home*, 108–45.

273. "Apartment House for Frank F. Fisher," *Chicago Architectural Forum*.

274. Commission on Chicago Landmarks, *Landmark Designation Report for the Fisher Studio Houses*, 6.

275. Ibid.

276. Ibid., 7.

277. Ibid.

278. Ibid.

279. Edgar Miller claimed to have designed the front façade and outside curving staircase, which Rebori accepted without modification. Cahan, Williams and Vertikoff, *Edgar Miller and the Handmade Home*, 52.

280. Mendell, "City Is Suing."

Conclusion

281. Ragdale, "Residency," https://www.ragdale.org/residency.

Bibliography

Archival Materials

Anderson, Sherwood. Papers. Special Collections, Newberry Library.

Dil Pickle Records. Special Collections, Newberry Library.

Drury, John. Unpublished, undated manuscript about Towertown. John Drury Papers. Special Collections, Newberry Library.

Fuller, Henry Blake. Unpublished diary. Allison Classical Academy, 1875–76. Henry Blake Fuller Papers. Special Collections, Newberry Library.

Grant, Frederic Milton, Letter to C.J. Bulliet, April 17, 1936. Smithsonian Institution, Archives of American Art.

———. Letter to Nita Herczel of the Union League Club of Chicago, November 4, 1958. Archive of the Union League Club of Chicago.

———. Photographs and identifying information of abstract musical transcription oil paintings. Archives of the Union League Club of Chicago.

———. Unpublished essay, December 8, 1958. Archives of the Union League Club of Chicago.

Little Room Records. Special Collections, Newberry Library.

Moody, Harriet. Papers, 1899–1930. Special Collections, University of Chicago Library.

———. Papers, 1906–1932. University of Wyoming Library.

Palmer, Elizabeth Dickerson. "An Account of the Eagle's Nest Colony" (unpublished and undated). Lorado Taft Field Campus Records, Northern Illinois University Archives, UA 32, Box 1, Folder 3.

Taft, Lorado. Papers. Special Collections, University of Illinois.

Volk, Leonard, and Douglas Volk. Papers. Special Collections, University of Illinois (1872–1953).

Books

Anderson, Margaret. *The Fiery Fountains*. New York: Hermitage House, 1951.

———. *My Thirty Years' War*. New York: Covici-Friede, 1930.

———. *The Strange Necessity*. New York: Horizon, 1969.

Anderson, Sherwood. *Memoirs*. New York: Harcourt-Brace, 1942.

Andreas, Alfred Theodore. *History of Chicago, from 1857 until the Fire of 1871*. Chicago: Higginson, 1885.

Beck, Frank O. *Hobohemia*. Chicago: C.H. Kerr Publishing, 2000.

The Book of the Fine Arts Building. Chicago: Fine Arts Building, 1911.

Bruegmann, Robert. *The Architects and the City: Holabird & Roche of Chicago, 1880–1918*. Chicago: University of Chicago Press, 1997.

Buechele, Thomas C., and Nicholas C. Lowe. *The School of the Art Institute of Chicago*. Charleston, SC: Arcadia Publishing, 2017.

Butcher, Fanny. *Many Lives—One Love*. New York: Harper and Row, 1972.

Cahan, Richard, Michael Williams and Alexander Vertikoff. *Edgar Miller and the Handmade Home*. Chicago: Cityfiles Press, 2009.

Chicago Department of Cultural Affairs. *Capturing Sunlight: The Art of Tree Studios*. Chicago: City of Chicago, 1999.

Corn, Wanda M. *The Great American Thing: Modern Art and National Identity, 1915–1935*. Berkeley: University of California Press, 1999.

De la Croix, St. Sukie. *Chicago Whispers: A History of LGBT Chicago Before Stonewall*. Madison: University of Wisconsin Press, 2012.

Dedmon, Emmett, and Sarah Brown Boyden. *Our 50th Year from the Top of the Tavern Club*. Chicago: Tavern Club, 1978.

Duffey, Bernard. *Chicago Literary Movements, 1890–1925*. Chicago: Newberry Library Conference on American Studies, 1952.

Eddy, Arthur Jerome. *Cubists and Post-Impressionists*. Chicago: A.C. McClurg, 1914.

———. *Two Thousand Miles on an Automobile, Being a Desultory Narrative of a Trip Through New England, Canada and the West*. Philadelphia: J.B. Lippincott, 1902.

Festival of Religious Art: Religious Art by Artists of Chicago and Environs. Exhibition Program, Renaissance Society, 1931.

Fuller, Henry Blake. "At St. Juda's." *The Puppet Booth: Twelve Plays*. New York: Century, 1896.

———. *Bertram Cope's Year*. Chicago: Alderbrink Press, 1919.

———. *The Cliff Dwellers*. New York: Harper Brothers, 1893.

Gerdts, William H. *The Friedman Collection: Artists of Chicago*. New York: Spanierman Gallery, 2002.

G.P.A. Healy Centenary Exhibition (exhibition program). Chicago: Art Institute of Chicago, 1913.

Greenhouse, Wendy, and Susan Weininger. *Chicago Painting, 1895–1945: The Bridges Collection*. Springfield: University of Illinois Press and Illinois State Museum, 2004.

Hanson, Harry. *Midwest Portraits*. New York: Harcourt-Brace, 1923.

Harris, Neil, ed. *The Chicagoan, A Lost Magazine of the Jazz Age*. Chicago: University of Chicago Press, 2008.

Healy, George P.A. *Reminiscences of a Portrait Painter*. Chicago: McGlurg and Company, 1894.

Hecht, Ben. *A Child of the Century*. New York: Simon & Schuster, 1950.

———. *A Thousand and One Nights in Chicago*. Chicago: University of Chicago Press, 2009.

Jacobson, J.Z. *Art of Today: Chicago 1933*. Chicago: L.M. Stein, 1932.

Jones, Wilbert, Kathleen Willis-Morton and Maureen O'Brien. *Chicago's Gold Coast*. Charleston, SC: Arcadia Publishing, 2012.

Kennedy, Elizabeth. *Chicago Modern 1893–1945: Pursuit of the New*. Chicago: Terra Foundation for the Arts and University of Chicago Press, 2004.

Kramer, Dale. *Chicago Renaissance: The Literary Life in the Midwest, 1900–1930*. New York: Appleton-Century, 1966.

Kuh, Katharine. *My Love Affair with Modern Art*. New York: Arcade Publishing, 2006,

Kushner, Marilyn Satin, and Kimberly Orcutt, eds. *The Armory Show at 100: Modernism and Revolution*. New York: New-York Historical Society, 1913.

Lord, Isabel Garland. *A Summer to Be: A Memoir by the Daughter of Hamlin Garland*. Lincoln: University of Nebraska, 2008.

Lowden, Frank O., and Wallace Heckman. *Lorado Taft's Indian Statue "Black Hawk."* Chicago: University of Chicago Press, 1912.

Ness, Zenobia, and Louise Orwig. *Iowa Artists of the First Hundred Years*. Des Moines, IA: Wallace-Homestead, 1939.

Newlin, Keith. *Hamlin Garland: A Life*. Lincoln: University of Nebraska Press, 2008.

Olson, Liesl. *Chicago Renaissance: Literature and Art in the Midwest Metropolis*. New Haven, CT: Yale University Press, 2017.

Peterson, Marina, and Gary McDonogh, eds. *Global Downtowns*. Philadelphia: University of Pennsylvania Press, 2012.

Pinkerton, Jan, and Randolph H. Hudson. *The Chicago Literary Renaissance*. New York: Facts on File, 2004.

Prince, Sue Ann, ed. *The Old Guard and the Avant-Garde: Modernism in Chicago, 1910–1940*. Chicago: University of Chicago Press, 1990.

Regnery, Henry. *Creative Chicago: From the Chap-Book to the University*. Chicago: Chicago Historical Bookworks, 1993.

Revisiting the White City: American Art at the 1893 World's Fair. Washington, D.C.: National Museum of American Art and National Portrait Gallery, Smithsonian Institution, 1993.

Selzer, Adam. *Chronicles of Old Chicago: Exploring the History and Lore of the Windy City*. New York: Museyon, 2014.

Seymour, Ralph Fletcher. *Some Went This Way: A Forty-Year Pilgrimage among Artists, Bookmen and Printers*. Chicago: R.F. Seymour, 1945.

Sharp, Ed. *Old House Handbook for Chicago and Suburbs*. Chicago: Chicago Review Press, 1979.

Simeone, Beth Baker. *The Art of Oregon: Influence of Eagle's Nest Art Colony and Rediscovered Collection They Left Behind*. Oregon, IL: Blurb, 2016.

Smith, Alson J. *Chicago's Left Bank*. Chicago: Henry Regnery, 1953.

Stamper, John W. *Chicago's North Michigan Avenue: Planning and Development, 1900–1930*. Chicago: University of Chicago Press, 1991.

Stilson, Jan. *Art and Beauty in the Heartland: The Story of the Eagle's Nest Camp at Oregon, Illinois, 1898–1942*. Bloomington, IN: AuthorHouse, 2006.

Taft, Ada Bartlett. *Lorado Taft, Sculptor and Citizen*. Greensboro, NC: Mary Taft Smith, 1946.

Taft, Lorado. *The History of American Sculpture*. New York: MacMillan, 1903.

Taft, Maggie, and Robert Cozzolino. *Art in Chicago: From the Fire to Now*. Chicago: University of Chicago Press, 2018.

Townsend, Kim. *Sherwood Anderson: A Biography*. Boston: Houghton Mifflin, 1987.

Walton, William. *World's Columbian Exposition Official Illustrated Publication, Art and Architecture*. Philadelphia: George Barrie, 1893.

Weller, Allen Stuart. *Lorado Taft: The Chicago Years*. Champaign-Urbana: University of Illinois Press, 2014.

World's Columbian Exposition Official Catalogue. Chicago: W.B. Conkey, 1893.

Ziegler, J.W. *World's Columbian Exposition*. Chicago: Monarch Book Company, 1893.

Zorbaugh, Harvey Warren. *The Gold Coast and the Slum: A Sociological Study of Chicago's Near North Side*. Chicago: University of Chicago, 1929. Reprint, 1983.

Dissertations and Theses

McGuire, Athalae. "Eagle's Nest Association." Master's thesis, Northern Illinois University, 1964.

Sparks. Esther. "A Biographical Dictionary of Painters and Sculptors in Illinois, 1808–1945." PhD dissertation, Northwestern University, 1971.

Williams, Lewis W., II. "Lorado Taft: American Sculptor and Art Missionary." PhD dissertation, University of Chicago, 1958.

Periodical Literature

American Art News 13, no. 29 (April 23, 1915): 5.

Anderson, Margaret. "Announcement." *Little Review*, issue 1 (March 1914).

"Apartment House for Frank F. Fisher." *Chicago Architectural Forum* (May 1937).

"Art Gallery Designed by Frank Lloyd Wright." *International Studio* 39 (February 1910).

Bowley, Devereux. "The Montmartre Look: Sol Kogen's Old Town Fling." *Inland Architect* (January 1978).

Chandler, Josephine Craven. "Eagle's Nest Camp, Barbizon of Chicago Artists." *Art and Archaeology* 12, no. 5 (November 1921).

"Chicago's New Club of the Arts—The Housewarming of the Cliff-Dwellers." *Harper's Weekly*, May 15, 1909.

Dell, Floyd. "At the Institute." *Friday Literary Review*, April 4, 1913.

Harper's Weekly, no. 1917 (September 16, 1893).

Little Review 3, no. 6 (September 1916).

"The Little Roomers in 'Captain Fry's Birthday Party.'" *The Bookman* (August 1912).

Matsoukas, Nick J. "The Kogen-Miller Studios," *Western Architect* (December 1930).

Meier, M.W. "A Theatrical Laboratory for Testing Plays." *Popular Mechanics* (December 1917).

Mix, Shelden A. "Burton Place, The Hand Made Street." *Chicago Magazine* (Spring 1966).

Monroe, Harriet. "Eagle's Nest Camp—A Colony of Artists and Writers." *House Beautiful* 16, no. 3 (August 1904).

"Ox-Bow at 100." *American Craft Magazine* (April–May 2010).

Reed, Earl H., Jr. "Edgar Miller, Design-Craftsman." *Architecture* (August 1932).

Roberts, Edith. "There's No Place Like Burton Place." *Chicago Magazine* (March 1956).

"Tree Studios." *Architectural Record* 51 (1922): 259.

Newspapers

Artner, Alan G. "In Celebrating Tree Studios' Past, Exhibit Can Also Impact the Present." *Chicago Tribune*, July 20, 1999.

———. "The Kogen History, Told in the Spirit of Preservation." *Chicago Tribune*, August 24, 1975.

Chicago Daily Tribune. "Students Burning Futurist Art and Celebrating Cubists' Departure." April 17, 1913.

———. "Studio Building Is Planned for 155 Carl Street." August 21, 1927.

Chicago Record-Herald. "May Bar Youngsters from Cubists Show." March 27, 1913.

Chicago Tribune. "The Cubist Art." April 2, 1913.

———. "Jesus Torres Obituary." June 14, 1948, C5.

———. May 2, 1867.

———. November 1, 1893.

———. October 24, 1915.

Construction News. "A Marked Advance in Studio Designing." November 22, 1913.

Bargelt, Louise. "Old Apartment House Answers to Modernizing." *Chicago Daily Tribune*, April 29, 1934, C4.

Bulliet, Clarence J. "Artists of Chicago Past and Present, No. 62, Frederic Milton Grant." *Chicago Daily News*, April 25, 1936.

———. "Artists of Chicago Past and Present, No. 96, Oliver Dennett Grover." *Chicago Daily News*, July 22, 1939.

Davis, Susan O'Connor. "Genuinely Civilized Oddballs," *Hyde Park Herald*, July 3, 2014.

Flavin, Genevieve. "Aztecs' Glory Finds Rebirth in Torres' Art." *Chicago Tribune*, November 16, 1947, S11.

Ford, Ann. "Artist Colony One Big Happy Family." *Chicago Tribune*, November 15, 1942.

Gapp. Paul. "Death of Bohemia." *Chicago Tribune*, February 14, 1988.

———. "No Longer on Top." *Chicago Tribune*, September 23, 1990.

Gordon, Alfreda, "Bohemia with a Haircut." *Sunday Times* (Chicago), March 24, 1940.

Jewett, Eleanor. "Color Work of F.M. Grant Wins Praise." *Chicago Tribune*, May 27, 1931.

———. *Chicago Tribune*, May 11, 1952.

Keegan, Anne. "Artists in Residence: Sandwiched Between the Medinah Temple and a Gaggle of Shops is an Oasis for Painters and Sculptors." *Chicago Tribune*, March 7, 1993.

Kogen, Rick. "Last Call at Ric's; A Final Toast to the Watering Hole Ric Riccardo Left Chicago." *Chicago Tribune*, September 15, 1995.

Levitt, Aimee. "The Migration of the Hipster, A Chicago History 1898–Present." *Chicago Reader*, October 2, 2013.

———. "Return of the Armory Show: Artistic Murder! Pictorial Arson! Total Degeneracy!" *Chicago Reader*, April 1, 2013.

Lieberman, Mary. *Chicago Evening American*, March 14, 1922.

Malkind, Sheila. "Always an Artist." *Chicago Reader*, April 22, 1993.

Mendell, David. "City Is Suing to Save Landmark Building." *Chicago Tribune*, August 27, 1999.

Poore, Nancy. "Imagination Keys Revamping of Two New North Homes." *Chicago Tribune*, February 7, 1965, E16.

Prescott Courier. "Chicago's Arts Club Is Saved." May 14, 1991.

Reitman, Ben. *Chicago Times*, August 23, 1937.

Shepard, Seth. "Drabness Gone in This Neighborhood." *Chicago Daily News*, November 30, 1940.

Strykowski, Sheri. "A Woman's World." *Chicago Tribune*, November 20, 1992.

Government Official Publications

Commission on Chicago Landmarks. Landmark Designation Report for the Fisher Studio Houses, March 10, 1992.
———. Landmark Designation Report for the West Burton Place Historical District, April 7, 2016.
———. Tree Studios—Preliminary Staff Summary of Information, 1980.
Historic American Buildings Survey, Columbian Exposition Store Buildings, National Park Service, 1963.
National Register of Historical Places. "West Burton Place Historical District." U.S. Department of the Interior, National Park Service, 2007.

Internet Website Resources

Administrative History of the Three Arts Club Records. Special Collections. University of Illinois at Chicago Library.
Bohan, Ruth L. "Pauline Palmer." Illinois Art Project. https://www.illinoisart.org/pauline-palmer.
Dryer, Joel. Illinois Art Project. "The First Chicago Art Exhibition—1859." https://www.illinoisart.org/first-chicago-art-exhibit.
"Eagle's Nest Artist Colony." Village of Oregon, Illinois. https://www.discoveroregonillinois.com/discoveroregon/eagles-nest-art-colony.
"Giverny: The Colony of American Artists." Terra Foundation for the Arts. https://www.giverny.org/museums/american/colperm.
Highleyman, Liz. "Margaret Anderson and Jane Heap: Literary Lesbian Lovers." *Lavender* (January 17, 2008). https://www.lavendermagazine.com/archives/uncategorized/margaret-anderson-and-jane-heap-literary-lesbian-lovers.
Ox-Bow School of Art & Artist Residency. "History." https://www.ox-bow.org/our-story.
Ragdale. "Residency." https://www.ragdale.org/residency.
Steffes, Patrick. "Bertrand Goldberg in Towertown, Part 1: Bertrand's Commune." https://www.forgottenchicago.com/features/bertrand-goldberg-in-towertown-part-1-bertrand-goldbergs-commune.
Whitaker, Jan. "Anatomy of a Restaurateur: Harriet Moody." *Restaurant-ing Through History*, June 16, 2011. https://www.restaurant-ingthroughhistory.com/2011/06/16/anatomy-of-a-restaurateur-harriet-moody.

Index

About the Author

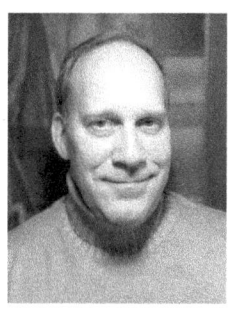

K eith M. Stolte has a bachelor of arts degree in history from the University of Chicago and has, since 1998, practiced law in the fields of intellectual property and unfair competition litigation. He resides at the Carl Street Studios, one of the artist colonies featured in this book, together with Dr. Brian Ortiz, his life partner of twenty years.

Visit us at
www.historypress.com